MW01118611

ACCESS TO JUSTICE

SOCIOLOGY OF CRIME, LAW AND DEVIANCE

Series Editors: Mathieu Deflem (Volumes 6–12)
Jeffrey T. Ulmer (Volumes 1–5)

Recent Volumes:

Volume 1:	Edited by Jeffrey T. Ulmer, 1998
Volume 2:	Edited by Jeffrey T. Ulmer, 2000
Volume 3:	Legal Professions: Work, Structure and Organization – Edited by Jerry Van Hoy, 2001
Volume 4:	Violent Acts and Violentization: Assessing, Applying and Developing Lonnie Athens' Theory and Research – Edited by Lonnie Athens and Jeffrey T. Ulmer, 2002
Volume 5:	Terrorism and Counter-Terrorism: Criminological Perspectives – Edited by Mathieu Deflem, 2004
Volume 6:	Ethnographies of Law and Social Control – Edited by Stacey Lee Burns, 2005
Volume 7:	Sociological Theory and Criminological Research, Views from Europe and United States – Edited by Mathieu Deflem, 2006
Volume 8:	Police Occupational Culture: New Debates and Directions – Edited by Megan O'Neill, Monique Marks and Anne-Marie Singh, 2007
Volume 9:	Crime and Human Rights – Edited by Stephan Parmentier and Elmar Weitekamp, 2007
Volume 10:	Surveillance and Governance: Crime Control and Beyond – Edited by Mathieu Deflem, 2008
Volume 11:	Restorative Justice: From Theory to Practice – Edited by Holly Ventura Miller, 2008

SOCIOLOGY OF CRIME, LAW AND DEVIANCE VOLUME 12

ACCESS TO JUSTICE

EDITED BY

REBECCA L. SANDEFUR
Stanford University, Stanford, USA

JAI

United Kingdom – North America – Japan
India – Malaysia – China

JAI Press is an imprint of Emerald Group Publishing Limited
Howard House, Wagon Lane, Bingley BD16 1WA, UK

First edition 2009

Reprints and permission service
Contact: booksandseries@emeraldinsight.com

British Library Cataloguing in Publication Data
A catalogue record for this book is available from the British Library

ISBN: 978-1-84855-242-5
ISSN: 1521-6136 (Series)

INVESTOR IN PEOPLE

CONTENTS

LIST OF CONTRIBUTORS

Nigel J. Balmer	Legal Services Research Centre, London, and Faculty of Laws, University College London, UK
Ab Currie	Research and Statistics Division, Department of Justice, Ontario, Canada
Stephen Daniels	American Bar Foundation, Chicago, IL, USA
Jennifer Earl	Department of Sociology and Center on Information Technology and Society, University of California, Santa Barbara, CA, USA
Bryant G. Garth	Southwestern Law School, Los Angeles, CA, USA
Joanne Martin	American Bar Foundation, Chicago, IL, USA
Masayuki Murayama	School of Law, Meiji University, Tokyo, Japan
Kwai Hang Ng	Department of Sociology, University of California, San Diego, CA, USA
Pascoe Pleasence	Legal Services Research Centre, London, and Faculty of Laws, University College London, UK
Mary R. Rose	Department of Sociology and School of Laws, University of Texas at Austin, Austin, TX, USA
Rebecca L. Sandefur	Department of Sociology and (by courtesy) School of Law, Stanford University, Stanford, CA, USA

Tania Tam Legal Services Research Centre, London, UK

Mary Nell Trautner Department of Sociology, University at Buffalo – SUNY, Buffalo, NY, USA

Kathryne M. Young Stanford University, Stanford, CA, USA

ACCESS TO JUSTICE: CLASSICAL APPROACHES AND NEW DIRECTIONS

INTRODUCTION

Around the world today, access to justice enjoys an energetic and passionate resurgence. It is an object both of scholarly inquiry and political contest, and both a social movement and a value commitment that motivates study and action. Though the recent resurgence makes much seem new, in fact access to justice has been a topic of policy advocacy and empirical research since the early 20th century (e.g., Smith, 1919). One legacy of early work is scholars' and practitioners' tendency to conceptualize access as a social problem that is faced by lower status groups, such as poor people. Another legacy is a penchant for reducing, in a whole variety of ways, questions of justice to matters of law. Given this orienting framework, classical access to justice research focuses heavily on empirically documenting how law falls short of its supposed promise. At the same time, classical research often relied on an expansion of law – more or more affordable lawyers, more or more welcoming courts and hearing tribunals, wider participation on juries, new and better rights – as *the* policy solution to injustice or inequality.

This volume heralds new directions in access to justice research. The chapters include cutting-edge work from scholars in law, political science, social psychology, sociology, and sociolinguistics. Their work reflects a high degree of sophistication in empirical analysis, and, as importantly, evidences a deeper engagement with social theory than past generations of scholarship. The richer conceptual frameworks employed by contemporary access scholars create more sophisticated research questions that in turn inform a more nuanced policy agenda. This research – on rights knowledge and police procedure, race and jury deliberation, tort reform and access to lawyers, self-interest and public service, ordinary people's experience with everyday troubles – reveals new discoveries about law and social process and provides foundation for a deeper understanding of access to justice that can inform wiser, more effective policies.

In distinct and complementary ways, each contribution moves access to justice research forward.

Among the most promising developments in contemporary access research is scholars' attention to the perspectives of the public and their experiences with justice on the ground. As Currie notes in his report on a recent large-scale survey of the Canadian public's experience with civil-law problems, "[s]o many aspects of ordinary daily activities are lived in the shadow of the law [that] it should not be at all surprising" that most of the population experiences significant problems "that have civil legal aspects" (this volume, p. 2). Civil justice problems are in many contemporary societies so common as to be "nearly normal features of everyday life" (Currie, this volume, p. 5 and Table 1). These often very mundane problems – with neighbors, merchants, government agencies, employers, or children's schools – can cause serious and wide-reaching consequences if not resolved, leading to additional justice problems, to the breakdown of relationships, to loss of employment or housing, to distrust of the legal system, and to impaired physical and mental health (Currie, this volume; Pleasence, Balmer, & Buck, 2006; Sandefur, 2008b). These problems are costly not only for the people who experience them, but also for the broader community that may lose their active participation and which provides for social services, public benefits, and other kinds of support.

Though these problems have legal aspects, people often do not think of them as legal, and they show an enormous creativity in their search for solutions (Earl, this volume; Nader, 1980; Pleasence et al., 2006; Sandefur, 2007b, 2008a, 2008b). Rather than turning to courts or lawyers, people are much more likely to turn to elsewhere for help or to attempt to resolve problems on their own. People also often do nothing about problems that they nevertheless recognize and consider serious (Currie, this volume; see also Earl, this volume, and Sandefur, 2007b). For more than two-fifths of reported problems in Currie's Canadian study, people took no action at all to try to resolve them. When people did nothing, their most frequently reported reasons for doing so had little to do with the financial costs of possible actions; rather, people did nothing to try to resolve a problem because they were uncertain about their rights, thought that nothing could be done, or thought trying to resolve the problem would take too much time (*ibid.*, Table V; see also Pleasence et al., 2006; Sandefur, 2007b). Currie's work, by documenting the enormous scale and wide scope of public experience with civil justice problems, reveals "justice *writ large* ... not limited to the formal laws and system of justice, [rather] justice as a social institution" (Currie, this volume, p. 2).

The second chapter pushes further the frontiers of research on public experience with civil-law troubles, using a "seeming defect" of many civil justice surveys to produce new knowledge about the volume and severity of public experiences with them (Pleasence et al., this volume, p. 43). Civil justice surveys are typically retrospective, asking respondents to recall events that occurred in the past. Drawing on techniques for modeling people's "forgetting curves" for life events, Pascoe Pleasence and his colleagues find that people are more likely to remember those problems that they believed were most important to resolve, that involved the most money, that caused the most adverse consequences in their lives, and for which they sought help. Overall, they find evidence that existing retrospective surveys substantially underestimate the frequency with which people encounter justice problems. For England and Wales, for example, they estimate that on the order of 2.7 times more serious and difficult to resolve civil-law problems occur than are reported. Respondents' failures of autobiographical memory lead to biased estimates of both the incidence of different kinds of problems and of their severity. This bias is problematic not only for scholars interested in understanding, but also for governments trying to design civil justice policy. Researchers may someday move toward large-scale longitudinal surveys of public experience with justice problems, a methodological innovation what would overcome some of the limitations of current research. Today, working at the cutting edge of the state of the art, Pleasence and his colleagues provide a valuable tool for estimating the true incidence and severity of these troubles "at the intersection of civil law and everyday adversity" (Sandefur, 2007b, p. 113).

As legal realists observe, "as a practical matter, individuals have only the legal rights of which they are aware and which they can hope to enforce or use" (Daniels and Martin, this volume, p. 3). In an innovative empirical study of procedural rights consciousness, Kathryne Young explores Americans' general knowledge about their constitutional rights in police searches and interrogations and how they use this knowledge to discern their rights in specific situations. Given the enormous amount of both fictional and factual media attention to crime and the police in the United States, Americans are unsurprisingly familiar with some of the "fundamentals of [US] criminal procedure," such as Miranda warnings and a right to counsel for criminal defendants (Young, this volume, p. 81). However, "it is this very familiarity that may lead people to draw erroneous conclusions about their constitutional rights" (*ibid.*). From data collected through asking people to respond to vignettes describing common encounters between citizens and the police, Young identifies elements of a lay jurisprudence of constitutional rights. This jurisprudence can lead people – with great confidence yet serious and consequential misunderstanding – to reason themselves out of exercising rights that they in fact possess. Young argues that the lay jurisprudence she discovers is more harmful than a simple lack of knowledge, concluding that "at least in some situations, citizens would be better off acting in complete ignorance of their procedural rights than trying" to use what knowledge they do have "to discern" their rights (Young, this volume, p. 83).

When poor people in the United States seek to exercise their rights, a substantial amount of the civil legal services available to assist them is provided through lawyers' work in organized civil pro bono programs, in which individual lawyers or law firms donate their time to provide services (Sandefur, 2007a, 2009). Stephen Daniels and Joanne Martin argue that a "necessary consequence" of this "privatization of legal services for the poor" is an "ad hoc institutionalization" organized principally by lawyers' and law firms' "self-interest" (this volume, p. 147). Their analysis demonstrates that lawyers' pro bono work is neither "free, nor purely charitable in nature. There is ... a market based on some exchange that distributes these resources. Demand does not drive th[is] market; ... the interests and priorities of those providing the resources" do so (Daniels and Martin, this volume, p. 149). These interests and priorities affect both which services will be provided and how they will be produced and delivered. The result is a civil legal aid system driven by provider, rather than consumer, interests.

Masayuki Murayama's piece on legal services in Japan also explores how different models of legal services delivery may affect the public's access. He argues that the Japanese market for private practice legal services is organized less by cost than by lawyers' and citizens' attempts to reduce their anxieties about each other. In comparative terms, Japan's legal profession is small relative to the country's population, about 1/20th the size of the United States'. While the United States has one lawyer for every 285 members of the public, Japan has one lawyer for every roughly 5,500 people (*ibid.*, p. 168). In many countries lawyers accept and, indeed, often solicit walk-in clients. In contrast, Japanese attorneys neither seek out nor "compete to obtain clients," and are often unwilling to take on new ones unless they are referred by someone the lawyer already knows (*ibid.*, pp. 171–173). Citizens, in their turn, are anxious about whether lawyers will be willing to receive them. In this context, neither a citizen's "general knowledge of the law," nor her level of education, nor her income predicts whether someone who experiences civil-law problems will consult an attorney about them; rather, it is whether someone has "personal experience and connections" with lawyers or courts that affects who takes their problems to lawyers (*ibid.*, p. 173). Rather than proposing to change the way this market operates, Murayama suggests a supplement to it: the expansion of existing legal advice centers. These centers, run by bar associations, provide relatively inexpensive, fixed-fee consultations to walk-in clients. By "allay[ing] people's discomfort" this additional means of matching potential clients to attorneys would, Murayama suggests, "open windows of the otherwise closed market of legal services" (*ibid.*, p. 194).

In a study of the impact of changes in law on access to lawyers, Mary Nell Trautner finds that personal injury lawyers alter the way they select from prospective cases not because of what a new law says, but rather in response to shifts in public opinion that they believe attend the legal change. In a number of countries, personal injury claims, sometimes called torts, are typically pursued in the context of contingent fee, or "no win, no fee" arrangements, in which a lawyer is paid out of the judgment or settlement from her client's case. When such lawyers lose a case, they not only do not get paid for their work, but are out-of-pocket for any expenses incurred preparing it for trial. Unsurprisingly, lawyers working in contingent fee arrangements select which cases to take and which to refuse with considerable care. In the United States, this segment of the legal services market has been reshaped in some states by the implementation of "tort reform." These legal changes have variously placed limits on the amount of money plaintiffs can recover in damages, on whom can be held liable for injuries, on the kinds of evidence that can be used to show harm and negligence, and on where and when such cases must be filed. In a creative vignette study of the impact of tort reform on how lawyers screen potential product liability cases, Trautner concludes that personal injury lawyers are responsive less to change in law per se than to "perceived changes in public attitudes and beliefs" (this volume, p. 226). "[T]ort reformers have been successful in linking corporations and victimhood in a narrative" that lawyers believe the public – who populates juries – had embraced. Reform thus encourages lawyers to shift their focus from considering whether potential clients can be construed as victims of negligent corporations to considering whether those same corporations will be seen by juries as victims of runaway tort claims (*ibid.*).

One of the challenges to justice in outcomes like trial verdicts and to equal participation in justice activities, such as jury service, is the fact that what looks like institutions' equal treatment of different groups can create unequal participation or unequal outcomes. Ng's chapter advocating for Spanish-language courtrooms and Rose's chapter on the sociology of the jury both address this issue. In formal legal settings like courts, lay people often have difficulty figuring out how to communicate their wishes and needs in ways that court personnel understand (Conley & O'Barr, 1990; Sandefur, 2008a, pp. 346–352); this difficulty is compounded when lay people do not speak the language of the court. In the United States, Spanish speakers are the largest language minority, accounting for 96% of interpreter needs in federal courts (Ng, this volume, p. 102). Drawing on practices in the Canadian justice system, Kwai Ng proposes the limited use of Spanish-language courtrooms in which all personnel would communicate directly in Spanish during parts of the trial as a "pragmatic measure" to deal with the perennial shortage of qualified interpreters (*ibid.*, p. 115). Ng's approach, like Murayama's, is characteristic of the new policy-oriented access research, which takes not only people as they are but legal systems as they actually operate as the starting point for designing equalizing policies.

In her study of the race and the jury, Mary Rose identifies two puzzles of equal participation: the limited success of attempts to diversify jury pools and the ambiguous relationship between juries' racial make-up and the verdicts they produce. Despite government attempts to expand participation on juries, "race remains a good predictor of who serves and who does not serve, especially in the early stages of the jury selection process when courts" assemble the initial pool of people from which particular jurors are chosen for specific cases (Rose, this volume, p. 135). Rose argues that attempts to open up juries have not worked because both scholars and policy makers know very little about the reasons why people do not show up to serve. Rose observes that "if large numbers of people are simply not being 'asked' to serve on juries" then the remedy is to ask them. However, attrition from service likely reflects more complicated processes, such as the influence on potential jurors' behavior of neighborhood norms about deference to law and courts' inadequate compensation for the very real hardships, including "lost income [and] unsupervised children," that can be imposed by jury service (*ibid.*, p. 129). If these are the reasons people do not serve, educational outreach and tougher summons enforcement will not be sufficient; rather, government must "invest more resources [to support jury service] so that the state demonstrates the same commitment that it asks from its citizens" (*ibid.*).

Rose shows that it remains unclear how racial representation on juries affects the outcome of trials. Research suggests that jury composition affects *how* juries deliberate, but so far has documented a much less clear relationship between racial composition and *what* juries decide. "Greater racial diversity on juries seems … to alter the entire context in which individual jurors hear evidence, think about issues, arrive at their own tentative conclusions, and imagine presenting their opinions to others" (*ibid.*, p. 134). At the same time, however, few studies find evidence that racial composition affects the final verdicts that juries produce. This finding does not mean that racial representation is irrelevant to justice, but rather we have yet to understand how race and racial diversity work in group deliberation. With respect to this puzzle, the literature has come to a dead end; to resolve it, research on juries needs to rethink the process at issue. In particular, Rose concludes, scholars need to move beyond documenting individuals' attitudes and judgments to look more carefully at group deliberation. Rose's engagement with core questions in social psychology opens up a new direction in jury research and, if policy makers are attentive, in justice policy.

A similar engagement with deep questions and common themes across subdisciplines motivates Jennifer Earl's call for a new sociology of troubles. Earl observes that many subfields study people's experiences with trouble – the literatures on social movements, social problems, industrial relations, and organizational conflict, for example – yet each approaches that study with little reference to the other, "breaking trouble up by forms of redress and researching those forms of redress in isolation" (this volume, p. 232). Thus, we have empirical research about whether disputes with neighbors are taken to law or not, or whether people who experience environmental catastrophes join social movements or not, or how driving while intoxicated comes to be seen as a social problem worthy of public attention, but little research that speaks to the fascinating questions of which kinds of troubles call forth which kinds of responses, or how people choose between forms of redress, or why the most common response to many troubles, in every subfield that studies them, is doing nothing at all. Earl calls for an integration of these subfields around their common interest, in troubles, an intellectual shift that would permit scholars to answer these broader questions.

The volume closes with a comment from Bryant Garth, who early in his distinguished career led a generation of access to justice research that combined visionary idealism with critical empirical analysis. Garth importantly reminds scholars and practitioners of the centrality of power and power relationships in any analysis of law, a centrality that is often obscured in the contemporary access to justice movements of both more and less developed nations. In the former, today's public conversations about access often rely on individual volunteerism and lawyers' pro bono service as a remedy to systemic problems like poverty, violence, racism, or gender inequality; in the latter, international development initiatives promote a rule of law that draws heavily on a rights model, particularly a model that privileges property rights. Both at home and abroad, Garth argues, "the key to advancement of any access to justice agenda ... is its relationship to critical scholarship informed by the theories and methods of social science, especially sociology," for "[l]aw without the sociology of law easily slips into the reiteration of legitimating rhetoric" (Garth, this volume, p. 258).

Classical access to justice research was often highly compelling, but it was also often very myopic. Its narrow vision has shaped both understanding and practice, leading scholars to produce research that goes no further than documenting that law betrays someone's ideals, leading lawyers and others "to think that" the only good solutions "to social problems" are "legal solutions," and encouraging practitioners, researchers, and opinion leaders to join in a chorus of "simplistic exhortations" about the importance of fulfiling "the unmet legal needs of ... vague categories" of people, like the disadvantaged (Garth, this volume, p. 258; see also, Abel, 1985; Galanter, 1974; Genn, 1993; Mayhew, 1975; Marks, 1976; Sandefur, 2008a, 2008b).

New, more promising directions in access to justice research are reflected in this volume. Scholars and practitioners both must step back from law to understand justice. They must do so empirically, by examining law's antecedents, complements, and alternatives, and conceptually, by drawing on the rich theories provided by the social sciences. Access researchers are almost always motivated by a wish to improve the world. Consequently, their interests include the application of their research insights in practice. They must strive for the same analytic clarity and methodological sophistication that characterizes the best pure research. Good understanding is valuable both for its own sake and because it is essential to good policy.

REFERENCES

Abel, R. L. (1985). Law without politics: Legal aid under advanced capitalism. *UCLA Law Review*, *32*, 474–642.

Conley, J. M., & O'Barr, W. M. (1990). *Rules versus relationships: The ethnography of legal discourse*. Chicago, IL: University of Chicago Press.

Galanter, M. (1974). Why the 'haves' come out ahead: Speculations on the limits of legal change. *Law and Society Review*, *9*, 95–160.

Genn, H. (1993). Tribunals and informal justice. *Modern Law Review*, *56*(3), 393–411.

Marks, F. R. (1976). Some research perspectives for looking at legal need and legal services delivery systems: Old forms or new? *Law and Society Review*, *11*, 191–205.

Mayhew, L. H. (1975). Institutions of representation: Civil justice and the public. *Law and Society Review*, *9*, 401–429.

Nader, L. (Ed.) (1980). *No access to law: Alternatives to the American judicial system*. New York: Academic Press.

Pleasence, P., Balmer, N., & Buck, A. (2006). *Causes of action: Civil law and social justice* (2nd ed.). London: TSO.

Sandefur, R. L. (2007a). Lawyers' pro bono service and American-style civil legal assistance. *Law and Society Review*, *41*, 79–112.

Sandefur, R. L. (2007b). The importance of doing nothing: Everyday problems and responses of inaction. In: P. Pleasence, A. Buck & N. Balmer (Eds), *Transforming lives: Law and social process* (pp. 112–132). London: TSO.

Sandefur, R. L. (2008a). Access to civil justice and race, class and gender inequality. *Annual Review of Sociology*, *34*, 339–358.

Sandefur, R. L. (2008b). Experience with civil justice problems: Strategies and consequences. Paper presented at the Seventh Legal Services Research Centre International Research Conference, Greenwich, England, June 19.

Sandefur, R. L. (2009). Lawyers' pro bono service and market-reliant legal aid. In: R. Granfield & L. Mather (Eds), *Private lawyers in the public interest*. New York, NY: Oxford University Press.

Smith, R. H. (1919). *Justice and the poor* (Carnegie Foundation for the Advancement of Teaching Bulletin No. 13. 2nd ed.). Boston: The Merrymount Press.

Rebecca L. Sandefur
Editor

THE LEGAL PROBLEMS OF EVERYDAY LIFE

Ab Currie

ABSTRACT

This chapter examines the prevalence of justiciable civil justice problems experienced by Canadians, the ways in which people respond to them and the consequences of experiencing these kinds of problems. The results show that experiencing justiciable problems is a nearly normal feature of the everyday lives of a large proportion of the population in a modern society. Particularly, important features of justiciable problems are the prevalence of multiple problems, the clustering of justiciable problems and the linkages between justiciable, health and social problems. The results suggest that justiciable problems may be a part of broader patterns of social exclusion. One implication of this research is that access to justice services may not only address legal problems but, by doing so, may have the effect of forestalling processes of social exclusion of which civil law problems are a part.

INTRODUCTION

This is a study of the legal problems that, for the most part, people do not take to the formal justice system to resolve. It looks at legal problems, but

Access to Justice
Sociology of Crime, Law and Deviance, Volume 12, 1–41

ISSN: 1521-6136/doi:10.1108/S1521-6136(2009)0000012005

not from the narrow lens of problems that come to the attention of some aspect of the formal justice system or are assumed to require the services of a lawyer. Rather, it takes as a starting point the much broader lens of the legal problems that are experienced by the public in their daily lives. This does not mean that these problems are less important than the ones that are resolved in the courts or by legal counsel. It is now a familiar theme in the literature of access to justice that many problems encountered in people's everyday lives have legal aspects, potential legal consequences and potential legal solutions. However, the legal option may not be the best or most sensible approach to resolving the problem. These problems may represent the "little injustices" (Nader, 1980) that are a part of everyday living for many people and they are important because people care about them. If we are interested in justice *writ large*, in justice as a social institution, not limited to the formal laws and system of justice, this is the terrain that is relevant.

THE INCIDENCE OF JUSTICIABLE PROBLEMS

Two defining features of modern societies are first, that civil laws are pervasive in the activities of everyday life and, second, that justiciable problems experienced by the population are ubiquitous. Civil laws regulate relations of the market such as the sale and purchase of goods and services, commercial transactions and lending and debt. Conditions relating to employment and the loss of employment, and those relating to occupying rental housing are situations where regimes of civil law touch the security and well-being of a large segment of the population. For the poor, access to shelter and income to which others have access through the market, are regulated by civil laws. The law regulates intimate personal relations between domestic partners, defines responsibilities related to the care of children and with respect to managing the affairs of those no longer able to do so competently on their own.

So many aspects of ordinary daily activities of life are lived in the shadow of the law, it should not be at all surprising that a study of the extent or incidence of civil justice problems should reveal that a large proportion of the population should experience problems that have a legal aspect. Two recent large-scale surveys carried out in Canada confirm that common feature shared with other similar countries, the ubiquitous nature of civil justice problems. A survey carried out in 2004 with a sample of 4,501 adult Canadians estimated that 47.7% of the population had experienced one or more problems within the three-year period covered by the survey

(Currie, 2006). The survey, on which this chapter is based and which was carried out in 2006 with a sample size of 6,665, estimated that 44.6% of adult Canadians had experienced one or more justiciable problems within a three-year period (Currie, 2007).

The results of the two Canadian surveys are roughly similar to studies carried out elsewhere, to the extent that they are comparable. All the surveys in Table 1 share the same general approach pioneered by the comprehensive legal needs study carried out in the United States and the paths to justice research conducted by Hazel Genn in the United Kingdom (Genn, 1999). However, most used somewhat different types and numbers of problems in the problem identification part of the questionnaires. The surveys cover different time periods within which respondents could report having experienced problems, and employ different methods for gathering the data. Each of these factors can have an effect on the estimated incidence of problems.

Regardless of the differences in methods and in the exact levels of justiciable problems measured, the strength of this body of research lies in the overall consistency of the results. A growing number of studies carried out in different countries demonstrate that justiciable problems that are characterized by those who experience them as serious and difficult to resolve are common features of everyday life. It is, therefore, important to examine the nature, extent and consequences of this social phenomenon, well described by Sandefur (2007) as the intersection of civil law and everyday adversity.

Using data on the year of occurrence of the problem, it was possible to adjust the data from the 2006 Canadian survey to estimate the incidence of problems occurring over a 15-month period. The estimated proportion of individuals experiencing one or more justiciable problems for this time period was 21%. This figure is somewhat more comparable to the results of other surveys with shorter time frames, such as the New Zealand study noted in Table 1.

THE 2006 SURVEY OF CIVIL JUSTICE PROBLEMS

The analysis is based on a random sample of 6,665 adult Canadians, 18 years and older, carried out in February and March 2006. Interviews were conducted by telephone. The objective of the research was to estimate the prevalence of civil justice problems in Canada, to examine how people respond to problems of this sort and the consequences of experiencing

Table 1. International Comparisons of the Prevalence of Justiciable Problems.

Study, Country, Date of Data Collection	Time Frame (years)	Percent Experiencing One of More Problems (%)	Methodology
American Bar Foundation, United States, 1994[a]	1	47 (low income) 52 (moderate income)	Telephone interviews
Hazel Genn, England and Wales, 1997[b]	5	40	In-person interviews
Hazel Genn and Alan Paterson, Scotland, 1998[c]	5	26	In-person interviews
Pascoe Pleasence et al., England and Wales, 2001[d]	3 1/2	36	In-person interviews
Pascoe Pleasence, England and Wales, 2004[e]	3 1/2	33	In-person interviews
Legal Services Agency, New Zealand, 2006[f]	1	29	In-person interviews
B. van Velthoven and M. ter Voort, Netherlands, 2003[g]	5	67	Internet questionnaire
Tony Dignan, Northern Ireland, 2005[h]	3	35	In-person interviews
A. Currie, Canada, 2004[i]	3	48	Telephone interviews
A. Currie, Canada, 2006[j]	3	45	Telephone interviews
Murayama et al., Japan, 2005[k]	5	19.5	In-person interviews
Sato et al., Japan, 2006[l]	5	36.5	In-person interviews

[a]ABA Consortium on Legal Services and the Public (1994a, 1994b).
[b]Genn (1999).
[c]Genn and Paterson (2001).
[d]Pascoe Pleasence and Alexy Buck, Nigel Balmer, Aoife O'Grady, Hazel Genn and Marisol Smith, Causes of Action: Civil Law and Social Justice, Legal Services Commission, 2004.
[e]Pleasence et al. (2006).
[f]Legal Services Agency (2006).
[g]B.C.J. van Velthoven and M. ter Voort, Paths to Justice in the Netherlands. Paper presented at the Fifth International Legal Services Research Conference, Cambridge, 2004; Department of Economics Research Memorandum, 2004.04, University of Leiden.
[h]Dignan (2006).
[i]Supra endnote 3.
[j]Supra endnote 4.
[k]Murayama et al. (2005).
[l]Sato, Takahashi, Kanomata, & Kashimura (2007).

problems. The survey instrument consisted of five major sections. A problem identification section asked respondents if they had experienced any of 76 specific problems carefully designed to have legal aspects. The set of problems was based on questionnaires used in other national surveys and on the experience gained from a similar survey carried out in Canada in 2004. Respondents were asked to indicate if within the three years prior to the interview they had experienced problems that were "serious and difficult to resolve". Subsequent sections of the questionnaire asked respondents what steps they had taken to resolve problems, about connections between problems where people experienced multiple problems and about the social impacts of experiencing legal problems. Respondents were also asked questions covering basic socio-demographic information. The civil justice problems examined in this research are self-reported by respondents as opposed to problems that are counted because they come to the attention of the formal justice system. The self-report methodology is an important feature of this research. The implications of this fundamental methodological feature will be discussed in greater detail later.

The percentage of individuals experiencing one or more justiciable problems translates into what, on the surface, appears to be strikingly large estimates of the absolute numbers of people experiencing problems. Based on the January 2006 Statistics Canada estimate of the Canadian population aged 18 years of age and older, approximately 25.9 million, about 11.6 million Canadians experienced one or more justiciable problems within the three-year survey period. Table 2 shows the percentage of respondents reporting one or more problems, the sample number and the estimated number in the population experiencing one or more problems in each of the 15 problem categories covered by the 2006 survey.

The numbers in brackets in column three represent the confidence interval of the estimate at the 5% level of statistical significance.

THE SIGNIFICANCE OF THE NEARLY NORMAL

Reporting the incidence of justiciable problems using absolute numbers introduces a level of concreteness that is absent with percentages. The numbers presented in Table 2 are large, so large, in fact, that they give the appearance of being nearly normal features of everyday life. There is no doubt that the numbers represent statistically reliable counts of the problems that respondents reported. However, they give pause for reflection about what the numbers, representing problems that are serious and difficult

Table 2. The Incidence of Civil Justice Problems in Canada.

Problem Category	Percent of Respondents Reporting at least One Problem in the Category (%)	Number of Respondents	Estimated Number of People in the Population (95% Confidence Interval)
Consumer	22.0	1,469	5,698,000 (5,641,900–5,754,100)
Employment	17.8	1,184	4,619,200 (4,561,500–4,676,900)
Debt	20.4	1,356	5,263,600 (5,201,700–5,532,500)
Social assistance	1.2	78	310,800 (295,600–326,000)
Disability benefits	1.0	66	259,000 (245,195–272,800)
Housing	1.7	116	440,300 (422,600–458,000)
Immigration	0.6	40	155,400 (144,800–187,000)
Discrimination	1.9	130	492,100 (473,400–510,800)
Police action	2.0	133	518,000 (498,500–537,500)
Family: Relationship breakdown	3.6	239	932,400 (906,300–958,500)
Other family	1.4	93	362,600 (346,300–378,900)
Wills and powers of attorney	5.2	348	1,346,800 (1,315,500–1,378,100)
Personal injury	2.9	192	751,100 (727,600–774,600)
Hospital treatment or release	1.6	108	414,400 (397,100–431,700)
Threat of legal action	1.2	82	310,800 (295,900–325,700)

to resolve, truly represent. The reader should keep in mind that the numbers represent estimated numbers of problems occurring over three years.[1]

A brief glance at the magnitude of some other justice numbers is an interesting although limited first attempt to test the reality presented by the numbers of civil justice problems. In 2005 there were 2.6 million incidents involving the *Criminal Code*, drug and other federal statutes. There were about 550,000 adults charged with offences in these categories.

This represents about 2.4% of the adult population of Canada (Statistics Canada, 2006). The results of the General Social Survey indicate that about one-third of the adult population reported that they were a victim of some type of crime in 2004 (AuCoin & Beauchamp, 2007). This would amount to roughly 8 million Canadians. Among all forms of victimization, there were over 2 million incidents involving violence (AuCoin & Beauchamp, 2007, p. 1). If the estimated numbers of civil justice problems are converted to a 15-month period to be more comparable to these annual numbers, about 2.5 million Canadians experienced one or more serious and difficult consumer problems, about 2 million experienced at least one employment problem and about 2.3 million experienced a serious debt problem. About 410,000 people experienced a relationship breakdown problem that was serious and difficult to resolve, presumably where the resolution was not consensual. The numbers of serious-and-difficult-to-resolve civil justice problems begin to look reasonable on the surface against the other *justice* numbers.

More fundamentally, to have credibility, the results of the research must stand or fall on the paradigm assumptions and the methodology that has produced them.

The reader unfamiliar with the paradigm assumptions underlying the approach to measuring civil justice problems and the methodology that follows might rightly ask: what has been measured and how serious is it? Thus a brief discussion of the literature that forms the genealogy of this research will be informative.

Much of the legal needs research from the 1930s (Clark & Corstvet, 1938) to the 1970s (Curran, 1977) equated legal need to the problems for which people seek the advice of a lawyer (Pleasence et al., 2001). However, during the 1970s a critique of the lawyer-centered approach emerged that significantly broadened the definition of legal problems from problems that require the services of a lawyer to problems that are legal in nature but for which the formal justice system is only one, and perhaps not the best, option for resolving it (Lewis, 1973). From this critique a body of paradigm assumptions (in the sense used by Merton, 1968) emerged that have guided most research beginning with the 1994 American Bar Association Comprehensive Legal Needs study.

- People may not recognize that the problems they experience have a legal aspect or a potential legal solution.
- People may experience a variety of barriers (financial resources, knowledge about what to do, a strong sense of self-efficacy) in accessing assistance to resolve justiciable problems.

- While justiciable problems are legal in nature, the formal justice system may not be the most appropriate or effective way to resolve the problem.

Thus the Comprehensive Legal Needs Study carried out in the U.S. in 1994 defined legal need as

> specific situations in which members of households were dealing with that raised legal issues – whether or not they were recognized as such or taken to some part of the civil justice system. (ABA Consortium on Legal Services and the Public, 1994a, 1994b, p. 16)

Similar to the American definition, Hazel Genn in the paths to justice research defines a justiciable "event" as

> a matter experienced by a respondent which raised legal issues, whether or not it was recognized by the respondent as being "legal" and whether or not any action taken by the respondent to deal with the event involved the use of any part of the civil justice system. (Genn, 1999, p. 12)

In the definition, Professor Genn uses the word "event" in preference to the word problem. However, elsewhere it seems clear that a justiciable "event" is equivalent to a problem or a potential problem where she writes that "questions included on the screening questionnaire covered the widest possible range of potentially justiciable problems, not merely the more obvious events that people would recognize as being potentially 'legal' problems" (Genn, 1999, p. 15).

The paradigm assumptions underlying the entire body of contemporary research on justiciable or legal problems have one main implication for methodology. The basic data on the incidence of problems must be gathered by means of survey research in which people self-report the occurrence of problems with legal content.[2] The basic form that the research takes is similar to all the studies noted in Table 1. A screening section presents a comprehensive set of problems carefully designed to have legal content. Thus the legal content of problems is not problematic. In order to limit problems to those that are serious or non-trivial, threshold language is used in the questionnaire, asking respondents to identify problems that were "difficult to resolve"[3] or problems that were "serious and difficult to resolve".[4] An important feature of this method is that self-reported problems that are serious and difficult to solve are subjective judgments by respondents. The subjectivity gives rise to a degree of caution in interpreting the data on incidence of problems and, even more so, when the occurrence of justiciable problems is so ubiquitous as to approach a normal state of affairs. Given the subjectivity inherent in the method, the robustness of the threshold language for identifying truly serious problems is a concern.

In the present study, respondents were asked two questions near the end of the interview in order to further examine the level of seriousness they attached to the problems they reported in the problem identification section of the questionnaire. Respondents were asked how difficult the problem had made their daily lives and how much they had wanted to resolve the problem. Responses to each of the questions was scored on a four-point scale ranging from extremely difficult to not difficult at all and extremely important to not important at all, respectively.

Overall, 58.9% of respondents said that the problem had made their day-to-day lives somewhat to extremely difficult and 86.7% said that resolving the problem was somewhat to extremely important. This second look represents the subjective assessments of respondents, as are the meanings attached to the threshold language in the screening questionnaire. It has both the virtue and the vice of looking at the problems from the point of view of the people experiencing them. Nonetheless, it gives a reassuring assessment of the robustness of the threshold language.

Table 3 shows the percentages of respondents who indicated that the problem was somewhat or extremely disruptive and who said it was somewhat to extremely important to resolve the problem, separately for the 15 problem types.

These responses could be applied to the incidence levels of problems initially established using the problem identification section of the questionnaire, reducing the incidence of problem types.[5] However, on strictly logical grounds, a problem need not be disruptive of one's day-to-day life to be a serious or potentially serious legal problem. Similarly, strictly speaking, it is not necessary that a respondent wants to resolve a problem for it to be serious or potentially serious. There is a degree of elasticity in the incidence of problems due to the fact that problem identification is based on subjective responses. However, it seems clear that the methodology produces reasonably robust results. The ubiquitous quality of civil justice problems is a real feature of modern life. The fact that problems are so frequent as to be nearly normal is more a cause for concern than for dismissing them as merely the problems of everyday life.

WHAT PEOPLE DO ABOUT CIVIL JUSTICE PROBLEMS

Overall, only 11.7% of all problems in this survey were resolved in a court or administrative tribunal. Thus it is of interest, in research of this type,

Table 3. The Perceived Seriousness of Civil Justice Problems.

Problem Type	Problem was Disruptive to Daily Life				Important to Resolve Problem			
	Extremely or very (%)	Somewhat (%)	Not very or not at all (%)	Number	Extremely or very (%)	Somewhat (%)	Not very or not at all (%)	Number
Consumer	12.6	29.9	57.5	1,463	47.5	33.7	18.8	3,402
Employment	33.8	34.8	37.4	1,413	63.9	24.2	11.9	1,821
Debt	18.7	30.9	50.4	1,432	55.4	28.5	16.1	1,737
Social assistance	37.5	39.6	22.9	48	62.5	12.5	25.0	24
Disability pensions	60.4	29.2	10.4	48	83.3	16.7	0.0	36
Housing	31.2	36.6	32.2	93	65.8	26.3	7.9	114
Immigration	35.3	47.1	17.6	34	92.8	7.2	0.0	42
Discrimination	38.5	31.9	29.6	91	41.9	25.6	32.5	93
Police action	27.5	29.4	43.1	102	45.2	38.7	16.1	93
Relationship breakdown	41.2	44.0	14.8	243	86.3	6.9	4.8	219
Other family law problems	52.9	39.7	7.4	68	93.8	3.1	3.1	96
Wills and powers of attorney	28.0	40.4	31.6	322	81.9	11.9	6.2	480
Personal injury	53.1	31.3	15.6	160	86.5	10.5	3.0	201
Hospital treatment or release	55.4	24.1	20.5	83	86.0	8.0	8.0	75
Threat of legal action	21.6	35.3	43.1	51	40.0	30.0	30.0	30

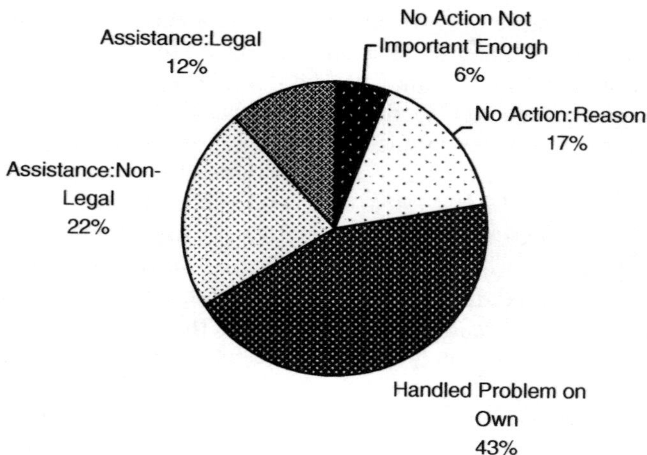

Fig. 1. Responses to Justiciable Problems.

to examine how people attempt to resolve their legal problems and how well they manage. Fig. 1 presents the basic types of responses made by respondents to their justiciable problems.

In the largest percentage of cases, 44.0%, respondents said they solved the problem on their own with no other form of assistance. The second most frequent response, 22.1%, was to seek help from a source other than a legal professional. Respondents sought legal assistance in only 11.7% of problems. In total, respondents said they took no action to resolve 22.2% of all problems. This included 16.6% in which no action was taken because the respondent faced some barrier or inhibition in taking action and 5.7% in which the respondent felt that the problem was not serious enough.[6]

Because most people do not obtain professional advice to deal with their problems it is important to know something about the kinds of problems that are related to the different responses, the types of people who respond in different ways and the success those people have in dealing with problems.

I Took No Action Because the Problem Wasn't Important Enough

Overall, respondents said they chose not to attempt to resolve the problem, thinking that it was unimportant in about 5.7% of all problems. The type of problem that respondents were most likely to feel was not important enough to attempt a resolution were problems related to police action. Respondents took no action because the problem was not important enough in 11.7% of all police action problems. This was followed by problems related to discrimination, in which respondents said that 9.9% of problems of this type were not important enough to attempt to find a solution. The percentage of respondents for whom the problem was not important enough to attempt a solution was above the average of 5.7% for three other problem types. These were employment problems, 7.4%, consumer problems, 6.8% and problems related to hospital treatment and release, 5.8%. In total, the five problems for which a greater than average percentage of respondents experiencing problems of that type, made up 71% of all problems falling into the "no action, not important enough" group. In all the other problem types a smaller than average percentage of respondents said the problem was not important enough.[7]

Young people aged 18–29 years and members of visible minority groups were the only two groups not likely to respond to problems, thinking that the problem was not important enough. The results of the binary logistic regression examining predictors of this response are presented in Table 4. The relationship between fairness and experiencing a problem is expressed as an odds ratio.[8] Notably, younger people are twice as likely as all others, with an odds ratio of 2.0, to take no action because of a perception that the problem is unimportant. Intuitively, an odds ratio of about 2.0, indicating that respondents in one category are twice as likely as all others to be in some other category, is substantively significant.

I Took No Action, But I Had a Reason

A second group of respondents took no action to resolve the problem, but failed to act because of a variety of perceived barriers. Table 5 shows the barriers to action reported by the respondents.

Table 4. Predictor Variables for Taking No Action: Not Important Enough.

Predictor Variable	Estimate	χ^2 and Probability	Odds Ratio (Confidence Interval of the OR)
Intercept	2.6	$\chi^2 = 76.2, p = <.0001$	
Age18–29	0.69	$\chi^2 = 7.4, p = .007$	2.0 (1.2–3.2)
Visible Minority	0.40	$\chi^2 = 7.5, p = .006$	1.5 (1.1–2.0)

Note: The reference category is all other problems.

Table 5. Barriers to Action.

Reasons for Not Taking Action	Number	Percent (%)
Thought nothing could be done	317	33.6
Was uncertain of my rights	99	10.5
Didn't know what to do	22	2.3
Thought it would take too much time	94	10.0
Though it would damage relationships with the other side	83	8.8
Thought it would cost too much	60	6.4
Thought the other side was right	47	5.0
Was too afraid to take action	25	2.7
Thought it would be too stressful	49	5.2
Other reasons	146	15.5
Total	942	100.0

Note: This represents a count of problems for which respondents indicated barriers to action and not a count of individual respondents.

Taking all problem types into account, respondents took no action for one of the reasons in Table 5 in 16.5% of all problems on average. There were six problem types for which respondents took no action more than the average. The two problem types for which respondents most frequently took no action because of a perceived barrier were, first, discrimination and second, police action. The percentages of problems for which this response occurred are significantly greater than the average of 16.6; 39.6% for problems related to discrimination and 36.9% of problems related to police action. These are the same two problems for which respondents were most likely not to take action because the problem was not important enough. Respondents were more likely than the average not to take action for a reason in four other types of problems. In order of the magnitude of difference from the average, these were 19.3% of employment problems, 19.2% of debt problems, 18.6% of problems relating to hospital treatment and release, 17.8% of consumer problems, 17.1% of immigration problems and 16.7% of problems involving disability pensions. In total, eight problems for which a greater-than-average percentage of respondents experiencing problems of that type, made up 97% of all problems falling into the "no action, for a reason" group.

Four vulnerable groups were likely to fail to respond to problems because of some perceived or actual barrier to accessibility of assistance. These were immigrants, Aboriginal people, people with less than high school education and people with incomes of less than $25,000 (Table 6).

Table 6. Predictor Variables for Taking No Action: Barriers to Accessibility of Assistance.

Predictor Variable	Estimate	χ^2 and Probability	Odds Ratio (Confidence Interval of the OR)
Intercept	1.6	$\chi^2 = 72.9$, $p = <.0001$	
Immigrants	0.53	$\chi^2 = 29.2$, $p = <.0001$	1.7 (1.4–2.1)
Aboriginal	0.65	$\chi^2 = 16.6$, $p = <.0001$	1.9 (1.4–2.6)
Less than high school	0.60	$\chi^2 = 17.0$, $p = <.0001$	1.8 (1.3–2.4)
Less than $25,000 per year	0.27	$\chi^2 = 5.3$, $p = .02$	1.3 (1.0–1.7)

Note: The reference category is all other problems.

I Took Care of It On My Own

The most frequent response to problems was to attempt to deal with it on one's own. Self-help was the response to 44.0% of all problems. The percentage of respondents who chose the self-help option exceeded the average in four problem types. These were debt, 59.4%, consumer problems, 58.7%, problems related to social assistance, 55.1% and problems related to hospital treatment and release, 48.8%. Taken together, these four problems for which a greater-than-average percentage of respondents experiencing problems of that type, made up 71% of all problems falling into the "no action, for a reason" group.

Analysis of demographic variables related to being a self-helper suggests that middle age[9] and middle income[10] respondents were most likely to choose the self-help option. The relationships were statistically significant although very weak. These relationships were not statistically significant in the multivariate analysis.

Respondents in the self-help group were less likely to feel that the outcome of the problem was unfair, 39.5%, than fair, 58.7%. This contrasts with the two groups where respondents took no action in which respondents were more likely to perceive the outcomes to have been unfair. In addition, the self-helpers were relatively unlikely to have abandoned attempts to resolve their problems. Only 6.8% of the self-help group reported having abandoned attempts to resolve problems compared with the 13.2% and 15.3% who took "no action because it was not important" and took "no action for a reason" groups, respectively.

Respondents who indicated they had attempted to resolve the problem on their own were asked if, in retrospect, they thought the outcome of their problem would have been better if they had obtained some form of assistance. About 42% of the self-help group thought that assistance would have improved the outcome for them.[11] This was most pronounced for respondents with immigration problems. Respondents with immigration or refugee problems who attempted to help themselves indicated that assistance would have improved the outcome for 72.7% of all problems. Following closely were respondents with problems in the other family law category. Self-help respondents indicated that some assistance would have improved the outcome in 71.4% of all other family law problems. In descending order, respondents felt that, in retrospect, assistance would have resulted in a better outcome in 62.5% of problems involving disability benefits, 55.0% of personal injury problems, 54.5% of problems stemming from police action, 52.5% of employment problems, 48.1% of problems related to wills and powers of attorney, 47.8% of discrimination problems, 46.7% problems related to hospital treatment and release, 44.4% of social assistance problems, 42.3% of consumer problems, 41.4% of housing problems, 38.8% of relationship-breakdown problems and 36.8% of problems related to the threat of legal action.[12]

Overall 43.4% of the self-helpers said they felt, in retrospect, that some assistance would have improved the outcome of their justiciable problem. When asked what sort of assistance they thought would be most useful, 66.6% of all responses included "someone to explain the legal aspects of the problem and to help with forms, letters and documents". The second most frequent mention was a lawyer, 47.7%. A lay advocate to deal with the problem on behalf of the respondent was the least frequent response, 21.3%. Even though respondent's judgments about the best course of action cannot be regarded as authoritative, it seems that public legal information and minor assistance could play an important role in assisting people resolve justiciable problems.[13]

Non-Legal Assistance

Respondents sought non-legal assistance for 22.1% of the problems they had experienced. There were eight problem groups in which respondents were more likely to seek non-legal help than the average. The problem type for which respondents said they sought non-legal assistance was, somewhat surprisingly, personal injury, 42.2%. This was followed by employment, 35.8%, wills and managing the affairs of a relative unable to do so on his or her own, 35.7%, housing problems, 33.6%, disability pensions, 33.3%, other family law problems, 23.5%, problems related to social assistance benefits and hospital treatment and release, 24.5%. The seven problems for which a greater-than-average percentage of respondents experiencing problems of that type (the average of 22.1% that sought non-legal assistance) made up 70% of all problems falling into the "sought non-legal help" group.

It is surprising that respondents sought non-legal help for problems in several of the problem categories. For instance, it might be expected that people would be less likely than average to seek non-legal help and more likely to seek the advice of a lawyer for personal injury problems. Similarly, for problems related to wills and managing the affairs of infirm relatives, matters for which powers of attorney are required, one would not expect that people would be more likely than the average to seek non-legal assistance. This might reflect the reality that legal and non-legal aspects of problems are very much interrelated and that in some cases people did not think of the problem in legal terms. It could also reflect a lack of knowledge about what to do about a problem. Similarly, one would not expect this to be the case for family law problems.[14] However, in this case, the course of action in certain cases might depend on the stage of the problem. People might well seek out non-legal sources of advice in the early stages of attempting to resolve the problem. The survey did not collect sufficient detail about the sequence of different sources of advice and therefore this aspect cannot be explored further.

The groups that were most likely to seek non-legal help were the disabled, middle age and middle-income people. The odds ratios indicate that the relationships are quite weak (Table 7).

Similar to the self-help group, the people seeking non-legal assistance were less likely to feel that the outcomes of problems were unfair, 37.8%, than fair, 60.0%. They were not very likely to abandon attempts to resolve problems, 6.6%.

Table 7. Predictor Variables for Seeking Non-Legal Assistance.

Predictor Variable	Estimate	χ^2 and Probability	Odds Ratio (Confidence Interval of the OR)
Intercept	1.5	$\chi^2 = 66.7, p = <.0001$	
Disabled	0.41	$\chi^2 = 21.8, p = <.0001$	1.5 (1.3–1.7)
Age 45–64	0.40	$\chi^2 = 7.2, p = .007$	1.5 (1.1–1.9)
Income $45,000 to $64,000	0.18	$\chi^2 = 3.7, p = .05$	1.2 (1.0–1.4)

Note: The reference category is all other problems.

The non-legal assistance group sought information, advice and assistance from a variety of sources. Labour unions and government offices were the most frequent sources, followed closely by friends and relatives (Table 8). The Internet and print material were reported rather infrequently. Whether people who approached government offices and unions actually received printed or human contact assistance is unknown. However, these results may mean that people have a strong inclination to seek assistance from familiar sources or sources offering face-to-face contact.

The people who sought non-legal advice were, overall, highly satisfied with the assistance they received. Satisfaction was measured on a four-point scale ranging from "very satisfied" to "not satisfied at all". Combining all problems, respondents were very or somewhat satisfied with the non-legal assistance received for 89.9% of all problems. Table 9 shows the percentage of respondents reporting they were satisfied with the assistance received, combining the very or somewhat satisfied responses, and those who were to some degree dissatisfied.

Table 8. Sources of Non-Legal Assistance.

Source of Assistance	Number	Percent (%)
Unions	317	20.0
Government offices	241	18.3
Friends and relatives	216	13.7
Other organizations	83	5.3
Police	63	4.0
Support groups	30	1.9
Internet	9	0.5
Libraries/books	3	0.2
Other sources	616	36.1
Total	1,578	100.0

Table 9. Satisfaction with Assistance.

Type of Assistance	Satisfied	Not Satisfied
Non-legal assistance	89.9% (152)	10.1% (17)
Legal assistance	76.6% (49)	23.4% (15)

Note: $\chi^2 = 19.6$, $p = .001$. Total for non-legal assistance = 169, legal assistance = 64.

Sought Legal Assistance

Respondents sought legal advice for 11.7% of all problems. It is not unexpected that respondents were far more likely than the average to seek legal advice for family law: relationship breakdown problems. People took this form of action for 48.8% problems related to relationship breakdown. Respondents sought legal advice for 47.1% of other family law problems. Respondents reported that they sought legal advice in 35.3% of problems in which they were served with a summons or received a threatening letter from a lawyer representing another party. The 35% figure seems low in this type of circumstance. Legal advice was the response by respondents in 21.2% of problems relating to wills and powers of attorney, 20.4% of problems resulting from police action, 16.8% of housing problems, 16.7% of problems relating to disability pensions and in 15.5% of personal injury problems and, finally, in 14.3% of problems relating to immigration and refugee matters. The nine problems for which a greater than average percentage of respondents experiencing problems of that type made up 50% of all problems falling into the sought legal help group. The lower percentage of problems for which respondents sought legal assistance more often than the average compared with other response groups is explained by the fact that people tend not to seek legal advice for the most frequently occurring problem types: consumer, debt and employment problems.

As a group, the disabled were statistically more likely to seek legal assistance. Problems with disability pensions were one of the problem types from which respondents are more likely than average to seek legal assistance. Second, people receiving social assistance were likely to seek legal assistance. However, social assistance is not a problem-type for which people were likely to seek out legal help. It is possible that people on social assistance are more likely than others to use legal assistance because they are eligible for legal aid. Finally, respondents with small families, no children or one child, were likely to seek legal assistance. Although there are variations by problem type, combining all problems, higher income is not, as one might have expected, related to the use of legal assistance (Table 10).

Interestingly, people who chose legal assistance as a response to problems were less likely to feel that the outcome of problems was unfair, 41.6%, compared with 56.2% who felt that the outcome was fair. Table 11 presents the data on perceived fairness of outcomes for all response groups.

As well, referring back to Table 9, a higher percentage of respondents who received legal assistance were not satisfied with the assistance they had received, compared with people who received non-legal assistance.

Table 10. Predictor Variables for Seeking Legal Assistance.

Predictor Variable	Estimate	χ^2 and Probability	Odds Ratio (Confidence Interval of the OR)
Intercept	2.3	$\chi^2 = 95.3$, $p = <.0001$	
Disabled	0.24	$\chi^2 = 4.7$, $p = .03$	1.3 (1.1–1.6)
Receiving social assistance	0.21	$\chi^2 = 3.4$, $p = .05$	1.2 (1.0–1.5)
No children or one child	0.27	$\chi^2 = 5.1$, $p = .02$	1.3 (1.0–1.6)

Note: The reference category is all other problems.

Table 11. Responses to Problems and the Unfairness of Outcomes for All Response Groups.

Outcome	Problem Responses				
	Took no action not important (%)	Took no action reason (%)	Handled it on my own (%)	Non-legal assistance (%)	Legal assistance (%)
Fair	39.5	31.8	58.6	60.0	56.2
Unfair	55.6	64.4	39.5	37.8	41.6
Not sure	4.9	3.8	1.9	2.2	2.2

Note: $\chi^2 = 159.9$, $p = <.0001$.

This is consistent with the results of a study carried out by the Canadian Forum on Civil Justice that found that some respondents felt that their situation had become worse after a lawyer had become involved in the case (Stratton & Anderson, 2006).[15] This effect may be explained by the fact that the legal process can be lengthy with people experiencing a further loss of control and some exacerbation of the collateral damage to their lives.

Although some respondents indicated they did not take action because they felt the problem was unimportant, a much higher percentage of respondents in this problem-response group felt that the outcome of problems that had been resolved were unfair, 55.6%, rather than fair, 39.5%. Compared with respondents who took some action to resolve the problem, a higher percentage felt that the outcome was unfair. Overall, 53.9% of all problems had been resolved at the time of the interview and, on average, for 44.3% of these, respondents perceived the outcome to be unfair. It is interesting that the percentage of resolved problems for which respondents felt the outcome to be unfair was larger for the "did nothing, not important enough" response group is higher than the average. This may be taken as some indication that the problem was not entirely unimportant after all.[16]

MULTIPLE PROBLEMS

Problems frequently do not occur in isolation. A significant percentage of respondents had experienced multiple problems within the three-year period. Table 12 shows the percentage of respondents with multiple problems.

In addition, the risk of experiencing justiciable problems appears to be cumulative. That is, the risk of additional problems increases as the number of problems already experienced increases. Table 13 shows the proportions likely to experience additional problems given that a certain number have

Table 12. Respondents Experiencing Multiple Problems.

Individuals Reporting One or More and Higher Order Numbers of Problems		Individuals Reporting Specific Numbers of Problems	
No problems	55.4% (3,964)	No problems	55.4% (3,964)
One or more	44.6% (2,971)	One problem	18.3% (1,215)
Two or more	26.4% (1,756)	Two problems	8.8% (581)
Three or more	17.6% (1,175)	Three problems	5.7% (378)
Four or more	12.0% (797)	Four problems	3.4% (236)
Five or more	8.4% (561)	Five problems	2.4% (161)
Six or more	6.0% (400)	Six problems or more	6.0% (400)

Table 13. Cumulative Risk of Experiencing Justiciable Problems.

Number of Problems Already Experienced	Probability of Experiencing Additional Problem
One	Two problems .323
Two	Three problems .394
Three	Four problems .384
Four	Five problems .406
Five	Six problems .410
Six	Seven problems .417
Seven	Eight problems .385
Eight	Nine problems .434
Nine	Ten problems .400

already occurred. The proportion of respondents who experienced one problem who then had a second problem is 0.323.[17] Since a simple proportion can be interpreted as risk, we can say that the risk of experiencing a second problem, having already experienced one problem is 0.323.

The progression is not perfectly linear. However, the probability of experiencing three problems if the individual already has two increases to 0.394 compared with the probability of 0.323 of having a second problem for respondents who have already experienced one problem. After three problems the risk of each additional problem varies but, with a few exceptions, remains higher than the risk of moving from one problem to two. This provides some evidence that experiencing civil justice problems may have a momentum. Problems tend to generate more problems, suggesting the trigger and cascade effect that is the core dynamic of the process of social exclusion.

The term social exclusion describes more than a condition in which people experience a cluster of interrelated problems. According to Giddens (1998), social exclusion may also be viewed as a process by which people fall away from the social mainstream, from lives of self-sufficiency into lives of dependency.[18] If this is the case, then problems related to debt, social assistance, disability pensions and housing should tend to occur more frequently as the overall number of justiciable problems increases. This appears to be true. Whereas 20.4% of all respondents indicated they had experienced at least one debt problem of some type, 62.7% of respondents with at least three problems and 78.5% of all respondents who reported six or more problems reported a debt problem. Debt appears to be an overwhelming problem for respondents with multiple problems. However, Fig. 2 shows the same pattern for other problems types related to social exclusion such as welfare benefits, disability pensions and housing. One or more housing problems, for example, was reported by 1.7% of the total sample. About 8.1% of respondents who had three or more problems and 15% of respondents with six or more problems had a housing problem.

The pattern of the increasing frequency of experiencing problems with social assistance and disability pensions with multiple problems is the same. Among all respondents 1.2% reported one or more social assistance problems. This increases to 4.9% of respondents among those reporting at least three problems and to 10.3% of respondents who experienced six or more problems. In a similar pattern, 1.0% of all respondents reported at least one problem with disability pensions. This increases to 4.6% and 8.5%, respectively, for respondents with three or more and six or more problems (Table 14).

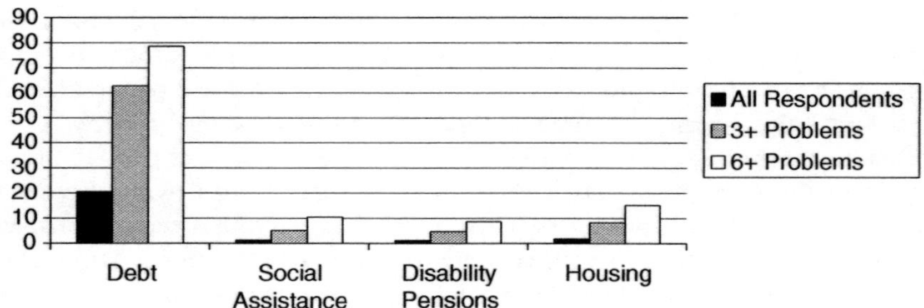

*The "n" values are as follows. Debt: all respondents with 1+ problems=1356, respondents with 3+ problems=737, respondents with 6+ problems=314. Social Assistance: all respondents with 1+ problems=78, respondents with 3+ problems=58, respondents with 6+ problems=41. Disability Pensions: all respondents with 1+ problems=66, respondents with 3+ problems=54, respondents with 6+ problems=34. Housing: all respondents with 1+ problems=116, respondents with 3+ problems=95, respondents with 6+ problems=60.

Fig. 2. Multiple Problems and Problems Related to Social Exclusion.

Table 14. Problems Related to Social Exclusion: Patterns of Increase.

Number of Problems	Debt		Social Assistance		Disability Pensions		Housing	
	%	% increase	%	% increase	%	% increase	%	% increase
At least one	20.4	–	3.5		2.6	–	5.4	–
Three or more	62.7	200	4.9	40	4.6	77	8.1	50
Six or more	78.5	25	10.3	110	8.5	85	15.0	85

It is also true that respondents report that the situation surrounding unresolved problems has become worse as they experience increasing numbers of problems. Fig. 3 shows the percentage of unresolved problems for which respondents said that the situation surrounding an unresolved problem has become worse according to the number of problems experienced. Whereas 9.9% of people with one unresolved problem said the situation had become worse, 17.2% of respondents with seven or more problems indicated that the situation had become worse likewise.

Problem Clusters

Previous research has focused on the clustering of justiciable problems. Not only do problems tend not to occur in isolation, in fact, they tend to occur

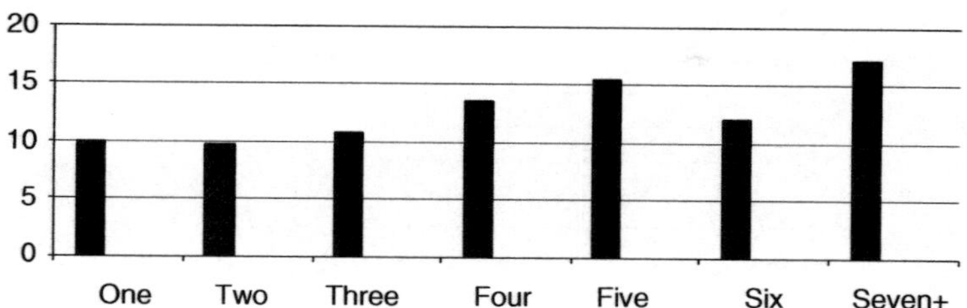

*The "n" values for the number of problems are: 1 = 39, 2 = 41, 3 = 48, 4 = 33, 5 = 27, 6 = 18 and 7+ = 66.

Fig. 3. Percent of Problems for Which Respondents Indicated That Situations with Unresolved Problems Had Become Worse.

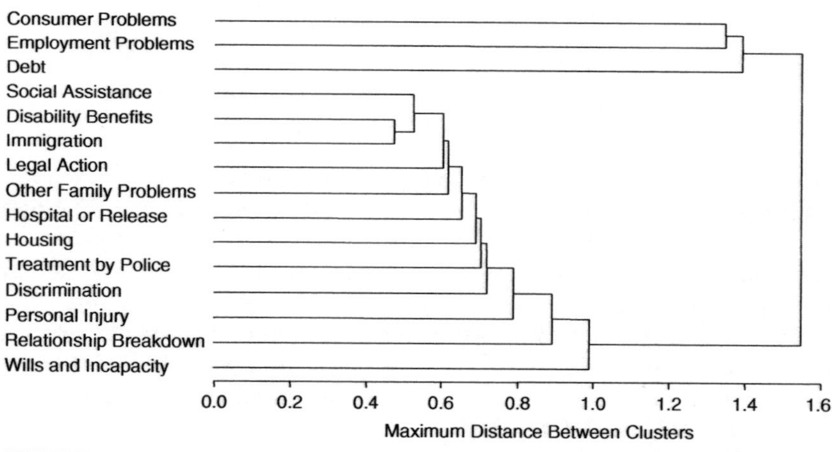

N = 1434

Fig. 4. Dendrogram for Cluster Analysis Three or More Problems.

according to distinct patterns. Analyses of data collected in 2001 and 2004 by Pleasence has identified a number of problem clusters, connecting family law problems and domestic violence, homelessness and police action and an economic cluster linking consumer, debt and several other problem types (Pleasence, Balmer, & Buck, 2006).[19] A standard cluster analysis was performed on the data (Romesburg, 1984).[20] The tree diagrams shown in Figs. 4 and 5 present the results of the cluster analysis.

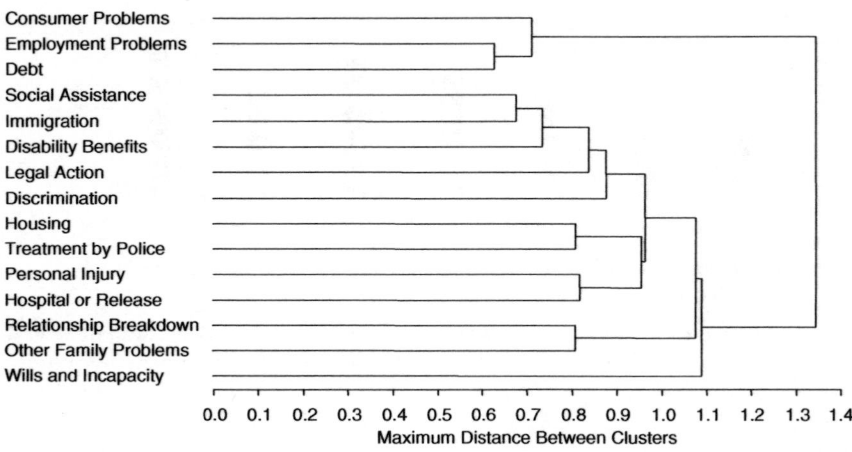

Fig. 5. Dendrogram for Cluster Analysis Five or More Problems.

The cluster analysis including all multiple problems (two or more problems) does not distinguish a very clear pattern of clustering. The only clear pattern of clustering links consumer, employment and debt problems. Consumer and employment problems are most closely linked. These two are linked in a cluster of three problem types with debt problems. Immigration problems are linked with disability benefits problems. In turn, this pair is linked with problems related to social assistance. Otherwise the tree diagram seems to grow progressively as the remaining problem types are added, showing little evidence of clustering.[21]

Fig. 5 shows the results of a similar cluster analysis carried out using respondents reporting five or more problems. Clusters appear much more distinctly for this high order multiple-problem group.[22] The same cluster of debt, employment and consumer problems appear clearly. Again, immigration, disability pensions and social assistance problems appear as a cluster. However, for the multiple-problem groups, the threat of legal action appears as part of the cluster. This could be linked either to appeals related to aspects of the refugee or immigration process, or to problems related to obtaining social services and disability pensions. Problems related to housing and those stemming from police action are linked in the tree diagram showing the results of the cluster analysis of multiple-problem respondents. The exact nature of the linkage is unclear. It is possible this represents a set of general background circumstances in which the people most likely to report housing problems live in lower socio-economic status neighbourhoods and are more likely to come into contact with the police.

Personal injury problems and problems related to hospital treatment and release are clearly related. These are linked to the housing and police action problems and, in turn, to the cluster containing social assistance and disability benefits problems. Finally, relationship-breakdown problems and other family law problems form a primary link for multiple problem respondents. These two problem types are connected more generally with other types of problems. Finally, problems related to wills and powers of attorney appear to stand apart from the others.

This shows clearly that the clustering of justiciable problems becomes more pronounced for people experiencing multiple problems, especially higher order multiple problems. This draws attention to the process of social exclusion, a process by which people may experience multiple, linked problems that follow on from one another forming "Gordian knots" of disadvantage. Problems are all the more difficult to solve because of the mutually reinforcing nature of the individual problems in the cluster. The fact that clustering appears more clearly with multiple-problem respondents provides further evidence of social exclusion.

Trigger Problems

The standard cluster analysis displayed earlier links problems using statistical methods. The causal connections among the problem types making up clusters are inferred theoretically. Pleasence et al. point out

> [p]roblem types do not have to cause or follow on from one another in order for a connection between them. Connections can also stem from coinciding characteristics of vulnerability to problem types, or coinciding defining circumstances of problem types. (Pleasence et al., 2006)[23]

However, the extent to which problems are connected is important because of the possibility that one problem can trigger another, and in turn, at least in some cases potentially set off the cascade effect of multiple problems that produces social exclusion. Respondents with at least two problems were asked if they felt that one of the problems had been a trigger for the other(s).[24] In 29.2% of the problems reported, respondents felt that one problem had been a trigger for subsequent problems.[25] In other words, there had been a causal relationship between the problems. Table 15 shows the frequency with which

Table 15. Percentage of Problems Identified as Trigger Problems by Problem Type.

Problem Type	Percentage of Problems
Relationship breakdown	56.9 (70)
Employment	48.3 (141)
Police action	36.4 (16)
Personal injury	35.6 (21)
Discrimination	30.8 (16)
Wills and powers of attorney	30.7 (27)
Consumer	28.5 (67)
Debt	23.0 (63)
Housing	21.4 (9)
Social assistance	21.2 (7)
Other family law problems	19.6 (9)
Threat of legal action	17.4 (4)
Disability pensions	17.1 (6)
Hospital treatment and release	13.9 (5)

the various problems within the 15 categories were reported as triggers for other problems. Relationship-breakdown problems were the most frequently mentioned trigger problems, followed by employment problems. Surprisingly, perhaps, debt problems rank eighth as trigger problems. This might be because the majority of debt problems involved relatively small amounts of money and although not trivial in the minds of respondents were unlikely to have consequences in other areas of life.

The patterns of trigger and consequence problems within and between problem categories are complex. Fig. 6 presents a visual representation of the major trigger and consequence patterns. The diagram is based on links with a frequency of five or more in order to make the visual presentation reasonably simple. The arrows turning back on the boxes represent problem categories representing trigger and consequence linkages involving specific problems within problem categories. The arrows between the boxes represent triggers and consequences between problem types. The arrows indicate the direction of the trigger–consequence links. The numbers besides the arrows represent the number of times a problem of that type was reported to be a trigger problem. In order to keep the diagram reasonably simple, only linkages with counts of five or more are included.

Problems in 10 of the 15 problem types produced trigger effects within and between problem categories. Problems related to social assistance, disability pensions, immigration, hospital treatment and release and housing

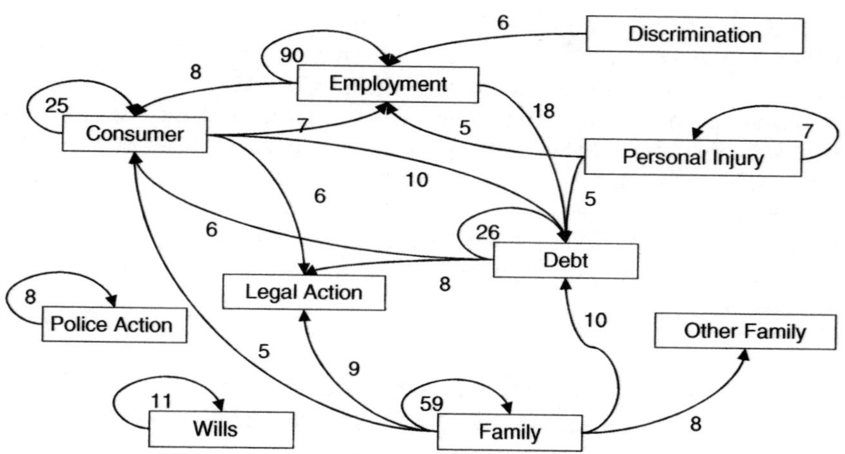

Fig. 6. Trigger Effects among Problem Types.

were not triggers for other problems in this sample. The largest number of trigger effects occurred within problem types, with 227 incidents reported across all categories. Employment problems had the greatest number of trigger effects, a total of 90. Other problem types that were triggers within the same problem categories were: family: relationship breakdown (59), consumer (25), debt (26), wills and powers of attorney (11), police action (8) and personal injury (7).

Respondents reported about half as many triggering events between problem categories as within problem categories, 150 in all. Debt problems as triggers for consumer problems was the most frequently reported causal connection: debt →consumer (6). This was followed by trigger and consequence linkages between employment→debt (18), relationship-breakdown→ debt (10), relationship-breakdown→legal action (9), relationship-breakdown→other family (8), employment→consumer (8), debt→legal action (8), discrimination→employment (6), personal injury→employment (8), consumer→employment (5), consumer→legal action (6), relationship-breakdown→consumer (5) and personal injury→debt (5).

Problems related to police action and those involving wills and powers of attorney were self-contained, with no linkages to other problem types. Other family problems were related only to relationship-breakdown problems. Discrimination problems were related only to employment problems. The threat of legal action was a consequence of three problems, family: relationship-breakdown, debt and consumer but has no triggering effect.

Problem Clusters Based on Trigger Problems

Although the standard cluster analysis did not produce clearly defined problem clusters, it is possible, having identified problem triggers, to revisit problem clustering around trigger problems. Approaching the data this way, there were five identifiable clusters. The largest cluster of problem types was triggered by family law: relationship-breakdown. Debt, threat of legal action, other family law problems and consumer clustered around relationship-breakdown. Another cluster was triggered by consumer problems, legal action and debt. Another, triggered by personal injury involves employment and debt problems.

NOT IN LEGAL SILOS, SOCIETAL IMPACTS OF JUSTICIABLE PROBLEMS

Because life is more seamless than compartmentalized, justiciable problems occur in clusters, not only with types of justiciable problems, but also with types of problems that do not have clearly legal aspects. Other research suggests there are many connections between justiciable and other kinds of problems.[26]

For a large percentage of respondents, experiencing a justiciable problem adversely affected their general quality of life. As noted earlier in the discussion about the robustness of the threshold language for discerning serious problems, respondents were asked whether the problem(s) had made their daily lives difficult. Almost 60% indicated that this was a consequence of having experienced justiciable problems. About 11% said that the problems made day-to-day life extremely difficult, 14.7% said that their lives had been made very difficult and 33.2% reported day-to-day life was somewhat more difficult as a result of the justiciable problem.

In addition to adverse effects on the overall quality of life, respondents were asked if the justiciable problems they experienced had contributed to or caused adverse effects in several areas of life. These were consequences: for physical and mental health, for patterns of alcohol or drugs use, for the occurrence of violence in family and other areas of personal life and for feelings of personal safety and security. Overall, 38.1% of all respondents with one or more problems reported having a health or social problem that they attributed directly to a justiciable problem (Fig. 7).

Extreme stress or emotional problems were the most frequently cited impact of experiencing justiciable problems, with 36.6% indicating that they had experienced a problem of this nature. This was followed by physical

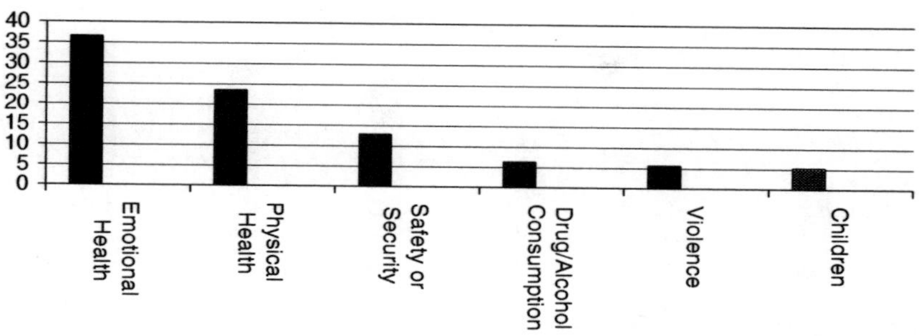

*Values of "n" are: Emotional health = 1037, physical health = 731, safety and security = 401, drug or alcohol consumption = 198, violence or threat of violence = 167, problems with children = 176.

Fig. 7. The Health and Social Impacts of Justiciable Problems, Percent of Respondents with Health and Social Problems Triggered by Justiciable Problems.

health problems, 23.5%, feelings of threats to one's security and safety, 12.9%, increased consumption of alcohol or drugs, 6.4%, threatened or actual violence, 5.7% and finally, problems with children, 5.3%.

Problem types: The percentage of respondents reporting a health or social problem related to a justiciable problem was considerably higher than the average for particular problem types. For example, respondents experiencing a problem in the other family law category reported that they experienced a health or social problem in 81.7% of all cases. Respondents experiencing problems in the relationship-breakdown category indicated that they had a health or social problem that could be related directly to the justiciable problem in 69.0% of all problems. Respondents reported a health or social problem related to 63.1% of all problems related to discrimination. Respondents reported a health or social problem in 37.8% of all consumer problems and in 43.0% of all problems related to debt.

HEALTH AND SOCIAL PROBLEMS AND THE NUMBER OF JUSTICIABLE PROBLEMS EXPERIENCED

Health and social problems that can be directly attributed to justiciable problems are closely related to the number of problems experienced.

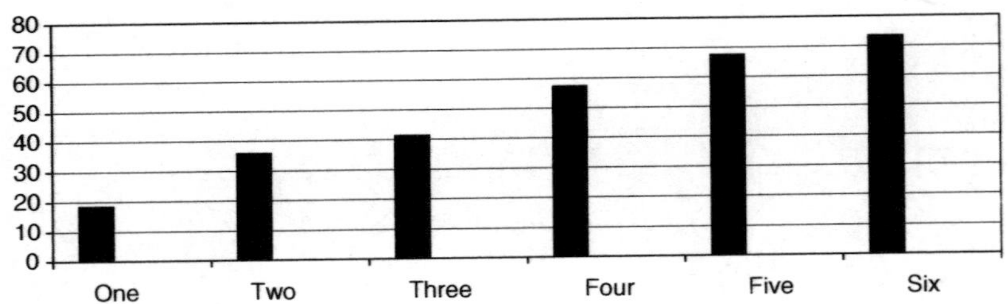

*values of "n" are: respondents with one problem triggering a health or social problem = 227, two = 209, three = 157, four = 136, five = 109, six = 295.

Fig. 8. Percent of Respondents Reporting a Health or Social Problem by Number of Justiciable Problems.

Fig. 8 shows the percentage of respondents reporting a health or social problem according to the number of justiciable problems they reported during the three-year period. Clearly, the likelihood of healthcare or social problem impacts of justiciable problems was very sensitive to the number of justiciable problems experienced.[27]

This suggests that social exclusion, viewed as an interlocking complex of justiciable and non-legal problems, was related to the increasing number of justiciable problems experienced.

VULNERABLE GROUPS AND THE EXPERIENCE OF HEALTH AND SOCIAL CONSEQUENCES

Respondents self-reporting as being disabled were 3.3 times more likely than the non-disabled to report all types of health and social problems combined as a consequence of justiciable problems.[28] It was assumed that the disability existed prior to the justiciable problem. Thus the link between justiciable problems and health and social consequences was assumed to represent a generalized high degree of vulnerability of the disabled to a range of consequences related to experiencing justiciable problems. As well, the unemployed,[29] people on social assistance[30] and people with incomes below $25,000 per year[31] were less than twice as likely as others to report health and social consequences. Several other groups also showed weaker tendencies to report health and social consequences of their justiciable problems. Respondents with three or more children were 1.4 times more likely than all respondents with children to experience consequences

Table 16. Predictors of Health and Social Consequences of Justiciable Problems.

Health and Social Consequences Combined	Estimate	χ^2	Probability	Odds Ratio (Confidence Interval of the OR)
Intercept	−1.8	71.1	.0001	–
Disabled	1.1	92.4	.0001	3.1 (2.1–5.0)
Social assistance	0.3	7.2	.007	1.3 (1.0–1.6)
45–64 years of age	0.1	10.2	.001	1.7 (1.3–2.1)
Unemployed	0.6	10.8	.001	1.8 (1.3–2.2)
Three or more children	0.5	10.5	.001	1.6 (1.2–2.1)

R^2 for the Regression Equation = .15

overall.[32] Members of visible minority groups[33] and people aged 45–64 years [34] were also slightly more likely than other respondents to experience health or social consequences of justiciable problems.

Binary logistic regression showed that being disabled, on social assistance, unemployed, having three or more children and being middle aged (45–64 years) – all have a statistically significant independent effect on experiencing health or social problems as a consequence of justiciable problems. The predictive power of the variables is relatively weak with the exception of disability (Table 16).

PERCEPTIONS OF THE FAIRNESS OF THE LAWS AND THE JUSTICE SYSTEM

Merely experiencing a justiciable problem was associated with an unfavourable attitude toward the law and the justice system regardless of subsequent negative or positive experiences in dealing with the problem. This was true even though the vast majority of people have no contact whatever with the formal justice system in the course of dealing with their problems. Respondents were asked to respond to the statement; "You feel that the laws and the justice system in Canadian society are essentially fair".[35] Overall, 67.8% of the public felt that the laws and the justice system were essentially fair. This increased to 71% for people reporting no justiciable problems, but was only 62.5% for people reporting one or more problems (Table 17).

Table 17. The Perceived Fairness of the Canadian Laws and Justice System.

Laws and the Justice System are Fair	No Problems		One or More Problems		Total	
	%	Partial cumulative %	%	Partial cumulative %	%	Partial cumulative %
Strongly agree	26.0	–	21.0	–	23.8	–
Somewhat agree	45.0	71.0	41.5	62.5	44.0	67.8
Somewhat disagree	15.0	–	18.5	–	16.6	–
Strongly disagree	8.3	23.3	16.5	35.0	12.0	28.6
Neither agree nor disagree + no answer	5.7		2.5		3.6	
Total	100 ($n = 3{,}694$)		100 ($n = 2{,}971$)		100 ($n = 6{,}665$)	

Note: $\chi^2 = 154.5$, $p < .0001$.

Remarkably, experiencing one or more problems in 13 of the 15 problem categories was also associated with a perception that the laws and the justice system were unfair. Table 18 shows the perceived fairness and unfairness of the justice system in relation to experiencing problems of distinct problem types. For this part of the analysis the fairness variable was transformed into a binary or two-category variable and run against the binary variable experienced no problems vs. experienced one or more problems in the category.

Respondents having problems related to police action were 3.7 times more likely than other respondents to feel that the laws and the justice system were unfair. On the lower end of the spectrum, respondents who experienced a consumer problem are only 1.6 times more likely to feel that the laws and the justice system are unfair.

Overall, combining all problem types, if the problem was resolved but the outcome was perceived to be unfair respondents were less likely to view the laws and the justice system as fair in comparison to those who felt that the resolution of their problem to have been fair. Table 19 shows that 66.9% of respondents who felt the outcome of their problem was fair also felt that the laws and the justice system are fair. The percentage feeling that the laws and justice system are fair declined to 57.9% for respondents who felt that the outcome of their problem or dispute was not fair.

As one might expect, being dissatisfied with the assistance received was also related to perceived fairness of the justice system. For this summary

Table 18. The Perceived Fairness of the Justice Laws and the Justice System and the Experience of Problem Types.

Problem Type	Odds Ratio (Confidence Limit of the Odds Ratio)	χ^2 and Level of Statistical Significance
Consumer	1.6 (1.4–1.8)	$\chi^2 = 50.1$, $p = <.0001$
Debt	1.7 (1.5–1.9)	$\chi^2 = 65.1$, $p = <.0001$
Wills and powers of attorney	1.7 (1.4–2.1)	$\chi^2 = 22.5$, $p = <.0001$
Employment	1.8 (1.6–2.1)	$\chi^2 = 80.6$, $p = <.0001$
Disability pensions	1.9 (1.1–3.1)	$\chi^2 = 6.2$, $p = .01$
Housing	1.9 (1.2–2.7)	$\chi^2 = 10.5$, $p = .001$
Discrimination	1.9 (1.3–2.7)	$\chi^2 = 12.3$, $p = <.0001$
Family law: Relationship breakdown	1.9 (1.5–2.6)	$\chi^2 = 23.2$, $p = <.0001$
Social assistance	2.1 (1.3–3.3)	$\chi^2 = 10.6$, $p = .001$
Hospital treatment and conditions of release	2.5 (1.7–3.9)	$\chi^2 = 23.5$, $p = <.0001$
Personal injury	2.5 (1.9–3.3)	$\chi^2 = 40.2$, $p = <.0001$
Threat of legal action	3.2 (2.1–5.0)	$\chi^2 = 30.6$, $p = <.0001$
Police action	3.7 (2.6–5.3)	$\chi^2 = 60.7$, $p = <.0001$
Other family law	Not statistically significant	
Immigration	Not statistically significant	

Notes: The odds ratio indicates the number of times more likely respondents will say experiencing one or more problems in a particular category will feel the laws and the justice system are unfair compared with all other respondents. The analysis was carried out on subset of 3,457 cases with the following "*n*'s" for each problem category; consumer = 1,022, employment = 914, debt = 896, social assistance = 22, disability pensions = 16, housing = 59, immigration = 14, discrimination = 42, police action = 72, relationship breakdown = 117, other family law problems = 33, wills and powers of attorney = 180, personal injury = 77, hospital treatment or release = 54 and threat of legal action = 26.

Table 19. Perceived Fairness of Resolved Problems and Perception of the Fairness of the Laws and the Justice System.

Perception of the Laws and the Justice System	Perceived Fairness of the Outcome of Problems That Had Been Resolved		
	Fair	Not fair	Not certain
Fair	66.9% (1,271)	57.9% (914)	% (44)
Unfair	31.2% (592)	39.5% (625)	% (39)
Not sure	1.9% (36)	2.6% (41)	% (4)
Total	100.0% (1,899)	100.0% (1,580)	100.0% (87)

Note: $\chi^2 = 39.1$, $p < .0001$.

analysis, the level of satisfaction with all 10 possible sources of assistance, scored with the same four-point scale as described earlier,[36] were summed to create an overall index ranging from 1 to 4, from very satisfied to very dissatisfied. Splitting this index into a binary variable, satisfied and not satisfied, it was run against the binary variable indicating whether respondents perceived the laws and the justice system to be fair or unfair. The outcome is shown in Table 20.

Finally, experiencing multiple problems is also associated with the perception that the justice system was unfair. Fig. 8 shows the percentage of respondents experiencing an increasing number of problems who perceived the laws and the justice system to be unfair (Fig. 9).

Fig. 8 shows a generally linear progression in which 24.5% of respondents reporting no problems felt that the laws and the justice system were unfair, increasing to 59.0% for respondents reporting seven or more problems.

The laws and the justice system have the symbolic power and value of all important social institutions, and embody the core values of society. Fairness is one of those values. Raymond Breton and his colleagues assert that "[F]airness is one of the yardsticks against which ... laws and

Table 20. Perceived Fairness of the Laws and Justice System and Satisfaction with Assistance.

Perception of the Laws and the Justice System	Satisfied with Assistance	Not Satisfied with Assistance
Fair	62.5% (122)	53.1% (17)
Unfair	37.5% (73)	46.9% (15)
Total	100.0% (195)	100.0% (32)

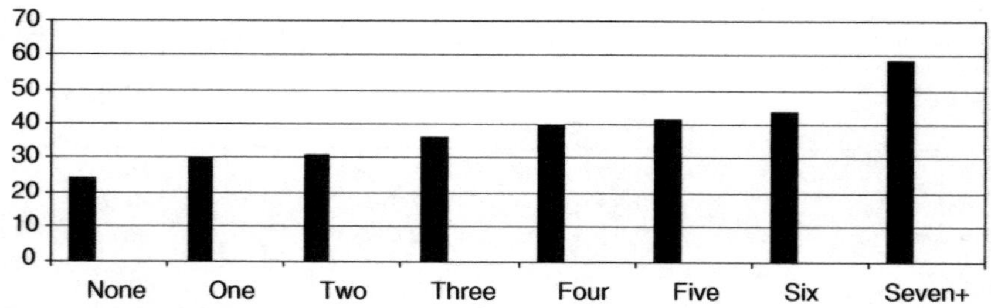

Fig. 9. Perceptions of Unfairness and Number of Problems.

regulations ... and the administration of justice ... are assessed. 'That's not fair!' is a definitive condemnation of the state of affairs in any domain of life."[37] Thus the laws and the justice system are a lightning rod for discontent that attract the negative attitudes of people who experience civil justice problems, even though they may never actually come into contact with the formal justice system. Because the justice system is a central social institution it is also one of the important dimensions along which people are integrated into the society.

CONCLUSION

The paradigm shift that took place in the 1970s and found its early expression in research in the 1994 Consortium on Legal Needs Research in the United States and in the 1997 Paths to Justice research in the United Kingdom focuses attention on a very broad framework for understanding the legal problems of the public. The results of the body of research that has grown in the wake of these two pioneering studies has documented that very large percentages of national and regional populations experience serious justiciable problems, and that problems are ubiquitous features of modern bureaucratic societies with extensive systems of civil law. It is frequently observed in the literature that justiciable problems are, from the point of view of the people who experience them, aspects of their everyday life. It might be easy, particularly from a conceptual vantage point outside the justiciable problems paradigm, to question why these "problems" should be viewed as deserving of attention, especially if that attention comes at a cost to the public purse, and not just as a sort of sociological truism, a natural consequence of societies characterized by extensive regimes of civil law.

This chapter provides some reasons why justiciable problems as they are documented in this and other research are worthy of attention. Justiciable problems are important because they can adversely affect the quality of modern life. They matter to the people who experience them. The vast majority of people who experience problems want to resolve them. For a smaller number of people, but still the majority, the justiciable problems they experience range from somewhat to extremely disruptive to their daily lives. Justiciable problems are experienced in the seamless mesh of people's day-to-day lives. Thus a number of health and social problems can develop as a consequence of experiencing justiciable problems.

Justiciable problems appear to be integral aspects of patterns of disadvantage, alternatively described as social exclusion. Experiencing justiciable problems has an additive effect or a momentum. People are increasingly likely to experience additional problems with each problem already experienced. Approximately one-fifth of the population represented by this study is likely to experience multiple problems. The larger the cluster of justiciable problems, the greater the likelihood of experiencing problems related to debt, housing, social services and disability benefits, problem types that may be among the signatures of social exclusion. The larger the number of problems experienced, the more likely that people will experience health and social problems that they attribute directly to the justiciable problems they have experienced and that are integral elements in the clusters of problems they experience.

People who experience justiciable problems were more likely to feel that the laws and the justice system are unfair. Fairness reflects a core value of justice as a social institution. The laws and the justice system seem clearly to be a lightning rod for discontent, even though the majority of people have had no contact with the justice system with respect to the problems they have experienced. The experience of justiciable problems may have implications for social cohesion, as well as for social exclusion. As a social institution, justice may be viewed as one of the institutions along which people are integrated into a society. The negative attitude toward the justice system, expressed as perceived unfairness, can be interpreted as a lack of social integration.

Of course, not everyone experiencing justiciable problems experiences adverse consequences. Most people appear to encounter a problem, deal with it and get on with life. However, this is not to say that even these people would not benefit from some level of assistance. A large percentage of the self-helpers in this study said, upon reflection, that some limited assistance would have improved the outcome of their problem.

It makes sense to look at need as a continuum, rather than as an "either/or" concept. A great deal or work remains before we can understand how the occurrence of one or two problems takes on the trigger and cascade effect characteristic of the process of social exclusion. With respect to the provision of assistance to help people resolve the justiciable problems they face, the results of this research suggest that a continuum of service approach that is characterized by early stage intervention and preventative approaches would be useful. A continuum of service approach can be easily visualized as a cone lying on its side, the full range of justiciable problems at the wide end and the problems that will be resolved by the formal aspects of the justice system at the narrow end. The continuum of service approach is one that provides the appropriate response to the problem at hand, through public legal education and information and advice to assist self-help, mediation and other forms of out-of-court dispute resolution, and legal representation – progressive forms of assistance as appropriate for the resolution of problems. The continuum of service approach requires citizen friendly, accessible places to seeks assistance – places that are the point of entry and the hub for referrals to a seamless network of access to justice services and to related social and healthcare services (Fig. 10).

This approach to research on justiciable problems views legal problems and concepts of justice and access to justice from the point of view of the people who experience them. This perspective locates access to justice in a broader policy framework than might be customary. Access to justice policy and services are linked to broader issues of public policy that reside outside the traditional justice domain. The provision of access to justice services can play a part not only in alleviating or preventing justiciable problems, but also a broader range of social and health problems. This is because experiencing justiciable problems is one aspect of a larger process by which social disadvantage is created, as justiciable problems trigger both other justiciable problems and a range of health and social problems. Access to justice services can therefore play an important role in building an inclusive society, diminishing social disadvantage, dependence and the related cost to

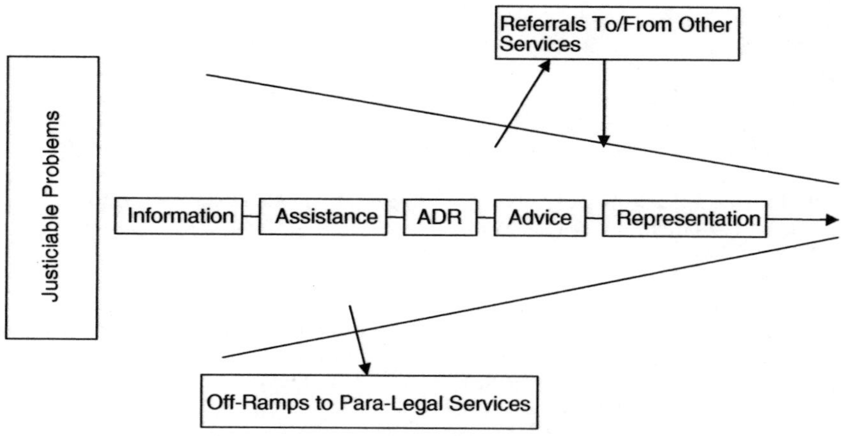

Fig. 10. A Continuum of Service Model of Access to Justice.

public services. Access to justice gives effect to full citizenship, assisting people without the means to do so themselves to resolve or avoid the problems that might limit their ability to enjoy the benefits that are the fundamental purposes of society.

NOTES

1. A three-year time period has advantages for data analysis because the larger numbers of problems and individuals allow for more robust statistical analysis.
2. This applies to survey research that can be generalized to large populations. Jon Johnsen suggests that action research studies using legally competent interviewers could more accurately assess the legal nature of problem situations. See Jon Johnsen, "Legal Needs Studied in a Market Context", in Francis Regan, Alan Paterson, Tamara Goriely, and Don Fleming, The Transformation of Legal Aid: Comparative and Historical Studies, Oxford University Press, Oxford, 1999. p. 216.
3. Pleasence et al., 2006, Appendix C, p. 290.
4. Questionnaire for the Causes of Action research, supra endnote 3; and Currie (2007).
5. See Currie (2007), Chapter 4 for a more detailed analysis.
6. Respondent's saying that the problem was not important enough to take action is certainly a contradiction with the threshold language of the questionnaire, "serious and difficult to resolve". These responses are used as a triviality screen and eliminated from the sample (See Genn, 1999, p. 13). However, respondents could incorrectly perceive a problem to be unimportant, only to discover later that it had serious unanticipated consequences. This is consistent with the paradigm assumption that people may not recognize the legal aspects of their problems. Thus, it seems reasonable to include these problems in all parts of the analysis.
7. The total "n" for this subgroup was 317. The χ^2 value for the source table was 1299.9, $p = <.0001$.
8. The odds ratio expresses the number of times more likely people experiencing one or more problems are to feel that the laws and the justice system are unfair.
9. Age 45–64, $\chi^2 = 6.4$, $p = .01$, Odds ratio = 1.2, Confidence interval of the odds ratio = (1.0 to 1.3).
10. Income \$45,000 to \$64,000, $\chi^2 = 7.6$, $p = .005$, Odds ratio = 1.3, Confidence interval of the odds ratio = (1.1 to 1.5).
11. $n = 2{,}442$.
12. Source table: $\chi^2 = 81.3$, $p = .0001$, $\phi = .18$.
13. $n = 1{,}051$.
14. This category includes becoming the guardian of a child, child apprehension by the state, getting independent legal representation for a child, actual or potential child abduction and child suspended from school unfairly.
15. See Stratton and Anderson (2006).
16. Supra endnote 33.

17. This is derived by dividing the number of respondents experiencing two problems (2) by the sum of respondents experiencing one problem (1) plus the number experiencing two problems (2), since those experiencing two problems have already experienced their first problem. Thus 2/(1+2) provides a true proportion. Similar calculations are made for calculating the risk of successive problems.
18. See Giddens (1998, p. 104).
19. Pascoe Pleasence et al., Causes of Action and Pascoe Pleasence, Causes of Action, 2nd Edition, pp. 65–72.
20. See Romesburg (1984).
21. This pattern resembles the chaining effect described in endnote 29, although the correction for chaining was used.
22. Cluster analysis was performed for respondents with two or more, three or more and four or more problems. Clear clustering patterns did not emerge for any but the group with five or more problems. Small numbers precluded cluster analysis on respondents with six or more problems.
23. Pleasence et al. (2006, p. 65).
24. The questionnaire did not attempt to identify time-ordered strings of problems or to ask respondents about causal chains of multiple problems. Experience from the 2004 survey was that asking year and month of the occurrence of problems to allow time ordering produced too much missing data at the month level. Thus the ability to create problem strings was limited. Therefore, in the 2006 survey respondents were asked to identify triggers. In this case, however, it was decided that asking respondents with higher order multiple problems about sequences was too complex and time-consuming for the telephone interview.
25. The specific wording of the questions was: "Do you feel that any of these problems are connected with one another? That is, one of them might have caused or contributed in some way to the other". Then: "If yes, which one of these problems would you say was the trigger problem?"
26. See Pleasence, Balmer, Buck, O'Grady, and Genn (2004) and Buck, Balmer, and Pleasence (2005).
27. One problem = 18.7% ($n = 227$), two problems = 36.0% ($n = 209$), three problems = 41.5% ($n = 157$), four problems = 57.6% ($n = 136$), five problems = 67.7% ($n = 109$), six problems = 61.6% ($n = 69$), seven or more problems = 78.5% ($n = 226$). $\chi^2 = 528.3$, $p = .0001$, $\phi = .42$.
28. $\chi^2 = 140.59$, $p < .0001$, confidence interval of the OR (2.7–4.0).
29. $\chi^2 = 18.5$, $p < .0001$, OR = 1.9, confidence interval of the OR (1.4–2.5).
30. $\chi^2 = 32.0$, $p < .0001$, OR = 1.7, confidence interval of the OR (1.4–2.0).
31. $\chi^2 = 32.0$, $p < .0001$, OR = 1.8, confidence interval of the OR (1.4–2.1).
32. $\chi^2 = 8.4$, $p < .004$, OR = 1.4, confidence interval of the OR (1.1–1.8).
33. $\chi^2 = 7.0$, $p < .0001$, OR = 1.3, confidence interval of the OR (1.1–1.5).
34. $\chi^2 = 13.3$, $p < .0001$, OR = 1.3, confidence interval of the OR (1.1–1.5).
35. Responses were recorded on a four-point scale ranging from strongly agree to strongly disagree with neither agree nor disagree accepted as a volunteered response.
36. Supra, endnote 54.
37. See Breton, Hartman, Lennards, & Reed (2004, p. 32).

REFERENCES

ABA Consortium on Legal Services and the Public. (1994a). Report of the legal needs of the low-income public, findings of the comprehensive legal needs study, Chicago, American Bar Association, Chicago.

ABA Consortium on Legal Services and the Public. (1994b). Report of the legal needs of the moderate- income public, findings of the comprehensive legal needs study, Chicago, American Bar Association, Chicago.

AuCoin, K., & Beauchamp, D. (2007). *Impacts and consequences of victimization, GSS 2004*. Juristat, Canadian Centre for Justice Statistics, Statistics Canada, Catalogue 85-002-XIE, Vol. 27, No. 1.

Breton, R., Hartman, N. J., Lennards, J. L., & Reed, P. (2004). *A fragile social fabric? Fairness, trust and commitment in Canada*. Montreal: McGill-Queen's University Press.

Buck, A., Balmer, N., & Pleasence, P. (2005). Social exclusion and civil law: Experience of civil justice problems among vulnerable groups. *Social Policy and Administration, 39*(3), 302–322.

Clark, E., & Corstvet, E. (1938). The lawyer and the public: An A.A.L.S. *Survey in Yale Law Review, 47*, 1972–1973.

Curran, B. (1977). *The legal needs of the public: The final report of a national survey*. Chicago: American Bar Association.

Currie, A. (2006). The civil justice problems experienced by low- and moderate-income Canadians: Incidence and patterns. *International Journal of the Legal Profession, 13*(3), 217–242.

Currie, A. (2007). *The Legal Problems of Everyday Life: Department of Justice: The Nature, Extent and Consequences of Justiciable Problems Experienced by Canadians*, Department of Justice, Ottawa.

Dignan, T. (2006). The Northern Ireland Legal needs survey. Paper presented at the Sixth International Legal Services Research Conference, Belfast.

Genn, H. (1999). *Paths to justice: What people do and think about going to law*. Oxford: Hart Publishing.

Genn, H., & Paterson, A. (2001). *Paths to justice Scotland: What people in Scotland do and think about going to law*. Oxford: Hart Publishing.

Giddens, A. (1998). *The third way*. Cambridge: Polity Press.

Legal Services Agency. (2006). Report on the 2006 National Survey of Unmet Legal Needs and Access to Services, Wellington, New Zealand.

Lewis, P. (1973). Unmet legal need. In: P. Morris, R. White & P. Lewis (Eds), *Social needs and legal action* (pp. 73–91). Oxford: Martin Robertson.

Merton, R. K. (1968). *Social theory and social structure (enlarged edition)*. New York: The Free Press.

Murayama, M., Minamikata, S., Hamano, R., Ageishi, K., Ozaki, I., & Sugino, I. (2005). Legal problems and their resolution: Disputing behaviour in Japan. Paper presented at the Annual Meeting of the Research Committee on the Sociology of Law, Paris.

Nader, L. (1980). *No access to law*. New York: Academic Press.

Pleasence, P., Balmer, N., & Buck, A. (2006). *Causes of action: Civil law and social justice* (2nd ed.). London: Legal Services Commission.

Pleasence, P., Balmer, N. J., Buck, A., O'Grady, A., & Genn, H. (2004). Civil law problems and morbidity. *Journal of Epidemiology and Community Health, 58*, 552–557.

Pleasence, P., Buck, A., Goriely, T., Taylor, J., Perkins, H., & Quirk, H. (2001). *Local legal need.* Research Paper 7, Legal Services Research Centre, London, pp. 8–11.

Romesburg, C. H. (1984). *Cluster analysis for researchers.* Belmont, CA: Lifetime Learning Publications.

Sandefur, R. L. (2007). The importance of doing nothing: Everyday problems and responses of doing nothing. In: P. Pleasence, A. Buck & N. Balmer (Eds), *Transforming lives: Law and social process* (pp. 112–132). London: Legal Services Commission.

Sato, O., Takahashi, H., Kanomata, N., & Kashimura, S. (2007). Citizen's access to legal advice in contemporary Japan: Lumpers, self-help seekers and third-party advice seekers. Paper presented at the Joint Annual Meeting of the Law and Society Association and the Research Committee on the Sociology of Law, Berlin.

Statistics Canada. (2006). *Canadian Crime Statistics.* Catalogue 85–205.

Stratton, M., & Anderson, T. (2006). *The social, economic and health consequences of a lack of access to the courts.* Ottawa: Department of Justice.

FAILURE TO RECALL: INDICATIONS FROM THE ENGLISH AND WELSH CIVIL AND SOCIAL JUSTICE SURVEY OF THE RELATIVE SEVERITY AND INCIDENCE OF CIVIL JUSTICE PROBLEMS

Pascoe Pleasence, Nigel J. Balmer and Tania Tam

ABSTRACT

Purpose – *Concerns about expenditure on legal aid in England and Wales have led to greater focus on 'value for money' and increased strategic targeting of resources. To inform targeting, the English and Welsh Civil and Social Justice Survey has been used to investigate the relative severity of different civil justice problem types. Thus, the survey has included a range of severity indices and related questions. However, this study takes a different approach in exploring how a seeming 'defect' of the survey, failure of autobiographical memory, may shed some of the clearest light on not just the issue of problem severity but also problem incidence.*

Access to Justice
Sociology of Crime, Law and Deviance, Volume 12, 43–65

ISSN: 1521-6136/doi:10.1108/S1521-6136(2009)0000012006

Methodology/approach – *We examine failures of autobiographical memory of civil justice problems and ask what they can tell us about problem severity.*

Findings – *We find that failures of autobiographical memory provide a useful guide to relative severity of civil justice problems of different types. They also provide a means to more accurately estimate the prevalence of problems.*

Originality/value of paper – *This paper is the first to examine the relative severity and incidence of civil justice problems through an analysis of recall patterns.*

INTRODUCTION

Although surveys form one of the principal investigatory tools of the social sciences, their utility can be limited by the accuracy of people's recall. However, although there has been much study of the factors affecting recall accuracy, findings have not been used to inform the narratives that flow from individual surveys. In this paper, we attempt such an application and demonstrate how recall failure can be used to explore the severity and incidence of civil justice problems.

The Policy Context

Recent years have seen unprecedented change in the delivery of legal aid services in England and Wales, following on from concerns about expenditure on legal aid that became prominent in the late-1980s (Legal Action Group, 1992). In keeping with what Glennerster, Hills, Travers, and Hendry (2000) have described as a 'third phase' of development of government social spending – characterised as a retreat from universality in welfare service provision flowing from an overwhelming of public resources – the change has involved various moves to 'target' spending on those most in need (Moorhead & Pleasence, 2003; Pleasence, Buck, Smith, Balmer, & Patel, 2004). As a consequence, the form and scope of legal aid means tests have been substantially reformed since the turn of the century (Buck & Stark, 2003; Lord Chancellor's Department, 2004). Also, predominantly in relation to civil legal aid, there has been increasing focus on both the types of problems that people actually face – as opposed to those that legal aid lawyers have focused on historically – and the types of people who are most vulnerable to experiencing them. The concept of 'legal need',[1] discussed in the 1989 government white paper *Legal Services: A Framework for the Future* (Lord Chancellor's Department, 1989), put at the heart of the 1995 white paper *Legal Aid: The Future of Publicly Funded Help in Solving Legal Problems and Disputes in England and Wales* (Lord Chancellor's Department, 1995) and enshrined in the Access to Justice Act 1999, has become central to the current legal aid reform programme. As real terms net civil legal aid expenditure has declined over the past decade (Department for Constitutional Affairs, 2005), the nature and philosophy of the civil legal aid scheme has therefore changed dramatically.

The policy focus on legal need within civil legal aid has manifested in a range of reforms. It has led, for example, to the introduction of a comprehensive 'Funding Code', setting out criteria for the grant of civil legal aid, aimed at directing resources to those cases with the greatest prospects of success and the greatest import (Pleasence, Buck, & Christie, 1999). It has also led to sustained efforts to expand provision of services in areas of 'social welfare' law, particularly through not-for-profit advice agencies, now a core component of the legal aid scheme (Lord Chancellor's Department, 1995).[2] It has led to a fundamental change in the way that civil legal aid services are procured, with the final stages of a journey from judicare to the procurement of cases in 'bundles that recognise the multiple nature of clients' problems' (Legal Services Commission, 2006, p. 7) now in train and, related to this, to the formal integration of legal services through Community Legal Advice Centres and Networks (Legal Services Commission, 2006). It has also led to a greater emphasis on taking services to those vulnerable, but 'difficult to reach', people who face physical, social and psychological barriers to accessing legal services (Buck, Tam, & Fisher, 2007; Pleasence, 2007).[3]

Although a substantial evidence base is emerging to inform much of the change that is taking place (e.g. Moorhead, Sherr, & Paterson, 2003; Pleasence, 2006), there are still some areas where that base is relatively under-developed. There is, for example, only limited understanding of the relative severity of different types of civil justice problem.

The Methodological Context

The English and Welsh Civil and Social Justice Survey (CSJS) has been used, on a number of occasions, to investigate the severity of civil justice problems. This has been in relation to both the relationship between problem severity and strategy – with more severe problems being linked strongly to a greater propensity for people to obtain advice (Pleasence, 2006) – and in relation to the relative severity of problem types. However, in the latter case, definitive conclusions have been difficult to extract.

Although the CSJS includes various indices of problem severity, respondents generally describe problems as severe, limiting the potential to differentiate between them. CSJS questions that explore the impact of problems on people's broad life circumstances have certainly helped to highlight the different ways that problems impact on people's lives (Pleasence, 2006; Pleasence, Balmer, Buck, Smith, & Patel, 2007),[4] but the impact of problems is clearly diffuse and causal pathways are not always apparent. Civil justice, as well as broader social, problems have also been observed to 'cluster' (Pleasence, Balmer, Buck, O'Grady, & Genn, 2004a; Moorhead, Robinson, & Matrix Research and Consultancy, 2006), further obscuring causal pathways and limiting ability to gauge relative severity. The cross-sectional nature of CSJS data, of course, acts as a structural limitation in this regard, as does the fact that surveys can be accurate only to the extent that respondents provide accurate answers to survey questions. Respondents to surveys must search their memory for responses that correspond to the questions asked (Mathiowetz, 2000), but the results of their searches may not always be reported accurately or result in events being recalled.

People may provide inaccurate answers to severity questions through, for example, concerns about the social desirability of answers, 'acquiescence' bias or lack of trust in confidentiality (e.g. Beatty, Herrmann, Puskar, & Kerwin, 1998; Weisberg, 2005). They may also fail to recall events and experiences relevant to questions, a problem that becomes greater the further back in time events and experiences have occurred (Sudman and Bradburn, 1973).

As a general rule, the further back in time an event has occurred, the less likely it becomes that a respondent will recall it. This poses a particular problem in the case of surveys of relatively rare events such as the CSJS; a problem that impacts on both the accuracy and the frequency of reports of civil justice problems.

However, it may be that this 'defect' of survey methodology, stemming from recall error, provides useful and otherwise unobtainable information about the nature of and relative severity of the problems studied through the CSJS.

As Tourangeau, Rips, and Rasinski (2000, p. 84) have illustrated clearly, memories of different types of things do not always exhibit similar 'forgetting curves' (i.e. patterns of recall error over time).[5] There seem to be several factors underlying this, but in general terms, as Tourangeau et al. have commented (p. 92),

> ... we are less likely to forget important events than unimportant ones; we are more likely to notice them in the first place and to discuss and think about them afterward. Thus, important events have the advantage of both more elaborate initial encoding and greater rehearsal after the fact; both factors probably contribute to greater retrievability.

It also appears that emotionally charged events are recalled more easily than neutral ones,[6] as are those that are atypical or infrequent (Thompson, Skowronski, Larsen, & Betz, 1996). So, as Loftus, Fienberg, and Tanur (1985) have described, in comparing the typical forgetting curve produced by Ebbinghaus (1913) with the curves associated with important events in people's lives, "people appear to 'lose' memories of hospitalizations and other important events more slowly and gradually" (p. 176).[7] Similarly, though more mundanely, larger purchases are recalled more frequently than smaller ones (Sudman & Bradburn, 1973) and, presumably, consumer problems associated with larger purchases more frequently than those associated with smaller ones.

Forward 'telescoping' of memories (i.e. recalling that events occurred more recently than they actually did) is also associated more with more important and salient events (Neter & Waksberg, 1964). This has the effect of making even more distinct the forgetting curves of more and less important/salient events.

Approaches to Modelling Memory Decay

The decay of memory can be modelled as a function of time (or retention interval) to produce forgetting curves. Models work on the presumption that respondents use information stored in their long-term memory when answering survey questions based on autobiographical information (Burton & Blair, 1991). Both exponential functions and power functions are commonly used to fit forgetting curves, often with very similar results. As yet, no approach has been found to be appropriate in all circumstances (Tourangeau et al., 2000). However, Rubin and Wenzel (1996) have argued that power functions generally provide a better fit than exponential functions. Bauer, Burch, Scholin, and Guler (2007, p. 913) have also suggested recently that power functions provide the best fit 'for a variety of data on forgetting' for adult respondents. Exponential functions may however provide a better fit for children's data (Bauer et al., 2007).

The Current Study

In this paper, we investigate the extent to which the forgetting curves of various categories of civil justice problems differ. We hypothesise that slower forgetting rates will be associated with problems that respondents said were more important to resolve, involved the most money, led to advice-seeking and led to the most adverse consequences. We also explore the forgetting curves of different problem types (i.e. problems falling into different areas of law), to discern the extent to which failure of recall might provide an objective means to determine relative severity. Finally, we estimate the extent to which surveys such as the CSJS under-report the incidence of civil justice problems as a result of recall failure.

METHODS

The English and Welsh Civil and Social Justice Survey

Data for the present study were drawn from the English and Welsh CSJS. The CSJS is a nationally representative (of residential households) survey of people's experience of civil justice problems and their responses to them. It was conducted, initially on a periodic basis, in 2001 and 2004 (Pleasence, 2006), but since January 2006 has been conducted on a continuous basis. In terms of detail, the CSJS is the most extensive survey of its kind so far undertaken. The survey has its distant origins in surveys of 'legal need' undertaken during the recession at the United States' Bar in the 1930s (Clark & Corstvet, 1938).[8] Its more recent origins, though, are in the two *Paths to Justice* surveys, carried out in England and Scotland in the late 1990s (Genn, 1999; Genn & Paterson, 2001). However, the CSJS has refined substantially the *Paths to Justice* approach. The focus of the CSJS has been shifted onto initial decision making, a wealth of demographic information has been added and, more generally, questions have been improved to address problems with the earlier surveys. The content of the survey is also continuously adapted to enable analysis to build upon emerging findings.

The 5,611 respondents to the 2001 survey were drawn from 3,348 residential households, randomly selected from across 73 postcode sectors throughout England and Wales. The eligible household response rate was 57 per cent and the cumulative in-scope adult response rate was 52 per cent.

The 5,015 respondents to the 2004 survey were drawn from 3,832 residential households, randomly selected from across 250 postcode sectors throughout England and Wales. The eligible household response rate was 79 per cent and the cumulative in-scope adult response rate was 57 per cent.

The 4,094 respondents to the continuous CSJS during 2006/2007[9] were drawn from 2,435 residential households, randomly selected from across 210 postcode sectors throughout England and Wales. The eligible household response rate was 76 per cent and the cumulative in-scope adult response rate was 55 per cent.

In all three surveys, respondents were interviewed face-to-face in their homes by professional interviewers. They were asked whether they had experienced a problem in the preceding 3.5 years (3 years for the continuous CSJS) that had been difficult to solve in each of eighteen distinct civil problem categories. Problem types are listed in Table 1, along with examples

Table 1. Discrete Problem Types Reported in the Survey, and Percentage/Number of Respondents Reporting One or More Problems of Each Type.

Problem Type	Examples of Sub-Types	2001		2004		2006/2007	
		%	N	%	N	%	N
Consumer	Faulty goods/services (e.g. building)	13.3	748	10.0	503	12.0	371
Neighbours	Antisocial behaviour	8.4	471	6.6	329	8.9	276
Money/debt	Financial mis-selling, disputed bills	8.3	465	5.6	279	5.5	169
Employment	Termination/terms of employment	6.1	344	5.2	260	5.3	165
Negligent Accidents	Road accidents, workplace accidents	3.9	217	4.9	244	3.6	112
Housing (rent)	Property disrepair, lease terms	3.8	215	2.7	137	3.2	98
Housing (own)	Rights of way, planning permission	2.4	135	2.4	121	2.0	61
Welfare bens.	Entitlement to/quantification of benefits	2.3	127	1.9	98	3.0	93
Relationship breakdown	Residence of children, division of assets	2.2	124	1.7	84	1.6	49
Divorce	–	2.2	122	2.1	106	2.2	68
Children	School exclusion, choice of school	1.9	108	1.5	75	1.9	59
Clinical negligence	Negligent medical or dental treatment	1.6	92	1.6	79	2.0	61
Domestic violence	Violence against respondent/children	1.6	88	0.8	42	0.8	25
Discrimination	Disability, race, gender, etc.	1.4	80	2.2	111	2.0	63
Police treatment	Assault/unreasonable detention by pol.	0.7	38	0.8	40	0.9	28
Homelessness	Experience/threat of homelessness	0.6	36	1.2	61	1.1	35
Mental Health	Conditions of hospital discharge	0.5	26	0.2	11	0.3	9
Immigration	Obtaining authority to remain in the UK	0.3	18	0.3	16	0.3	9

of constituent sub-categories and the proportion of respondents reporting having experienced one or more problem of each type. The questions were carefully constructed to limit the circumstances reported to those to which legal principles can be applied. In 2004 and 2006/2007, for the two most recent problems identified in each category, respondents were asked about how important it had been to resolve problems and about what impact problems had had on their lives. In 2001, for one randomly selected problem, respondents were asked how important it had been to resolve the problem. A range of demographic and household data was also collected.[10]

Modelling Memory Decay Using the CSJS

For each survey, the reference period was divided into quarters (3 months per quarter). For problem characteristics of interest (i.e. stated importance, money in dispute, resolution strategy adopted, problem type), the number of problems that concluded in each time period was counted. Counts in each time period were then divided by the maximum count in any time period to standardise all analyses (between a range of 0 and 1). A power function, shown in Eq (1), was fitted for each decay model (Rubin, 1982).

$$r_0 = at^{-b} \qquad (1)$$

where r_0 = retention rate, a = propensity to omit (i.e. percentage of problems reported), b = rate of memory decay, t = time.

Models were implemented using nonlinear regression, constrained to prevent *a*-values greater than 1. Given the relatively small number of time points, we present bootstrap estimates of confidence intervals for *b*-values, where estimates are made following repeated random samples of the same size as the original sample of data (Davison & Hinckley, 1997).

The non–time related propensity to omit events (*a*) is likely to apply where respondents choose not to report events, commonly due to the social desirability associated with the event. For example, we might expect domestic violence to be commonly underreported out of choice (*a*), rather than as a consequence of memory decay (*b*). However, we have no way of determining *a* using our survey data. We retain the term in analysis, although it is simply a measure of the tendency for the highest count to occur in the most recent time period and has no bearing upon decay.

For each survey, memory decay models were fitted for (1) the stated importance of resolving the problem, (2) the amount of money in dispute,

(3) problem resolution strategy, (4) the number of adverse consequences reported to have flowed from the problem and (5) the eighteen problem types.

Stated importance data stemmed from two questions. In 2001 respondents were asked whether it had been 'very important', 'fairly important', 'not very important' or 'not important at all' to resolve the problem. Two categories of perceived importance were formed by collapsing the first two and last two responses into single categories. In 2004, respondents were asked, 'How important would you say it was for you to resolve this problem?' A scale from 0 to 10 was presented to respondents on a 'show card', with 0 marked as 'not at all', 2 as 'mildly', 5 as 'moderately', 8 as 'markedly' and 10 as 'extremely'. Two categories of perceived importance were formed by collapsing responses from 0 to 5 (less important) and 6 to 10 (more important). This allowed for more problems to fall into each category.

The amount of money in dispute was derived from various questions enquiring into the nature of the problem. Amounts were split into three categories. These were up to £200, between £201 and £1,000, and more than £1,000.

Problem resolution strategies were derived from a series of questions enquiring into the actions that respondents took to resolve problems (Pleasence, 2006). Three strategy categories were used for analysis. These were 'did nothing', 'handled alone' and 'sought advice'. All formal advice was included in the last category, whether or not provided by a lawyer.

The number of adverse consequences that respondents perceived to have followed on from problems was obtained from the question, "Did or do you experience any of the[se] things ... as a result of [the] problem?" Respondents were presented with nine types of adverse consequence: physical ill health, stress-related ill health, relationship breakdown, personal violence, property damage, loss of a home, loss of employment, loss of income and loss of confidence.

The eighteen problem types are set out in Table 1.

If we had based our analysis on a count of problems that started in each time period, rather than concluded in each time period, we would have had more problems with which to fit the models. Not all problems had concluded by the time of interview. However, problems varied considerable in their duration, so the use of problem start dates would have left open the possibility that differences in forgetting curves were a reflection of differences in problem duration. This would have been a particular issue in relation to problem resolution strategy, where the duration of problems falling within the three categories differed dramatically. For example, in 2001, the average problem respondents handled alone lasted 5 months, whereas the average problem for which respondents sought advice lasted 12 months.

RESULTS

Tables 2–4 show fitted values for *a* (non–time related propensity to omit) and *b* (rate of memory decay) for (1) the stated importance of resolving the problem, (2) the amount of money in dispute, (3) problem resolution strategy, (4) the number of adverse consequences reported to have flowed from the problem and (5) the eighteen problem types set out in Table 1. The proportion of the variance explained by each model (R^2) is also shown.

Table 2. Modelling Memory Decay in 2001 Survey.

	a	*b*[a]	95% C.I. for *b*		R^2
			Lower	Upper	
Importance					
Less important	1	**0.58**	0.47	0.68	0.79
More important	1	**0.54**	0.45	0.62	0.81
Cost					
Less than £200	0.96	**0.80**	0.49	1.11	0.79
£200–£1,000	1	**0.54**	0.32	0.76	0.52
More than £1,000	1	**0.47**	0.25	0.70	0.53
Broad strategy					
Handled alone	1	**0.64**	0.55	0.74	0.86
Did nothing	1	**0.76**	0.68	0.83	0.96
Obtained advice	1	**0.53**	0.46	0.61	0.82
Problem type (ranked by *b*)					
Consumer	1	**0.79**	0.66	0.89	0.94
Neighbours	0.93	**0.76**	0.42	1.1	0.76
Money/debt	1	**0.75**	0.64	0.86	0.92
Children	1	**0.72**	0.49	0.95	0.65
Housing (rent)	1	**0.58**	0.39	0.78	0.67
Employment	1	**0.52**	0.38	0.65	0.62
Negligent accidents	1	**0.52**	0.4	0.63	0.68
Welfare benefits	0.77	**0.50**	0.17	0.83	0.38
Mental health	0.55	0.50	0.04	0.96	0.14
Clinical negligence	0.99	**0.44**	0.26	0.62	0.44
Domestic violence	0.93	**0.42**	0.26	0.59	0.53
Housing (own)	1	**0.41**	0.27	0.55	0.50
Homelessness	1	0.40	0.21	0.58	0.36
Discrimination	0.87	0.38	0	0.75	0.26
Relationship breakdown	0.86	0.33	0.04	0.62	0.19
Divorce	0.8	0.15	–0.03	0.33	0.15
Police	0.38	0.03	–0.39	0.45	0
Immigration	–	–	–	–	–

[a]*b* represents the rate of memory decay. Entries in bold indicate an R^2 of 0.4 or above.

Table 3. Modelling Memory Decay in 2004 Survey.

	a	b[a]	95% C.I. for b		R^2
			Lower	Upper	
Importance					
Less important	1	**0.70**	0.65	0.74	0.97
More important	1	**0.59**	0.52	0.66	0.91
Cost					
Less than £200	0.88	**0.91**	0.34	1.47	0.47
£200–£1,000	0.99	**0.46**	0.32	0.60	0.48
More than £1,000	0.70	0.36	0.16	0.56	0.29
Broad strategy					
Handled alone	1	**0.81**	0.74	0.88	0.96
Did nothing	0.92	**0.73**	0.39	1.07	0.75
Obtained advice	1	**0.49**	0.41	0.56	0.87
Adverse Consequences					
No adverse consequences of problem	1	**0.74**	0.70	0.78	0.98
1 adverse consequence	1	**0.55**	0.46	0.64	0.84
2 adverse consequences	1	**0.47**	0.40	0.54	0.81
3+ adverse consequences	1	**0.43**	0.32	0.55	0.66
Problem type (ranked by b)					
Money/debt	0.99	**0.99**	0.81	1.17	0.97
Welfare benefits	0.97	**0.92**	0.65	1.19	0.80
Police	1	**0.85**	0.74	0.97	0.94
Neighbours	1	**0.83**	0.71	0.95	0.88
Consumer	1	**0.78**	0.7	0.85	0.95
Clinical negligence	0.97	**0.68**	0.36	1	0.64
Employment	0.88	**0.60**	0.39	0.8	0.59
Children	1	**0.60**	0.31	0.89	0.48
Housing (rent)	1	**0.58**	0.2	0.95	0.65
Discrimination	0.99	**0.50**	0.42	0.58	0.64
Housing (own)	1	**0.45**	0.31	0.59	0.51
Relationship breakdown	0.71	**0.45**	0.13	0.78	0.28
Homelessness	0.84	0.42	0.28	0.56	0.31
Domestic violence	0.64	0.41	–0.02	0.84	0.16
Negligent accidents	1	0.28	0.15	0.41	0.38
Immigration	0.38	–0.06	–0.66	0.53	0.00
Divorce	–	–	–	–	–
Mental health	–	–	–	–	–

[a] b represents the rate of memory decay. Entries in bold indicate an R^2 of 0.4 or above.

The R^2 values are important, as they indicate the extent to which we are able to model memory decay in each instance. Where R^2 values are above 0.4, entries for b values are in bold. Most cases where R^2 values are lower than 0.4, indicating a poor fit for the model, can be attributed to sparsity of data.

Table 4. Modelling Memory Decay in 2006 Survey.

	a	*b*[a]	95% C.I. for *b*		R^2
			Lower	Upper	
Importance					
Less important	1	**0.89**	0.79	0.98	0.98
More important	0.98	**0.80**	0.69	0.91	0.97
Cost					
Less than £200	1	**0.77**	0.55	1	0.72
£200–£1,000	1	**0.78**	0.60	0.97	0.90
More than £1,000	1	**0.68**	0.58	0.79	0.91
Broad strategy					
Handled alone	1	**0.98**	0.89	1.06	0.99
Did nothing	0.98	**0.91**	0.77	1.05	0.94
Obtained advice	0.98	**0.75**	0.64	0.86	0.95
Adverse Consequences					
No adverse consequences of problem	1	**0.91**	0.85	0.97	0.99
1 adverse consequence	0.98	**0.82**	0.70	0.94	0.94
2 adverse consequences	1	**0.71**	0.53	0.88	0.82
3+ adverse consequences	0.94	**0.69**	0.44	0.94	0.73
Problem type (ranked by *b*)					
Immigration	0.93	**1.40**	0.10	2.69	0.45
Discrimination	0.99	**1.14**	0.78	1.49	0.94
Money/debt	1	**1.13**	0.96	1.31	0.97
Mental health	0.97	**1.05**	0.05	2.05	0.39
Homelessness	0.99	**1.05**	0.42	1.68	0.86
Welfare benefits	1	**1.01**	0.84	1.18	0.93
Housing (rent)	0.95	**0.98**	0.60	1.36	0.81
Consumer	0.99	**0.96**	0.80	1.13	0.97
Neighbours	1	**0.93**	0.81	1.05	0.95
Housing (own)	0.98	**0.72**	0.49	0.95	0.82
Employment	0.96	**0.72**	0.50	0.94	0.90
Domestic violence	0.92	0.49	0.03	0.95	0.34
Police	0.83	**0.49**	0.24	0.75	0.50
Relationship breakdown	0.93	0.51	0.25	0.77	0.37
Children	0.69	0.45	−0.17	1.06	0.16
Clinical negligence	0.86	0.30	0.06	0.53	0.19
Divorce	0.62	0.24	−0.03	0.52	0.17
Negligent accidents	0.86	0.23	0.03	0.57	0.19

[a]*b* represents the rate of memory decay. Entries in bold indicate an R^2 of 0.4 or above.

For example, there were only five problem types (consumer, neighbours, money/debt, employment and negligent accidents) which had an average of 6 or more problems per quarter time period across all three datasets. Four problem types (mental health, immigration, homelessness and unfair police treatment) had an average of three or fewer problems per period.

The problem of data sparsity is compounded where memory decay is not a significant factor affecting recall. Relatively rare events are likely, in such circumstances, to be somewhat irregularly distributed across time anyway. Of course, lack of fit where data are not sparse is a good indication that memory is relatively unaffected by the progress of time.

Higher values of b represent quicker rates of memory decay, and lower values concomitantly represent slower rates of memory decay.

Started Importance of Resolving Problems

Tables 2–4 suggest that forgetting curves are flatter for problems that people describe as being the most important to resolve. For these problems, b was observed to have values of 0.54, 0.59 and 0.80 in respect of the 2001, 2004 and 2006/2007 surveys, respectively. This compared to corresponding values of 0.58, 0.70 and 0.89 in the case of problems described as less important to resolve. For the 2004 survey, there was virtually no overlap of the 95 per cent confidence intervals. It would appear, therefore, that people are less likely to forget problems that they regard as more important to resolve as time passes. Fig. 1 illustrates this phenomenon using the 2001 survey data (the most populous).

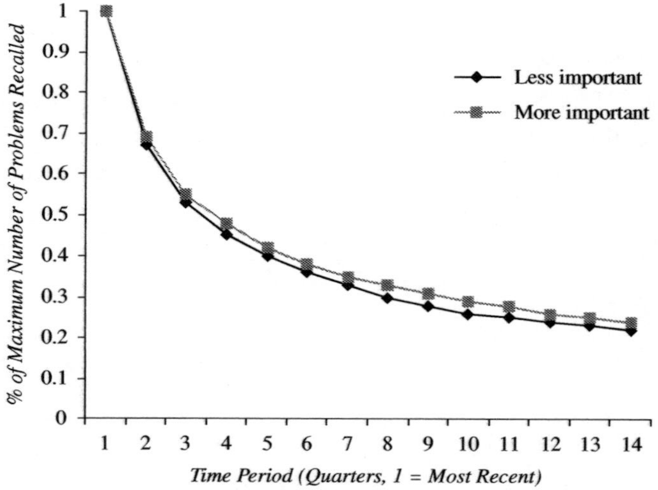

Fig. 1. Memory Decay by Problem Importance.

Amount of Money

Tables 2–4 also suggest that forgetting curves are flatter for problems that involve the most money. That is, people tended to recall more expensive problems most. For all three surveys, *b* values were lower for problems involving more than £1,000 (0.47, 0.36 and 0.68 in 2001, 2004 and 2006/2007, respectively) than for problems involving less that £200 (0.80, 0.81 and 0.77). The forgetting curves for the 2001 survey are set out in Fig. 2.

Findings for problems involving between £200 and £1,000 were more ambiguous; a problem compounded by the relative sparsity of data for this category in 2006/2007. However, in 2001 and 2004, the forgetting curve for this category of problem fell neatly between those for the other two categories.

The 2004 survey model for the more than £1,000 category fitted relatively poorly to the data, with an R^2 of just 0.29. This is likely to be down to sparsity of data. However, as indicated earlier, it may in part be a consequence of recall being relatively unaffected by the progress of time.

Problem Resolution Strategy

There was a clear difference in the forgetting curves of problems for which people sought advice and problems that people dealt with on their own.

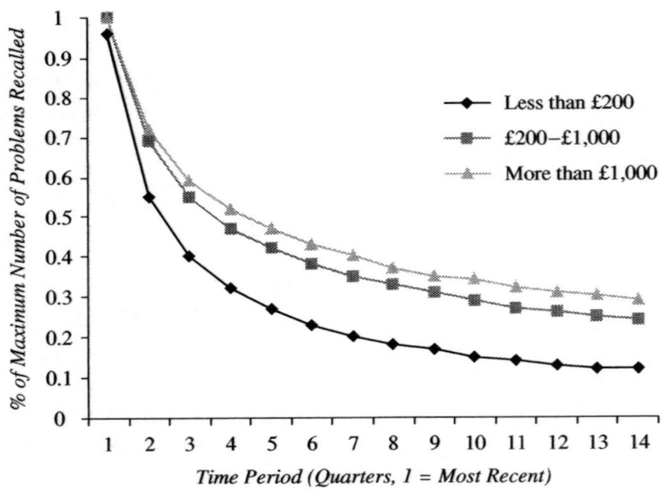

Fig. 2. Memory Decay by Problem Cost.

As is evident from Tables 2–4, time appeared to affect recall of problems for which people sought advice to a far lesser extent than problems people handled themselves. That is, people tended to forget problems they handled on their own quicker than problems for which they sought advice. Indeed, there was no overlap of the 95 per cent confidence intervals for the *b* values of these two problem categories in 2004 or 2006/2007 – indicating a clearly significant difference. Furthermore, Tables 2–4 also reveal a remarkable consistency in these particular forgetting curves.

Fig. 3, which sets out the forgetting curves derived from 2001 survey data, illustrates the extent of the effect of time on recall of problems for which different strategies are adopted. After 14[11] quarters, problems for which advice was obtained were recalled at almost twice the rate as problems people dealt with themselves. The difference was even greater in 2004 and 2006/2007.

However, part of the reason for the difference in recall patterns for problems for which advice is obtained and problems that people deal with themselves is that obtaining advice is itself a relatively infrequent and salient event that is likely to be subject to repeated rehearsal (and to lead to additional rehearsal of the memory of the underlying problem, as well as an increase in problem duration). Thus, some of the difference just outlined may be due to the strategy adopted to deal with problems, rather than the nature of the problems themselves. Nevertheless, the results are entirely

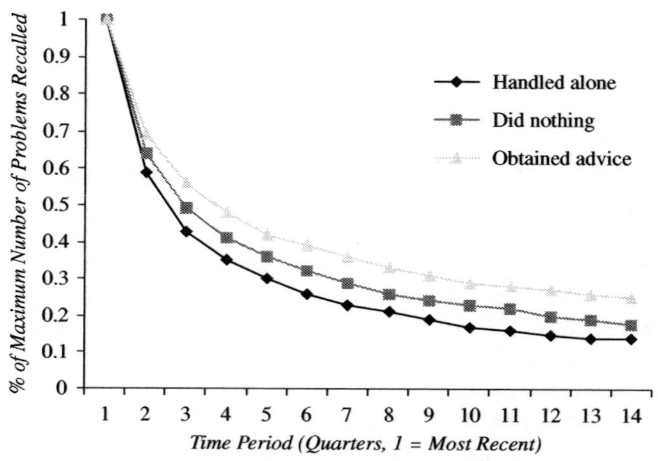

Fig. 3. Memory Decay by Problem-Solving Strategy.

consistent with the proposition that problems for which people obtain advice are more important to them than are other problems. The explanations are not contradictory.

Tables 2–4 also indicate that problems people take no action to resolve are prone to greater memory decay than problems about which people seek advice.

Adverse Consequences

Forgetting curves differed depending on the number of adverse consequences that were reported to have followed from civil justice problems. As Tables 3 and 4 indicate, forgetting curves became progressively flatter as the number of adverse consequences increased. That is, people tended to recall more problems that had adverse consequences for them. Although none of the differences were significant at the 95 per cent level, the consistency of the results is striking. In 2004, the *b* value reduced from 0.74 to 0.55 to 0.47 to 0.43 as the number of adverse consequences rose from zero to one to two to three or more. In 2006, the corresponding figures were 0.91, 0.82, 0.71 and 0.69.

As with problem resolution strategy, adverse consequences will themselves be salient events subject to repeated rehearsal and likely to trigger additional rehearsal of the memory of initial problems. In this case, though, adverse consequences can themselves be regarded as aspects of problem severity.

Problems Types

Tables 2–4 also set out *b* values for the 18 problem types that are the basic subject matter of the CSJS. So, as can be seen from Fig. 4, 2001 survey respondents appeared to recall distant problems concerning negligent accidents better than distant problems concerning consumer problems. The difference in forgetting curves was significant and was echoed by similar significant findings in relation to both 2004 and 2006/2007 data. The *b* values for negligent accidents were 0.44, 0.28 and 0.23 in 2001, 2004 and 2006/2007, respectively. The corresponding *b* values for consumer problems were 0.79, 0.78 and 0.96. Clinical negligence problems also appear to have a much flatter forgetting curve than consumer problems, with *b* values of 0.44, 0.68 and 0.30 in 2001, 2004 and 2006/2007, respectively.

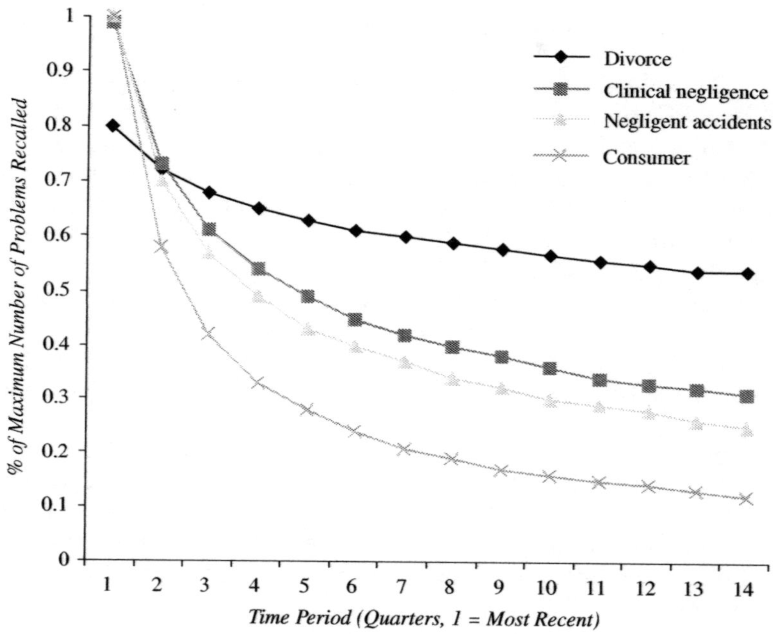

Fig. 4. Memory Decay by Problem Type.

As can also be seen from Fig. 4, divorce was associated with very low *b* values in 2001 and 2006/2007 and poorly fitting models (0.15 in 2001 and 0.17 in 2006/2007). No model could be fitted for the 2004 divorce data. Similarly, problems ancillary to relationship breakdown were associated with poorly fitting models and relatively low *b* values (0.33, 0.45 and 0.51 in 2001, 2004 and 2006/2007, respectively), as was domestic violence (0.42, 0.41 and 0.49). Thus, all types of family-related problems appeared to be relatively well recalled over time.

As can be seen from Tables 2–4, for a number of problem types – such as discrimination, homelessness and mental health – there was some fluctuation in *b* values relative to other problem types. In each of these three cases, 2001 and 2004 data suggested relatively flat forgetting curves, whereas 2006/2007 data suggested relatively steep curves. Accordingly – and in light of the relatively small numbers of problems available for analysis at problem type level, especially in relation to these rarer types of problem – it was not possible to establish as clear a picture of the relative severity of problems of different types as might have been hoped.

Incidence without Memory Decay

Civil justice problems are inevitably under-reported in surveys such as the CSJS as a consequence of memory decay. Had the numbers of problems reported in the most recent time period of 2001 been maintained across all periods (throughout the entire survey reference period), then there would have been 5,726 concluded problems, instead of the 2,116 concluded problems actually reported.[12] This is 2.7 times as many problems. The multiples were 2.7 and 3.3[13] in 2004 and 2006/2007, respectively.

In the case of consumer problems in 2001, if the numbers of problems in the most recent time period had been maintained across all periods, there would have been 1,974 concluded problems, rather than the 574 concluded problems actually reported. That equates to almost three and a half times as many problems.

In contrast, the reported incidence of some types of problem appears relatively unaffected by memory decay. So, for example, had the number of divorces or problems concerning mental health or unfair treatment by the police in the most recent time period of the 2001 survey been maintained across all periods, there would have been slightly fewer problems than the actual number reported.[14]

DISCUSSION

Memory failure poses one of the greatest problems for social surveys, impacting on both the representativeness of events reported and on estimates of incidence. As our results demonstrate, maybe two-thirds or more of civil justice problems that CSJS respondents would regard as falling within the scope of the survey go unreported. Incidence of civil justice problems is therefore likely to be much higher than CSJS estimates suggest. However, recall failure does not seem to impact evenly on the reporting of problems in different categories.

In line with previous findings, and our hypotheses, our results indicate that those civil justice problems respondents said were the most important to resolve, described as involving the most money, leading to advice being sought and reported to lead to the most adverse consequences are recalled over longer periods of time than other problems.

Although the results concerning stated importance and money are relatively straightforward to interpret – with consistent findings over the three surveys – there is a question about the extent to which the results concerning strategy and adverse consequences reflect memory of strategies and consequences, rather than of underlying problems. However, given previous findings in relation to problem severity and advice (Pleasence, 2006), it seems likely that the clear difference in forgetting curves associated with problems about which people seek advice and problems which people attempt to resolve on their own is attributable not only to advice itself being a relatively infrequent and salient event (i.e. likely to lead to repeated memory rehearsal) but also to the nature of the underlying problems.

In the case of adverse consequences, given that they are aspects of problem severity, the degree to which their recall may enhance recall of problems is less problematic. The additional rehearsal is down to greater problem severity rather than an associated behaviour.

In any event, it seems evident that forgetting curves are linked, to some extent, to the seriousness of problems. This opens up the possibility that they might be referenced in the targeting of public resources towards those with the greatest 'legal need'. However, while our hypotheses are supported by our results, the picture of relative severity of civil justice problem types is far from clear. So, although the results suggest that consumer problems are significantly less severe than problems going to the heart of family life, the standing of many problem types is uncertain. In part this is due to data sparsity. As shown in Fig. 1, incidence of some problem types was very low. However, in addition to data sparsity, lack of clarity results from the heterogeneous nature of many of the problem types included within the CSJS. For example, the types of problem included within the rented housing category range from harassment and eviction to difficulties getting a deposit back. Likewise, money/debt problems range from difficulties getting someone to pay money they owe to being the subject of a County Court judgment.

So, we will have to wait for more data to become available through the CSJS, or from elsewhere, before effective analysis at the problem sub-type level will become possible and a clear picture able to emerge.

For now, we have shown that analysis of recall patterns provides an indication of severity of civil justice problems. We have also provided a means by which to provide a much better estimate of the incidence of such problems.

In the latter case, our findings suggest that at least three-quarters of problems falling within the scope of the CSJS are not reported through it – a finding that goes some of the way to explaining why the incidence of problems reported through the CSJS seems low relative to the volume of advice reported to be provided by some advice organisations.[15] Of course, the problems that are not reported through the CSJS will not exactly mirror those that are reported. They will tend to be less serious, meaning that they will be perceived as less important to resolve, involve smaller sums of money, less often lead to advice being sought and have fewer adverse consequences. As our findings in relation to divorce suggest, major life events are unlikely to be substantially under-reported. However, policy makers should be aware that there may be more 'legal need' in the world than surveys suggest.

NOTES

1. Although the concept is an evolving and disputed one, it is concerned with those circumstances in which people facing 'justiciable' problems (Genn, 1999) are unaware of the legal context of those problems or, if they are aware of the context, are unable to assert their rights through law "for want of legal services of adequate quality or supply" (Royal Commission on Legal Services is Scotland, 1980, paragraph 2.10).

2. Early attempts to encourage solicitors to broaden practice into emerging areas of social welfare law, such as the introduction of the green form scheme, were less successful (Kemp & Pleasence, 2005, p. 287). As the Legal Action Group (1992) observed, solicitors maintained their focus on family and crime-related work. For a discussion on the differences between lawyer and non-lawyer services operating within the legal aid scheme, see Moorhead et al. (2003).

3. See, also, Sandefur's (2007) discussion of the barriers presented by people's past experience of dealing with problems.

4. See, also, similar analyses in, for example, Genn (1999), Genn and Paterson (2001), Coumarelos, Wei, and Zhou (2006), Dignan (2006) and Currie (2007).

5. Based on Bradburn, Rips, and Shevell (1987).

6. Events that are positively emotionally charged being those that are recalled for the longest time (Walker, Skowronski, & Thompson, 2003). The emotional impact of events can also influence the accuracy of recall (Nadeau & Niemi, 1995).

7. See, also, Loftus (1982).

8. For a history, see P. Pleasence et al. (2001).

9. Five quarters of data have been used in this analysis; four from 2006 and one from 2007.

10. For technical details, see Phelps, Hayward, and Hanson (2005).

11. 12 quarters in 2006–2007.

12. For which date data were available.

13. It is not clear why there is such a difference between these two figures, although two potential explanations can be put forward. First, incidence of problems has been rising since 2004, which would have the effect of seeing higher numbers of problems reported in more recent time periods. Also, the 2001 and 2004 surveys used a fixed and memorable date (1 January) as the start point for the survey reference period. The 2006 reference period commenced three years before the date of interview. Memories may have been difficult to locate against this less memorable date.

14. The multiples were 0.9, and 0.7 and 0.9, respectively.

15. The CSJS, for example, suggests a lower incidence of consumer problems than the volume of calls reported by Consumer Direct, a telephone advice service dealing with consumer issues – although many of Consumer Direct's calls will not concern 'justiciable' problems (Genn, 1999).

ACKNOWLEDGMENTS

The authors acknowledge the role of the Legal Services Commission in funding the English and Welsh Civil Justice Survey and the assistance of Zofia Bajorek in the preparation of the manuscript.

REFERENCES

Bauer, P. J., Burch, M. M., Scholin, S. E., & Guler, O. E. (2007). Using cue words to investigate the distribution of autobiographical memories in childhood. *Psychological Science, 18*(10), 910–916.

Beatty, P., Herrmann, D., Puskar, C., & Kerwin, J. (1998). 'Don't know' responses in surveys: Is what I know what you want to know and do I want you to know it? *Memory, 6*(4), 407–426.

Bradburn, N. M., Rips, L., & Shevell, S. (1987). Answering autobiographical questions: The impact of memory and inference on surveys. *Science, 236*, 157–161.

Buck, A., & Stark, G. (2003). Simplicity versus fairness in means testing: The case of civil legal aid. *Fiscal Studies, 24*(4), 427–449.

Buck, A., Tam, T., & Fisher, C. (2007). *Putting money advice where the need is: Evaluating the potential for advice provision in different outreach locations.* London: Legal Services Commission.

Burton, S., & Blair, E. A. (1991). Task conditions, response formulation processes, and response accuracy for behavioral frequency questions in surveys. *Public Opinion Quarterly, 55*, 50–79.

Clark, C., & Corstvet, E. (1938). The lawyer and the public: An A.A.L.S. survey. *Yale Law Journal, 47*, 1282–1285.

Coumarelos, C., Wei, Z., & Zhou, A. Z. (2006). *Justice made to measure: NSW legal needs survey in disadvantaged Areas*. Sydney: Law and Justice Foundation of New South Wales.

Currie, A. (2007). *The legal problems of everyday life: The nature, extent and consequences of justiciable problems experienced by Canadians.* Ottawa: Department of Justice.

Davison, A. V., & Hinckley, D. V. (1997). *Bootstrap methods and applications.* Cambridge: Cambridge University Press.

Department for Constitutional Affairs. (2005). *A fairer deal for legal aid.* London: Department for Constitutional Affairs.

Dignan, T. (2006). *Northern Ireland legal needs survey*. Belfast: Northern Ireland Legal Services Commission.

Ebbinghaus, H. (1913). *Memory: A contribution to experimental psychology* (originally published in 1885). New York, NY: Teacher's College.

Genn, H. (1999). *Paths to justice: What people do and think about going to law*. Oxford: Hart Publishing.

Genn, H., & Paterson, A. (2001). *Paths to justice Scotland: What people in Scotland think and do about going to law*. Oxford: Hart.

Glennerster, H., Hills, J., Travers, T., & Hendry, R. (2000). *Paying for health, education and housing*. Oxford: Oxford University Press.

Kemp, V., & Pleasence, P. (2005). Targeting civil legal needs: Matching services to needs. *Obiter*, *26*(2), 285–303.

Legal Action Group. (1992). *A strategy for justice*. London: Legal Action Group.

Legal Services Commission. (2006). *Making legal rights a reality: The legal services commission's strategy for the community legal service*. London: Legal Services Commission.

Loftus, E. F. (1982). Memory and its distortions. In: A. G. Kraut (Ed.), *The G. Stanley hall lecture series*. Washington D.C.: American Psychological Association.

Loftus, E. F., Fienberg, S. E., & Tanur, J. M. (1985). Cognitive psychology meets the national survey. *American Psychologist*, *40*(2), 175–180.

Lord Chancellor's Department. (1989). *Legal services: A framework for the future*. London: HMSO.

Lord Chancellor's Department. (1995). *Legal aid: The future of publicly funded help in solving legal problems and disputes in England and Wales*. London: HMSO.

Lord Chancellor's Department. (2004). *Lord chancellor's department consultation paper: Criminal defence service bill*. London: Lord Chancellor's Department.

Mathiowetz, N. (2000). Methodological issues in the measurement of work disability. In: N. Mathiowetz & G. Wunderlich (Eds), *Survey measurement of work disability*. Washington D.C.: Institute of Medicine.

Moorhead, R., & Pleasence, P. (2003). Access to justice after universalism. *Journal of Law and Society*, *30*(1), 1–10.

Moorhead, R., Robinson, M., & Matrix Research and Consultancy. (2006). *A trouble shared: Legal problems clusters in solicitors' and advice agencies*. London: Department for Constitutional Affairs.

Moorhead, R., Sherr, A., & Paterson, A. (2003). Contesting professionalism: Legal aid and non-lawyers in England and Wales. *Law and Society Review*, *37*(4), 755–808.

Nadeau, R., & Niemi, R. G. (1995). Educated guesses: The process of answering factual knowledge questions in surveys. *The Public Opinion Quarterly*, *59*(3), 323–346.

Neter, J., & Waksberg, J. (1964). A study of response errors in expenditures data from household interviews. *Journal of the American Statistical Association*, *59*, 17–55.

Phelps, A., Hayward, B., & Hanson, T. (2005). 2004 English and Welsh civil and social justice survey: Technical report, Legal Services Commission, London.

Pleasence, P. (2006). *Causes of action: Civil law and social justice*. Norwich: TSO.

Pleasence, P. (2007). Trust me, I'm a lawyer: Outreach advice and the integration of public service. *Focus*, *54*, 20–21.

Pleasence, P., Balmer, N. J., Buck, A., O'Grady, A., & Genn, H. (2004a). Multiple justiciable problems: Common clusters, problem order and social and demographic indicators. *Journal of Empirical Legal Studies*, *1*, 301–330.

Pleasence, P., Balmer, N. J., Buck, A., Smith, M., & Patel, A. (2007). Mounting problems: Further evidence of the social, economic and health consequences of civil justice problems. In: P. Pleasence, A. Buck & N. J. Balmer (Eds), *Transforming lives: Law and social process*. Norwich: TSO.

Pleasence, P., Buck, A., & Christie, J. (1999). *Testing the code: Final report*. London: Legal Aid Board.

Pleasence, P., Buck, A., Goriely, T., Taylor, J., Perkins, H., & Quirk, H. (2001). *Local legal need*. London: Legal Services Commission.

Pleasence, P., Buck, A., Smith, M., Balmer, N. J., & Patel, A. (2004). Needs assessment and the community legal service in England and Wales. *International Journal of the Legal Profession*, *11*(3), 213–232.

Royal Commission on Legal Services in Scotland (the 'Hughes Commission'). (1980). Report of the Royal Commission on Legal Services in Scotland, HMSO, Edinburgh.

Rubin, D. C. (1982). On the retention function for autobiographical memory. *Journal of Learning and Verbal Behaviour*, *21*(1), 21–38.

Rubin, D. C., & Wenzel, A. E. (1996). One hundred years of forgetting: A quantitative description of retention. *Psychological Review*, *103*, 734–760.

Sandefur, R. (2007). The importance of doing nothing: Everyday problems and responses of inaction. In: P. Pleasence, A. Buck & N. J. Balmer (Eds), *Transforming lives: Law and social process*. Norwich: TSO.

Sudman, S., & Bradburn, N. M. (1973). Effects of time and memory factors on response in surveys. *Journal of the American Statistical Society*, *68*, 805–815.

Thompson, C. P., Skowronski, J. J., Larsen, S. F., & Betz, A. L. (1996). *Autobiographical memory*. Mahwah: Erlbaum.

Tourangeau, R., Rips, L. J., & Rasinski, K. (2000). *The psychology of survey response*. Cambridge: Cambridge University Press.

Walker, W. R., Skowronski, J. J., & Thompson, C. P. (2003). Life is pleasant – And memory helps to keep it that way! *Review of General Psychology*, *7*(2), 203–210.

Weisberg, H. F. (2005). *The Total Survey Error Approach: A Guide to the New Science of Survey Research*. Chicago: University of Chicago Press.

RIGHTS CONSCIOUSNESS IN CRIMINAL PROCEDURE: A THEORETICAL AND EMPIRICAL INQUIRY

Kathryne M. Young

ABSTRACT

This article's overarching purpose is to serve as an initial theoretical and empirical step in applying rights consciousness inquiry to the criminal procedure context. First, building on previous work within the legal consciousness and rights consciousness traditions, I discuss the ways in which attention to criminal procedure can inform our understanding of rights consciousness and enumerate differences between the way rights consciousness approaches civil law and the ways it might approach criminal law. Additionally, I suggest that understanding the relationship between people's subjective impressions of procedures and procedures' legal and moral validity offers a novel means of studying procedure that I term "procedural rights consciousness." In the second part of the article, I report results of two studies designed as first empirical steps in applying rights consciousness as the first part suggests. My findings indicate that not only do people lack knowledge about their rights in criminal investigations but they also think about these rights in patterned ways that reflect a method of understanding law characterized by

Access to Justice
Sociology of Crime, Law and Deviance, Volume 12, 67–95

ISSN: 1521-6136/doi:10.1108/S1521-6136(2009)0000012007

"lay jurisprudence" reasoning, in which culturally prevalent "tenets" are applied to specific situations. This mechanism often leads people to erroneous conclusions about the rights they possess. The final part of the article sets out an agenda for further rights consciousness research.

INTRODUCTION

Rights consciousness research has spanned a plethora of substantive civil law areas, but has not been explored with respect to criminal law. This article's overarching aim is to provide a first theoretical and empirical step in this direction. First, I assess the state of rights consciousness research and suggest ways in which this literature offers a novel, productive approach to understanding and theorizing the criminal justice system, and criminal procedure in particular. I then report results from two studies that investigate this approach and discuss the implications of the results for rights consciousness research more generally. Finally, I sketch an agenda for future theoretical and empirical work at the intersection of rights consciousness and criminal procedure.

RIGHTS CONSCIOUSNESS IN THE CRIMINAL LAW CONTEXT

The Legal and Rights Consciousness Traditions

In the past two decades, legal consciousness has transitioned from an emerging area of research to an established subfield within the sociology of law. Centrally, research in this tradition comprises at least two closely interwoven strands: people's apprehension of the law and their willingness to mobilize it. Anthropological and sociological notions of law have been pivotal in theorizing the processes that form "commonsense understanding[s] of the way the law works" (Nielsen, 2004, p. 7). Legal consciousness is not a stagnant description of a person's "psychological state[,] but an outcome of social processes through which meanings and identities are collectively reconstructed" (Somers & Roberts, 2008, p. 23, citing Merry, 1990, p. 247). The way people see the world – their core beliefs, hopes, understandings, and suppositions about the way it works – cannot be separated from the way they see the law. Nor can law itself be disjoined from the social world.

Patricia Ewick and Susan Silbey (1998) have examined the fluidity of people's relationships to law, finding that orientations to law and legality vary with context. In *The Common Place of Law*, the authors identify three paradigms: people see themselves as "with the law," "before the law," or "against the law" (or some combination thereof), depending on situational factors. The same person who might orient "with the law" when evicting a non-paying tenant might orient "before the law" when she has to take a drug test for a government job. Relatedly, in her study of sexual harassment on public transit, Laura Beth Nielsen (2004) discovered four paradigms through which people understand the legality of harassing speech: "freedom of speech" (free speech is an American value that should be protected); "autonomy" (people should deal with harassment on their own); "impracticality" (the government cannot successfully control speech anyway); and "distrust of authority" (the government cannot be trusted to regulate speech fairly). Nielsen concludes that "people make connections from their past experiences – good or bad – which arise in part from the social positions they occupy – and that these experiences shape their understanding of the law" (Nielsen, 2000, p. 1087). The paradigms Nielsen describes, as well as those identified by Ewick and Silbey, suggest that there are systematic, and perhaps predictable, patterns in how people think about law and that, moreover, a person's orientation to law derives from her experiences and her social location (Nielsen, 2000).

People's willingness to use the law as a problem-solving tool is closely related to their understanding of law and legality (Merry, 1990). Social experience "creat[es] dispositions that come to colour future behaviour" and "affect[s] early, fundamental decisions about what options to explore and pursue," as well as whether people experience a problem as "justiciable" at all (Sandefur, 2007, p. 131; see also Engel and Munger's seminal work on legal consciousness and disability rights, 1996). Rebecca Sandefur (2007) has found, for example, that this mechanism contributes to socioeconomic differences in people's willingness to pursue legal solutions to their problems.

Sociological work on rights consciousness tends to be housed conceptually within the legal consciousness tradition and is the descendant of rights literatures in multiple disciplines. Stuart Scheingold's eminent work on the "myth of rights" has been particularly influential, reflecting a post-Civil-Rights-era (and post-Warren-Court-era) disaffection with rights litigation as a social reform tool. In Scheingold's view, rights-affirming court decisions are not self-implementing political victories legal triumphs do not assure equality for the disenfranchised, and meaningful implementation of these decisions requires further political struggle (Scheingold, 1974). Also formative has been Lawrence Friedman's "The Idea of Right as a Social and Legal Concept." In it, Friedman (1971) defines "consciousness of right" as a person's tendency to take advantage of her own rights – a description which, to a large extent, still encapsulates the field.

As Somers and Roberts (2008) point out, the literature has sometimes focused on natural rights, but more often addresses citizenship rights, those that a country grants as a matter of law.[1] This tendency is likely due in part (as Somers and Roberts suggest) to the latter's measurability and may also be due to social scientists' reluctance to make a normative appraisal of natural rights – a phenomenon akin to one Sandefur describes regarding access to justice (2008).[2] Particularly as it has developed over the past two decades, work on rights consciousness has assumed manifold forms, comprising topics such as attitudes and beliefs about the way rights work, the relationship between social characteristics and people's ideas of rights, technical knowledge about legal rights, and types and frequency of rights-claiming behavior.

One vein of rights consciousness literature focuses on the importance of individual identity in defining and claiming rights. In their analysis of disabled Americans' life stories, David Engel and Frank Munger (1996) demonstrate the great importance of identity and personal narrative in shaping how, and whether, people understand themselves as rights-holders, how they orient themselves toward law, and how their conceptions of a right can affect their identities even when they do not assert the right (see also Merry, 1990 regarding people's identities as rights-holders; Gilliom, 2001).

One important, closely related body of rights consciousness work – and one which overlaps a great deal with access to justice scholarship – is rights mobilization. This literature acknowledges that rights "are not self-enforcing but rather must be realized by individuals ... [R]ights are constructs, and the processes by which individuals come to understand themselves as suffering a harm to which some right may provide remedy is important to empirically understand" (Nielsen, 2007, p. xiv). This includes examining how rights are, and are not, claimed. Drawing on Scheingold's insight that rights are not self-enforcing, Felstiner, Abel, and Sarat (1980) describe the rights-claiming process from a claimant's perspective: first, a person perceives an incident as injurious ("naming");

second, she attributes this injury to something, or someone, outside herself ("blaming"); third, she voices her grievance and requests a remedy ("claiming"). Researchers have found that social circumstances, particularly socioeconomic status, affect whether people perceive an incident as justiciable – a factor highly relevant to how, and whether, rights mobilization occurs (see, e.g., Sandefur, 2007).

Rights Consciousness and the Criminal Justice System

The procedural justice tradition within social psychology is probably the closest researchers have come to examining rights consciousness in the criminal realm. A key insight from this literature is that if a person believes she is treated fairly in a legal proceeding, her satisfaction with the proceeding's outcome, good or bad, will be improved; conversely, negative assessments of procedural fairness lead to negative assessments of outcomes (see, e.g., Thibaut & Walker, 1978; Tyler, 1984; Molm, Peterson, & Takahashi, 2003). This finding has been replicated in many iterations and even with criminal defendants (Casper, Tyler, & Fisher, 1988). Procedural justice work has also examined people's attitudes toward institutions. Tom Tyler and Kenneth Rasinski (1991) have found that agreement with Supreme Court decisions is not a crucial component of people's attitudes toward the Court but that people who believe the Court uses fair decision-making procedures view it as more legitimate. Tyler (1984, p. 70) has also written extensively about the relationship between compliance and procedural justice, explaining that positive impressions of procedural fairness are a "key element in explaining support for legal authorities."

Critics have pointed out that procedural justice work tends to focus on perceptions of fairness at the exclusion of outcome fairness. This may distract researchers from "seriously confronting persistent and large social inequalities" (MacCoun, 2005, p. 189, citing Haney, 1991) that "by normative criteria might be considered substantively unfair or biased" (MacCoun, 2005, p. 189). Similarly, focusing on subjective impressions of procedural fairness diverts attention from procedures' substance. Just because a person believes she was treated fairly by police does not mean that her constitutional rights were upheld, nor that she was given a meaningful opportunity to exercise them.

Applied to criminal investigation and adjudication, rights consciousness offers a way to bridge the research gap between people's satisfaction and procedures' legality, drawing from the procedural justice literature while emphasizing substantive law and building on the insights of legal consciousness. For example: How well do subjects of government investigation understand their rights? How are these beliefs created, and what implications does this have for criminal justice? In encounters with police, are people more satisfied with procedures that they believe are mandated by law? When can people be manipulated to relinquish their rights? How is rights assertion shaped by identity and experience in the context of criminal investigation and adjudication? We might characterize the examination of these and related questions as "procedural rights consciousness."

Several key distinctions between criminal and civil law affect how rights consciousness might be applied to criminal procedure. The "naming-blaming-claiming" paradigm operates differently in the criminal context. Suppose a person's house is illegally searched by the police, without a warrant or probable cause, in violation of the Fourth Amendment to the United States Constitution. Any "claiming," first of all, is unlikely to happen unless the victim of the rights violation is accused of a crime. As Pamela S. Karlan (2007, p. 1916) points out, "law enforcement behavior that does not directly undergird criminal prosecutions – such as the harassment of innocent citizens or even the use of substantial physical force to arrest criminal suspects – is less likely to be litigated." Claims that arise from criminal prosecutions are generally used as shields and litigated as part of a defense strategy; the remedy sought is exclusion, not monetary compensation. Tort suits for the same constitutional violations are uncommon, and the few that are brought are rarely fruitful[3] (Meltzer, 1988, pp. 283–284). Since defendants (or perhaps more accurately, defense attorneys) wouldn't seek exclusion if there was nothing harmful to exclude, constitutional claims of this type are usually brought when a claimant has done something illegal, morally questionable, or otherwise worth concealing from a jury. Thus, constitutional issues in criminal procedure tend to be litigated by an unusual set of claimants, and one especially unlikely to arouse public sympathy. This may color popular perceptions about these kinds of constitutional claims.

Of people whose constitutional rights are violated during criminal investigations, it is impossible to know how many become claimants. For one, violations that do not lead to evidence (e.g., illegal drug searches where no drugs are found) may go unrecorded. Even those that do culminate in criminal prosecutions often end in plea bargains before a constitutional right is ever claimed. Nor do claimants generally include victims of illegal policing tactics that are intended to control people rather than investigate them – for example, verbal harassment. Thus, claimants may comprise just a small subset of those whose constitutional rights are violated during government investigation and adjudication.

Another major difference between criminal law and civil law situations is that in the former, it is often incumbent on an individual to assert a constitutional right during an interaction with police. Using a version of the example above, suppose a police officer knocks on a person's door and asks to conduct a warrantless search of her home. For her Fourth Amendment right to be preserved, she must assert it at this moment (by refusing the search) or during the search (by asking police to stop). She may not assert it retroactively. By contrast, in the civil context, such immediate assertions are rarely required. A victim of sexual harassment does not waive her right to bring a sexual harassment claim against her employer if she fails to protest *while* she is being harassed. Thus, rights knowledge may play a different role in criminal procedure than in civil law and is an important aspect of rights consciousness in the criminal context. (And individuals' knowledge, or lack of knowledge, may further narrow the subset of possible claimants.)

Additionally, the Sixth Amendment right to counsel applies in most types of criminal trials, but not in civil trials (*Lassiter v. Department of Social Services*, 1981). Availability of counsel may shape the claiming process. Since rights claimants in criminal cases generally have access to counsel, and since counsel is tasked with providing a defense to a particular crime, rights claims made in criminal cases may emerge less from a claimant's sense that she was "wronged" than as part of a trial strategy that includes minimizing the amount of inculpatory evidence the jury sees. This does not suggest that victims of rights violations in the criminal procedure context don't feel wronged or believe that they deserve compensation, but that there may be less correlation between rights claiming and a sense of victimhood in the criminal context than in the civil context.

In short, rights consciousness offers new and fertile ground for understanding criminal investigation and procedure. Conversely, drawing upon these areas of the law may deepen our understanding of rights consciousness. As is true in the civil realm, people's orientation to constitutional criminal procedure arises from fluid, dynamic processes between individuals' attitudes, beliefs, and identity, social inequalities, authorities' behavior, black-letter law, and the legal and social culture in which rights exist.

RIGHTS KNOWLEDGE AND LAY JURISPRUDENCE: A FIRST EMPIRICAL STEP

Motivation

> [C]omprehending the most basic functions of rights requires the empirical study of rights consciousness and claiming behavior ... This perspective, which is squarely within the law and society tradition, places the study of ordinary citizens' understandings of rights, and what action they take based on that knowledge, at the forefront of an empirical research agenda ... [This has] important implications for law's capacity to achieve social change and can lead to a better understanding of how rights can and should operate in a social and legal system.
>
> Laura Beth Nielsen, 2007, p. xi

Little work has been done that probes the relationship between the judiciary's interpretation of constitutional criminal procedure and citizens' understanding of their criminal procedural rights. In some areas of law, we might consider a disjunction between legal rules and popular understanding problematic mostly at an abstract level. For example, the average American's suppositions about how law governs corporate transactions might be quite wrong, and such erroneous assumptions would be unfortunate in the sense that we might hope for some alignment between the law itself and people's understanding of the world in which they live.

In criminal law, however, such misalignment would be problematic in a couple of additional ways. For one, the Court's use of concepts such as "reasonable" and "voluntary" in its criminal procedure doctrine suggest reliance on popular understanding. The Court must make normative assessments how people see their social world, and these assessments can be tested empirically. If the Court says, for example, that a "reasonable" person will behave a particular way in an encounter with police, but empirical testing shows that very few people will actually behave that way, we would begin to question the doctrine – for example, the Court's ability to make normative assessments along these lines or the wisdom of hinging constitutional doctrine on these sorts of concepts.

Misalignment between criminal procedure doctrine and popular understanding is also problematic because of the crucial role that knowledge plays in police–citizen interactions. In solving justiciable civil legal problems, people are unlikely to cite their own ignorance of the law as a reason for not taking legal action and may lack a meaningful sense of what they know and do not know (Sandefur, 2007, p. 130). In the criminal procedure context, a dearth of knowledge has many implications. People who lack legal knowledge may unwittingly, and irrevocably, waive constitutional rights – and they may not know that their own ignorance of their rights influences their decisions about how to interact with law enforcement. These interactions, in turn, have legal consequences. Research is needed to understand which rights people know, how people think about their rights, where these ideas come from, and what effects these beliefs have on people's actions.

The myriad rules that referee the United States' investigation and prosecution of its citizens for criminal acts are embodied largely in the Fourth, Fifth, and Sixth Amendments. Nearly all these protections have been held applicable to state governments through the Fourteenth Amendment. Absent a specific exception such as consent or exigency, a citizen must knowingly and voluntarily waive a right for the right to be relinquished.[4] Obviously, people are unlikely to assert rights that they don't believe they possess. This logic underlies the warning requirement set out by the United States Supreme Court in *Miranda v. Arizona* (1966); a meaningful waiver of the right not to incriminate oneself requires that suspects are aware of the right in the first place. Informing citizens of their rights at the outset puts all subjects – theoretically, at least – on equal footing.

The Court, however, has not adopted an analogous view of knowledge with regard to Fourth Amendment searches and seizures. It has held that a person does not need to be informed of her right to refuse a search and that even if she consents under the erroneous belief that she was required to submit to a search, any evidence that the search uncovers will not necessarily be excluded.[5] Thus, the onus is on a suspect to both *know* and *use* her Fourth Amendment rights. Justice Brennan's dissent in *Schneckloth v. Bustamonte* (1973, p. 277) criticized the Court for hinging its decision on the legal fiction of perfect knowledge: "It wholly escapes me how our citizens can meaningfully be said to have waived something as precious as a constitutional guarantee without ever being aware of its existence." Several scholars have echoed this view. Janice Nadler (2002, p. 213) writes that is it "not a secret" that "the Court's Fourth Amendment consensual encounter doctrine is founded upon a legal fiction." Nadler points to Wayne LaFave's famous criminal procedure treatise, which begins discussion of Fourth Amendment waiver with reference to "[t]he so-called consent search" (Nadler, 2002, p. 213, citing LaFave, 1996, p. 4). Others have suggested that the absence of a meaningful knowledge requirement creates an incentive for police officers to keep citizens from knowing their rights (e.g., Cloud, 2007).

Criticism of the consent search doctrine is particularly poignant given the sheer number of these searches. It is difficult to know precisely how many searches are based on consent alone, but estimates hover around 90% (Simmons, 2005, p. 773). Not only is it legal for police to knock on a citizen's door without suspicion and ask to search, but it yields widespread acquiescence (Burkoff, 2007; Chanenson, 2004). There may be a "normative impulse to submit to [state] power because police officers as enforcers of the law are presumptively right" (Lassiter, 2007, p. 1176). In some jurisdictions, consent searches are used regularly as a tool of law enforcement (Nadler, 2002, pp. 153–154), echoing other "preventative investigation" techniques (see Reiss, 1971).[6]

Less obviously, a lack of knowledge may affect how citizens use their Fifth and Sixth Amendment rights as well. For example, even after being Mirandized, a suspect may waive, or refuse to waive, her right to silence or counsel without understanding the legal consequences. She may not know, for example, that asking, "What is going to happen to me now?" counts as a willingness to speak to police without counsel (*Oregon v. Bradshaw*, 1983, pp. 1043–1044), or that non-Mirandized statements can be used to impeach her credibility at trial if she takes the stand (*Harris v. New York*, 1971).[7]

Despite the central role of rights knowledge in citizens' interactions with police, the degree to which ignorance actually facilitates waivers remains unknown. Only a tiny handful of empirical studies are on point, the majority of which were conducted within a decade of the Warren Court's seminal criminal procedure decisions. In Austin Sarat's 1975 survey of 220 Wisconsin adults, he found that "[l]ess than half know that an arrested person cannot be made to answer questions" and that "[o]ver 90% know that the police have to inform suspects of their rights" (Sarat, 1977, p. 479, citing Sarat, 1975). In an unpublished dissertation, Illya Lichtenberg found that of citizens who consented to a vehicle search following a traffic stop, "[m]ost were unaware of their legal right to refuse" (Chanenson, 2004, p. 454, citing Lichtenberg, 1999). However, Lichtenberg's conclusion was based on only 54 respondents – the small percentage who responded to solicitations. As Lichtenberg acknowledges, "this constitutes a relatively serious threat to validity" (Chanenson, 2004, p. 455, citing Lichtenberg, 1999).

In this section, I take two initial empirical steps in applying a rights consciousness framework to criminal procedure.

Data and Methods

Study 1 builds on the simple insight that in many situations, knowledge of a right is a precondition for its assertion. I ask how much knowledge people have about their criminal procedural rights and discuss the implications of my findings. Study 2 is a smaller, qualitative study in which I ask how people understand, and answer questions about, their constitutional rights.

To begin examining what constitutional rights people believe they possess, I created a survey consisting in part of 10 scenarios that raise Fourth, Fifth, and Sixth Amendment questions. All are based squarely on Supreme Court cases decided between 1978 and 2004, and all (insofar as is possible in constitutional criminal procedure) are matters of settled law. In none of the scenarios are police or other government officials required to inform an individual of the rights he or she possesses.[8] Questions and answers are listed in Appendix A. Three examples are listed below:

> **Q**: Police suspect Julie is growing marijuana in her house. Growing marijuana indoors requires special lamps that give off a lot of heat. From the sidewalk, police use a "thermal imaging device" (a machine that measures heat waves) to look at the heat coming from Julie's house. Are the officers allowed to do this without a warrant?
>
> [The answer is no. Without a warrant, officers are not allowed to use specialized technology to see inside a person's home; they may only use technology that is generally available to people, such as binoculars.]
>
> **Q**: Steve is charged with cruelty to animals, a misdemeanor in his state punishable by either fines or community service. Steve's case goes to trial in front of a jury, and Steve can't afford a lawyer. Does he have a right to have a lawyer provided?
>
> [The answer is no. The Sixth Amendment right to counsel applies in all felony cases, but does not apply in misdemeanor cases if the defendant could not face jail time for the offense.]
>
> **Q**: If police question you in violation of your rights, and you tell them where you've hidden an object, then they find your fingerprints on the object, can the fingerprints be used against you?
>
> [The answer is yes. If a suspect makes voluntary statements that lead police to physical evidence, the evidence is admissible even if *Miranda* was violated.]

Although some of the questions were tricky, none was particularly obscure, and all addressed situations reasonably likely to arise in the normal course of a police investigation. Nor is knowledge in these scenarios inconsequential. As discussed earlier, rights knowledge would enhance decision-making in these situations. In some scenarios, legal knowledge could affect the actions a person chooses to take. In others, it might simply afford a greater sense of control or agency.

The respondent population for Study 1 comprised 367 undergraduates: 258 from a public community college in Southern California and 109 from a private four-year university in Northern California. Respondents were students in history, psychology, sociology, and political science courses at the community college and students in sociology and American studies courses at the private university. Classes were selected based on instructor willingness to distribute the survey.

Study 2 was designed to further probe how people answer questions about their rights. I used a convenience sample of 25 individuals, ranging in age from their early 20s to their early 70s, and ranging in level of formal education from a high school diploma (in several cases) to a Ph.D. (in two cases). Each respondent was given the same yes-or-no questions used in Study 1[9] and was asked to explain the answers in an open-ended response. The content of responses was coded according to the method of reasoning used to answer a question.

Results

If respondents had no previous knowledge of the American legal system and guessed randomly, we would expect that about 50% (or 1,825) of the 3,650 answers given would be correct. If respondents had strong, or even moderate, knowledge of their rights, we would expect this number to be higher. Nearly all respondents were American citizens, and many reported prior exposure to the American criminal justice system: as jurors or suspects, through high school or college classes, or from friends or family members employed in law enforcement.

In Study 1, 1,461 of respondents' total answers were correct and 2,189 were incorrect. That is, respondents answered correctly about 1,461/3,650 (or 40%) of the time, and incorrectly about 2,189/3,650 (or 60%) of the time. For seven of the ten questions, fewer than half of respondents chose the correct answer. These figures are striking; not only did respondents not know how their constitutional rights applied in the scenarios, but their guesses were more likely to be wrong than right.[10]

In three of the scenarios, respondents' answers were extremely lopsided; more than 80% of respondents answered these three questions incorrectly (aside from these, the least evenly divided responses were 64.8% to 35.2% and 60.4% to 39.6%). In all three scenarios that received lopsided responses, respondents guessed that the law affords greater constitutional protection to criminal defendants than it actually does. Two of these questions dealt with Fourth Amendment rights: the legality of pen registries (police looking at the numbers a person has dialed from her home telephone) and the ability to raise Fourth Amendment claims (whether illegally-seized evidence can be used in court against someone whose person or property wasn't the object of the search); one dealt with Sixth Amendment rights: the availability of counsel in different types of misdemeanor cases. In each situation, respondents believed that certain fundamental constitutional ideas (here, the right to privacy and the right to counsel) would apply in particular cases to protect defendants. The results suggest that people may tend to overestimate the power of rights to protect criminal defendants. See Appendix B for a breakdown of respondents' answers to each question.

The lines of reasoning that led to erroneous answers likely varied by question. The Sixth Amendment errors were probably due to overbreadth; people know about the right to counsel generally and assume that it applies in all situations. Since most respondents lack specialized legal knowledge, perhaps this is not surprising. The question about pen registries can be seen as a form of overbreadth, as well; people may have assumed that a privacy right exists, then applied it too broadly. But people's erroneous answers are more troubling here, since the Court's decision in that case hinged on the idea that even if the defendant had a subjective expectation of privacy in the phone numbers he dialed from home, his expectation was not reasonable under societal standards (*Smith v. Maryland*, 1979). Respondents' pattern of answers highlights a possible problem in the doctrine. It suggests that in actuality, even after almost 30 years of settled law to the contrary, people *do* have an expectation of privacy in pen registries. And we might take the ubiquity of this expectation as strong evidence of its reasonableness. This tension illustrates the usefulness of empirical inquiry in understanding the beliefs and assumptions that undergird constitutional criminal procedure.

Responses in Study 2 were coded according to the type of reasoning that respondents used to answer each item. We might imagine a wide range of ways in which people might think about, and answer questions about, their rights. For example, their ideas about the law might align with their beliefs about what the law *should* say – a possibility suggested by Darley, Carlsmith, and Robinson (2001), who found that people tend to assume that the substance of the criminal law in their own states matches their beliefs about what the law should be. If a similar mechanism is at work with regard to constitutional rights, we might expect people to explain their answers in terms of their own values (e.g., "citizens should have the right to refuse searches," or "attorneys are important for trial"). Another possibility is that people could draw on their own experiences. If so, we would expect them to analogize between those experiences and the scenarios presented in the hypotheticals (e.g., "When I was pulled over by a cop, the same thing happened, so I think the officer can search" or "my brother is a lawyer and he told me about this"). People's likelihood of reasoning from this kind of analogy might depend on the extent of their previous contact with the criminal justice system. Alternatively, people could justify their responses by reasoning from a framework or ideology that reflects their overarching beliefs and understandings about governmental power (e.g., "Police seem to be able to do whatever they want, so I'm sure they can search the car" or "defense attorneys always find some way to get evidence thrown out, so I bet the letter won't come in").

The ways in which respondents actually explained their answers varied little, and one pattern was overwhelming: people tended to use a basic version of classic legal reasoning. They stated a broad legal principle (correct or not), then applied this rule to the facts in the scenario. Responses to the question about whether police need a warrant to measure heat emanating from a private home are illustrative. For example: " ... I believe that the evidence provided by the device would be said to provide 'probable cause;'" "Just because the cops are checking for heat is probably circumstantial. It wouldn't be enough to search the house;" "I'd think that if officers are inquiring about something inside of the house, they would need a warrant ... " Each response implicitly or (more often) explicitly invokes a principle that people believe is a legal "rule:" probable cause enables searches, circumstantial evidence cannot be used as justification for a search, and a warrant is necessary for police to gather evidence inside a home. As in this example, respondents' assertions about the law were sometimes correct, and sometimes not.

Where respondents identified a correct legal rule, they sometimes misapplied it. For example, consider the third question in the previous section, which asks whether, if a *Miranda* violation leads police to physical evidence, the physical evidence can be used in court. Although none identified it by name, many respondents accurately explained the exclusionary rule's underlying principle (evidence must be excluded if police obtain it as the result of a procedural violation), writing responses such as: "Although you'd think it should, I think that it can't count because she didn't know her rights," and "Because her rights were not read to her, nothing is valid." These respondents not only understood the reasoning behind exclusion, but correctly ascertained that the exclusionary rule would be a key doctrine at issue in this scenario. However, they applied the rule as a blanket matter, leading them to believe that a defendant would benefit from it here.

Notably, most respondents stated at least a few fundamentals of criminal procedure correctly. We might guess that this would not be true in other major areas of law (e.g., property, patents, contracts) and that respondents' familiarity with criminal procedure is due in part to the disproportionate representation of criminal justice issues in various media outlets. As will be discussed in the following section, it is this very familiarity that may lead people to draw erroneous conclusions about their constitutional rights.

Discussion

These studies offer a starting point for expanding rights consciousness research to the criminal procedure context and for thinking about procedural rights consciousness more generally. This vein of work has the potential to yield further insight about people's understanding of rights, about the influence of factors such as social location and identity on this understanding, and about how and when rights are claimed and acted upon.

From these two studies alone, it is impossible to discern whence people derive the legal "rules" they draw upon to decide whether a right exists in a particular circumstance. The rules' content and application, however, was somewhat predictable. This style of pseudo-legal reasoning can be understood as a kind of "lay jurisprudence,"[11] in which the "doctrine" comprises widespread cultural ideas and assumptions about the Constitution and the criminal justice system. By and large, the "rules" respondents cited align with what we might suppose are shared, general beliefs about criminal procedure that are rooted in American civic culture. For example, in determining whether "Steve" was entitled to legal representation in his misdemeanor trial, respondents wrote: "It's a criminal case; as such, one is entitled to a legal defender," "Everyone has the right to a lawyer, I think this is in the *Miranda* warning," and "All defendants have the right to a public defender in criminal trials by jury." These three respondents answered incorrectly, but their justifications drew upon a simplified (or, we might say, idealized) version of the holding in *Gideon v. Wainwright* (1963).

The consistency of reasoning across questions suggests that lay jurisprudence is a mechanism through which people understand and make decisions about their rights, drawing on a store of beliefs about the law and applying them to specific situations. These beliefs tend to reflect widespread ideas about the protection the Constitution affords. A lay jurisprudential approach to rights situations leads people to misunderstand the rights they possess. Put differently, when it comes to criminal procedure, a little knowledge can be a dangerous thing. This does not contradict the rights consciousness paradigms described by Nielsen and others, but rather builds on the literature's identification of systematic, and predictable, patterns in how people think about law.

In both studies, respondents were in greatest agreement when a question either evoked only one lay jurisprudential tenet, or evoked multiple, non-conflicting tenets. For example, in response to the question about the admissibility of physical evidence stemming from a *Miranda* violation, the only tenet readily available is the exclusionary rule principle. Respondents invoked this idea with near-unanimity, which led over 90% of them to answer incorrectly. The content of the open-ended responses in the second pilot study is consistent with this interpretation of the results. Typical responses included, "I think because it is a private place the police would have had no legal way of finding the letter," "It was obtained illegally so it can't count," and "The search was illegal and the letter was found in the illegal search." These responses reflect a lay jurisprudential approach. However, when lay jurisprudence reasoning could cut in two different directions, responses tended to be mixed. For example, the question about using a thermal imaging device to detect heat lamps evokes two popular tenets: (1) police need a warrant to search; (2) a "search" is a physical intrusion. Responses tended to align with one of these two ideas, and were divided accordingly.

Lay jurisprudential tenets were applied consistently across items as well. The survey contained two questions that dealt with potential violations of the Fifth Amendment's *Miranda* warning requirement. In one of these, a blanket application of the notion that *Miranda* violations mandate exclusion leads to a correct answer; in the other, it leads to an incorrect answer. Responses followed suit. This pattern was especially noteworthy with regard to the latter question, because respondents' answers followed lay jurisprudential reasoning even when respondents stated that they disagreed morally with the outcome to which their reasoning led. Representative responses include: "Although it seems like extremely bad practice, they read [the defendant] his rights and he decided to confess anyway," and "If the defendant does not ask to speak to an attorney and actively waives his rights he is screwed." This suggests that the mechanism Darley et al. describe with regard to the penal code (people think that law's content aligns with their own beliefs) may operate differently with regard to people's orientation to constitutional rights in the criminal realm – or that it may operate differently in situations that raise questions about procedural rights rather than questions about substantive law.

Moreover, these results suggest that in deciding whether to invoke rights and how to interact with authorities, people's actions may often be based on erroneous beliefs. Laypeople can hardly be expected to have an encyclopedic knowledge of criminal procedure, but it appears that at least in some situations, citizens would be better off acting in complete ignorance of their procedural rights than trying to discern what rights they have. In the Fourth Amendment context, "consent" may be as much of a myth as Justice Brennan, Janice Nadler, and others have suggested. Assuming we consider it problematic for people to relinquish rights out of ignorance rather than conscious choice,[12] this finding lends support to legal and policy proposals designed to make waivers more meaningful, such as a Fourth Amendment warning requirement analogous to the *Miranda* warnings.[13] In the Fifth and Sixth Amendment contexts, although the *Miranda* warnings give suspects a little information about the law, the warnings fall far short of ameliorating suspects' unfamiliarity. The warnings may have been adequate when *Miranda* was handed down in 1966, but more than four decades later, Fifth Amendment law is filled with clarifications, caveats, and exceptions. If we want to equip people with a meaningful opportunity to use their rights, the *Miranda* warnings may no longer go far enough. Indeed, the warnings may perpetuate the kind of lay jurisprudential tenets that can lead people to erroneous conclusions about how rights operate in particular situations and may lead people to assume that they know more than they actually do.

Finally, not only does lay jurisprudence lead people to err about the rights they possess, but it leads them to err in predictable ways. This finding underscores the concerns of MacCoun, Haney, and others regarding procedural justice research. Some law enforcement techniques already incorporate means of increasing compliance by making people feel more satisfied in police–citizen interactions. A meaningful opportunity to exercise constitutional rights may or may not correlate with these feelings of satisfaction. Thus, the ways people understand criminal procedure, and the assumptions they make about how the law works, may open the door to methods of policing designed to encourage waiver and render people vulnerable to manipulation and unwitting surrender of their rights.

AN AGENDA FOR FUTURE RESEARCH

The Relationship between Rights Consciousness and the Constitutional Landscape

Ideas and assumptions about social behavior are embedded throughout constitutional criminal procedure. Hinging the admissibility of evidence on "reasonableness" or "voluntariness," for example, suggests some consensus about the types of behavior that are reasonable or voluntary. Normative assessments are necessarily at the crux of these determinations. Empirical inquiry can help produce "a clearer picture of the existing constitutional landscape" (Meares & Harcourt, 2000, p. 735) by testing the validity, effects, and implications of normative judgments that underpin criminal procedure doctrine.[14] This kind of research has important implications for the understanding of rights consciousness more broadly – asking, for example, how people's orientation to rights maps onto the legal landscape, and whether awareness of rights engenders a willingness to claim them.

Rights Consciousness and Social Location in Constitutional Criminal Procedure

One crucial question for future research is how rights consciousness, including rights knowledge and rights assertion, operates along demographic lines such as race, class, and gender. This builds on existing work such as Nielsen's study of attitudes about street harassment, in which she found that paradigms for opposing the regulation of free speech varied by race and gender. For example, non-whites were more likely than whites to oppose regulation because they did not trust the government to regulate fairly.

Even if knowledge of rights is equally distributed among members of different socioeconomic levels, people may think about the justiciability of their rights in ways that are heavily influenced by their experiences and background (Sandefur, 2007; Engel & Munger, 1996). Annette Lareau's work on how social class shapes individual interaction styles offers a possible starting point. Lareau suggests that upper-middle class parents' interactions with their children differ from working class parents'. The former are socialized to interact with professionals, use institutions to their advantage, and voice requests for change when they are unsatisfied with treatment or outcomes they receive from authorities. In contrast, working class children are raised to be deferential and quiet around authorities and are discouraged from protesting unsatisfactory treatment or outcomes (Lareau, 2002). This "emerging sense of entitlement" (Lareau, 2002, p. 749) in children of professionals may be particularly relevant to interactions between citizens and the police, since police are such an acme incarnation of authority. For example, low-status individuals may be more likely to view police as occupying a higher status position than themselves. If questioned by police, they may be more likely to act in a manner that police associate with guilt. In contrast, a high-status individual may view police either as equals, or even as occupying an inferior social position. As a result, high-status individuals may engage with police by instinctively using techniques that render them less vulnerable to intrusive investigative tactics.[15]

Demographic differences in rights assertions could also stem from disparate senses of fairness and agency, grounded in the kinds of social and financial resources available to different groups. In discussing subjective perceptions of fairness, Sandefur (2008, p. 341) points out that current research "tells us much about what kinds of experiences people believe to be fair but rather less about which groups are more or less likely to encounter fair-feeling experiences." For example, an affluent white woman may refuse consent to a warrantless search without worrying about police retribution. This willingness to assert rights may stem from an implicit, perhaps even unconscious, awareness of her own control; if the officer acts illegally, the affluent woman will hire a good lawyer to argue on her behalf. A working-class black man in the same situation may feel less at liberty to refuse. He may perceive – perhaps accurately, and perhaps even unconsciously – that if police misbehave, he will have little legal or social recourse. He may assume that his best bet is to consent, even if he would rather refuse. John Gilliom (2001) has described a regime of governmental oversight, regulation, and scrutiny of welfare recipients, whereby people learn through experience that regardless of official regulations, authorities' discretion is virtually unfettered. Working-class people do not necessarily view law as more "prosecution-friendly," but may see themselves as more subject to government regulation and as possessing fewer rights, because their past experiences with authority have been brusque, invasive, and characterized by a lack of opportunity for personal agency.

Rights Consciousness and Rights Characteristics

Finally, future research might probe differences in rights consciousness with respect to different types of procedural rights. For example, within the universe of constitutional rights in criminal procedure, we might imagine at least two continuums. First, a right could be characterized as "latent" or "manifest" to varying degrees. The more latent a right is, the more incumbent it is upon the individual to assert the right – that is, exercise of a latent right is heavily dependent on a person's knowledge, action, or both. For example, suppose police pull a person over and ask her to step out of the vehicle. They have no probable cause, but say, "We need to search your trunk, all right?" Although the search requires consent, the person may not know she has a right to refuse. In order for her to exercise her right, she not only must know (or believe, or suppose) she has the right, but must be willing to claim or assert it. As such, her Fourth Amendment right in this situation falls toward the "latent" end of the spectrum. A more "manifest" right, on the other hand, requires little of the individual; regardless of the individual's action, the government must act in a way that acknowledges the right. The requirement that police read the *Miranda* rights and obtain a waiver before interrogating a person in custody is one example. The suspect need not enter the situation knowing she has a right to the *Miranda* warnings, nor does she need to request them. Such a rule would fall farther toward the "manifest" end of the spectrum. And, certainly, a procedural right might move from one place on this spectrum to another as the situation – and with it, the attendant law – changes.

On another spectrum, a right might range from "situational" to "ubiquitous." The most situational rights only exist under particular conditions. The right to an attorney is closer to this end of the spectrum. It only applies to criminal defendants, only to those charged with certain categories of crimes, and only when formal adversarial charges are brought against a person. Conversely, a more ubiquitous right applies in a broader variety of circumstances. For example, physical abuse by the police is a constitutional violation regardless of whether a person is a criminal defendant, where she is located, or whether, at the time of the beating, she asserts her Fourteenth Amendment right to due process. Fig. 1 suggests one way to conceptualize these two spectrums.

Certainly, the exact placement of any individual right on the spectrums can be debated. "A" and "B" above are possible placements for the examples given in the previous paragraph. "C" and "D" suggest placements for the right to refuse a warrantless search of one's home and the right to refuse a warrantless search of one's car, respectively. The latter falls closer to the "situational" end of the spectrum because criminal procedure doctrine contains a wide variety of situations in which an officer may conduct a warrantless search of a car. For example, if a car is lawfully stopped, police

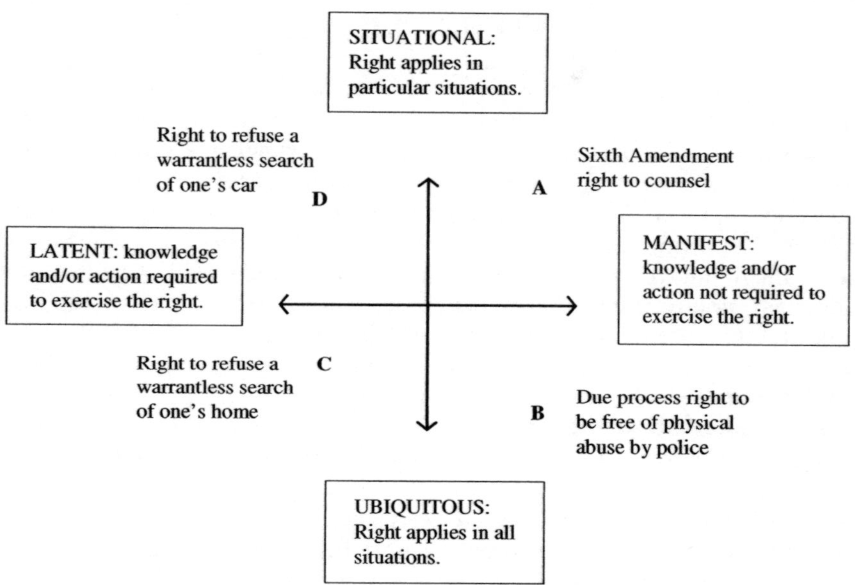

Fig. 1. Conceptual Spectrums for Constitutional Criminal Procedure Rights.

may always order the driver (*Pennsylvania v. Mimms*, 1977) and passengers (*Maryland v. Wilson*, 1997) out of the vehicle; if an arrest occurs, police may search the entire interior of the car, excepting the trunk and the engine compartments, and including any container, open or closed, regardless of size (*New York v. Belton*, 1981; *Thornton v. U.S.*, 2004). On the other hand, the rules for searches incident to arrest in suspects' homes are more restrictive. For example, closed containers outside the arrestee's "grabbable distance" cannot be opened simply because an arrest occured (see *Chimel v. California*, 1969).

These spectrums are intended to be descriptive, not normative. Nor are they exhaustive. Rather, they represent just one way we might parse legal rules and doctrine in order to better understand rights consciousness in the criminal context. We might ask: How does rights knowledge map onto these continuums? Are more latent, and more situational, rights difficult to exercise compared to more manifest, ubiquitous ones? Do characteristics of a right affect how people orient themselves in relation to it? What measures can be taken to assure that people are given an opportunity to meaningfully assert their rights?

CONCLUSION

The discussion and studies above illustrate the fruitfulness of examining criminal procedure as an aspect of rights consciousness research. Legal consciousness – and rights consciousness in particular – offers a useful means of understanding constitutional criminal procedure rights, raising questions about the rights citizens believe they possess, how these ideas are formed, their willingness to assert rights, and how their relationship to government authority affects, and is affected by, these beliefs. Additionally, investigation into procedural rights consciousness offers a way to build on procedural justice work, probing the relationship between procedures' legal content, people's subjective impressions, and normative questions about the legality and morality of particular procedures.

The studies above also suggest that people's understanding of their criminal procedural rights in particular situations is a product of "lay jurisprudence," in which they reason from generalized notions about constitutional and criminal law. This phenomenon often causes them to draw erroneous conclusions about their rights, and these conclusions are likely to have appreciable consequences when people are the subjects of government investigation. Understanding this mechanism may further prevent abuses of state power and point to procedural reforms that would allow citizens to exercise their constitutional rights in more meaningful ways.

More research is needed to completely explore rights consciousness in the criminal realm, including how naming, blaming, and claiming operate differently in civil, versus criminal, law. Work on rights knowledge and rights assertion, particularly with respect to demographic factors, is also an important component of rights consciousness in the criminal law context and offers fertile ground for future empirical and theoretical work.

NOTES

1. As Somers and Roberts (2008) acknowledge in describing a "right to have rights," the division between human and citizenship rights is not a clean one. For example, even if we stipulate that a man has no natural right not to incriminate himself, we could still debate whether his natural rights are violated if he is denied this right on the basis of his race while it is granted to others in his country. That is, a state may not need to grant a particular right, but if it chooses to grant the right, it must do so evenhandedly. Furthermore, we might argue that if a state grants a right to its citizens, it assumes a corresponding responsibility to make a good faith effort to effectuate the right in a meaningful way.

2. Sandefur (2008, pp. 340–341) incisively observes that sociological work on access to justice struggles with an inherent tension. On the one hand, empirical work on "justice" requires, to some extent, a list of justice's ingredients. On the other, such a list embodies a normative appraisal of the type for which social science may be ill-suited. In response, scholars have taken two approaches: either taking up equality as a working definition of justice – thus measuring behavior or outcomes (e.g., racial equality) against formal legal institutional standards, or skipping the question of substantive justice altogether and focusing instead on people's subjective experiences (e.g., outcome satisfaction).

3. It is also worth noting that some incidents we might understand as constitutional "violations" are not technically "violations" at all. For example, if police ignore a suspect's right not to incriminate herself, and they obtain inculpatory statements as a result, the Fifth Amendment is not actually violated until the statement is used against the defendant in court.

4. See, e.g., *Miranda v. Arizona* (1966) regarding the Fifth Amendment, *Schneckloth v. Bustamonte* (1973) regarding the Fourth Amendment, and *Edwards v. Arizona* (1981) regarding the Sixth Amendment.

5. Actual knowledge of one's right to refuse a search is merely one factor in the "totality of the circumstances" that courts analyze to determine whether consent to the search was voluntary.

6. For more on how consent searches operate, see Steven L. Chanenson's (1999) discussion of Illya D. Lichtenberg's unpublished dissertation, "Voluntary Consent of Obedience to Authority: An Inquiry into the 'Consensual' Police-Citizen Encounter." Lichtenberg studied consent searches stemming from highway traffic stops in Maryland and Ohio and found that of the 9,028 people who were asked for consent, 89.3% granted it.

7. Certainly, as a practical matter, informing a suspect of every applicable doctrinal nuance would be unfeasible, at least for policing in its current incarnation. But it is not unthinkable that police departments could have a "rights consultant" on hand for suspects who have questions about their rights but are otherwise willing to talk to police.

8. Some of the questions pose a hypothetical scenario and ask respondents whether police behavior was legal. Other questions are asked more directly: Are police allowed to do x?

9. Some questions used minor differences in phrasing, but the substance was unaltered.

10. It is important to note that the questions are a collection of difficult, but settled, non-peripheral constitutional questions, and were not intended as a representative sample of criminal procedure issues overall. For this reason, the results do not tell us that people are incorrect about 60% of the rights they possess, nor that they guess erroneously 60% of the time.

11. John Conley and William O'Barr (1990, pp. 44–45) have used this term to describe layperson reasoning in civil law problems.

12. This may seem obvious, but hinges on where the responsibility for rights knowledge rests. In oral argument in *United States v. Drayton* (2002), Justice Kennedy suggested that citizens should bear some responsibility to know their own rights, lest they assume the risk of missing an opportunity to exercise them: "An American citizen has to protect his rights once in a while ... that's a bad thing?"

Chief Justice Warren's opinion in *Miranda* exemplifies the opposite philosophy, in which the state bears responsibility for informing citizens in order to ensure they have an adequate opportunity to exercise their rights: "[A] warning at the time of the interrogation is indispensable to overcome its pressures and to *insure that the individual knows* he is free to exercise the privilege at that point in time" (*Miranda v. Arizona*, 1966, p. 469 (emphasis added)).

13. The Supreme Court has consistently declined to extend *Miranda*'s rights knowledge reasoning to other areas – most notably Fourth Amendment searches and seizures (Reich, 2003) (see, e.g., *Florida v. Bostick*, 1991).

14. For example, Janice Nadler (2002, p. 155) has observed that "[t]he question of whether a citizen feels free to terminate a police encounter depends crucially on certain empirical claims, as does the question of whether a citizen's grant of permission to search is voluntary;" Steven L. Chanenson (2004, p. 455) has written that empirical research is needed "to fill the yawning hole in our knowledge about consent searches." For further discussion of the paucity of empirical research in constitutional criminal procedure, see also Merritt (1999); Chanenson (2004); Meares and Harcourt (2000).

15. And this, of course, may be compounded by any favorable treatment that high-status individuals already enjoy from police due to race, class, or other status markers.

16. The original survey included 11 questions. I removed one from the analysis: "If the police interrogate you without reading you your *Miranda* rights, then you confess, can the confession be used against you in trial?" This question is ambiguous and imprecise; the confession could not be used against a defendant in the prosecutor's case-in-chief, but could be used against a defendant for other purposes in trial, such as impeaching the defendant's credibility if she takes the stand.

ACKNOWLEDGMENTS

I am deeply indebted to Becky Sandefur for many useful conversations and for her insightful feedback on multiple drafts. Thanks also to Bob Weisberg for inspiration and helpful suggestions, to Taylor Young for her research assistance, and to the Stanford Criminal Justice Center and the Stanford Graduate Fellowship program for financial support. I presented an earlier draft of this chapter at the 2008 meeting of the Pacific Sociological Association in Portland, Oregon.

REFERENCES

Burkoff, J. (2007). Search me? *Texas Tech Law Review*, *39*, 1109–1141.

Casper, J. D., Tyler, T., & Fisher, B. (1988). Procedural justice in felony cases. *Law and Society Review*, *22*(3), 483–508.

Chanenson, S. L. (2004). Get the facts, Jack! Empirical research and the changing constitutional landscape of consent searches. *Tennessee Law Review, 71*, 399–470.

Cloud, M. (2007). Ignorance and democracy. *Texas Tech Law Review, 39*, 1143–1169.

Conley, J. M., & O'Barr, W. (1990). *Rules versus relationships: The ethnography of legal discourse*. Chicago, IL: University of Chicago Press.

Darley, J. M., Carlsmith, K. M., & Robinson, P. H. (2001). The ex ante function of the criminal law. *Law & Society Review, 35*(1), 165–190.

Engel, D. M., & Munger, F. W. (1996). Rights, remembrance, and the reconciliation of difference. *Law and Society Review, 30*(1), 7–53.

Ewick, P., & Silbey, S. S. (1998). *The common place of law: Stories from everyday life*. Chicago, IL: University of Chicago Press.

Felstiner, W. L. F., Abel, R. L., & Sarat, A. (1980). The emergence and transformation of disputes: Naming, blaming, claiming. *Law and Society Review, 15*(3/4), 631–654.

Friedman, L. M. (1971). The idea of right as a social and legal concept. *Journal of Social Issues, 27*, 189–198.

Gilliom, J. (2001). *Overseers of the poor: Surveillance, resistance, and the limits of privacy*. Chicago, IL: University of Chicago Press.

Haney, C. (1991). The fourth amendment and symbolic legality: Let them eat due process. *Law and Human Behavior, 15*(2), 183–204.

Karlan, P. S. (2007). The paradoxical structure of constitutional litigation. *Fordham Law Review, 75*, 1913–1929.

LaFave, W. R. (1996). *Search and seizure: A treatise on the fourth amendment* (§ 8.1) (3d ed.). St. Paul, MN: West.

Lareau, A. (2002). Invisible inequality: Social class and childrearing in black families and white families. *American Sociological Review, 67*(5), 747–776.

Lassiter, C. (2007). Consent to search by ignorant people. *Texas Tech Law Review, 39*, 1171–1194.

Lichtenberg, I. D. (1999). Voluntary consent of obedience to authority: An inquiry into the 'consensual' police-citizen encounter. Unpublished dissertation.

MacCoun, R. J. (2005). Voice, control, and belonging: The double-edged sword of procedural fairness. *Annual Review of Law and Social Science, 1*, 171–201.

Meares, T. L., & Harcourt, B. E. (2000). Foreword: Transparent adjudication and social science research in constitutional criminal procedure. *Journal of Criminal Law and Criminology, 90*, 733–798.

Meltzer, D. J. (1988). Deterring constitutional violations by law enforcement officials: Plaintiffs and defendants as private attorneys general. *Columbia Law Review, 88*, 247–328.

Merritt, D. J. (1999). Constitutional fact and theory: A response to judge Posner. *Michigan Law Review, 97*, 1287–1295.

Merry, S. E. (1990). *Getting justice and getting even: Legal consciousness among working class Americans*. Chicago, IL: University of Chicago Press.

Molm, L. D., Peterson, G., & Takahashi, N. (2003). In the eye of the beholder: Procedural justice in social exchange. *American Sociological Review, 68*(1), 128–152.

Nadler, J. (2002). No need to shout: Bus sweeps and the psychology of coercion. *Supreme Court Review, 200*, 153–222.

Nielsen, L. B. (2000). Situating legal consciousness: Experiences and attitudes of ordinary citizens about law and street harassment. *Law and Society Review, 34*(4), 1055–1090.

Nielsen, L. B. (2004). *License to harass: Law, hierarchy, and offensive public speech*. Princeton, NJ: Princeton University Press.

Nielsen, L. B. (Ed.) (2007). *Theoretical and empirical studies of rights*. Burlington, VT: Ashgate Publishing Company.

Reich, M. (2003). United States v. Drayton: The need for bright-line warnings during consensual bus searches. *Journal of Criminal Law and Criminology*, *93*, 1057–1093.

Reiss, A. J., Jr. (1971). *The police and the public*. New Haven, CT: Yale University Press.

Sandefur, R. L. (2007). The importance of doing nothing: Everyday problems and responses of inaction. In: P. Pleasence, A. Buck & N. J. Balmer (Eds), *Transforming lives: Law and social process* (pp. 116–136). London, England: HMSO.

Sandefur, R. L. (2008). Access to civil justice and race, class, and gender inequality. *Annual Review of Sociology*, *34*, 339–358.

Sarat, A. (1975). Support for the legal system: An analysis of knowledge, attitudes, and behavior. *American Politics Quarterly*, *3*(1), 3–24.

Sarat, A. (1977). Studying American legal culture: An assessment of survey evidence. *Law and Society Review*, *11*(3), 427–488.

Scheingold, S. (1974). *The politics of rights*. New Haven, CT: Yale University Press.

Simmons, R. (2005). Not 'voluntary' but still reasonable: A new paradigm for understanding the consent searches doctrine. *Indiana Law Journal*, *80*, 773–824.

Somers, M. R., & Roberts, C. N. J. (2008). Toward a new sociology of rights: A genealogy of 'buried bodies' of citizenship and human rights. *Annual Review of Law and Social Science*, *4*, 385–425.

Thibaut, J., & Walker, L. (1978). A theory of procedure. *California Law Review*, *66*(3), 541–566.

Tyler, T. R. (1984). The role of perceived injustice in defendants' evaluations of their courtroom experience. *Law and Society Review*, *18*(1), 51–74.

Tyler, T. R., & Rasinski, K. (1991). Procedural justice, institutional legitimacy, and the acceptance of unpopular Supreme Court decisions: A reply to Gibson. *Law and Society Review*, *25*(3), 621–630.

Cases Cited

Argersinger v. Hamlin, 407 U. S. 25 (1972).
Bordenkircher v. Hayes, 434 U.S. 357 (1978).
California v. Greenwood, 486 U.S. 35 (1988).
Chimel v. California, 395 U.S. 752 (1969).
Edwards v. Arizona, 451 U.S. 477 (1981).
Florida v. Bostick, 501 U.S. 429 (1991).
Gideon v. Wainwright, 372 U.S. 335 (1963).
Harris v. New York, 401 U.S. 222 (1971).
Illinois v. Rodriguez, 497 U.S. 177 (1990).
Kyllo v. United States, 533 U.S. 27 (2001).
Lassiter v. Department of Social Services of Durham County, N.C., 452 U.S. 18 (1981).
Maryland v. Wilson, 519 U.S. 408 (1997).
Miranda v. Arizona, 384 U.S. 436 (1966).
Moran v. Burbine, 475 U.S. 412 (1986).
New York v. Belton, 453 U.S. 454 (1981).

Oregon v. Bradshaw, 462 U.S. 1039 (1983).
Pennsylvania v. Mimms, 434 U.S. 106 (1977).
Rakas v. Illinois, 439 U.S. 128 (1978).
Schneckloth v. Bustamonte, 412 U.S. 218 (1973).
Scott v. Illinois, 440 U.S. 367 (1979).
Smith v. Maryland, 442 U.S. 735, 744 (1979).
Thornton v. United States, 541 U.S. 615 (2004).
United States v. Drayton, 536 U.S. 194 (2002).
United States v. Patane, 542 U.S. 630 (2004).
United States v. Pollard, 959 F.2d 1011, (D.C. Cir.), cert. denied, 506 U.S. 915 (1992).

APPENDIX A. SURVEY QUESTIONS[16]

Q: If you put your trash in sealed bags out on the curb for pickup, can the police come and look through it whenever they want?
A: Yes. No reasonable expectation of privacy exists in garbage that a person has put out for collection. *California v. Greenwood.*

Q: Without a warrant or any suspicion, are police allowed to look at the phone numbers you've dialed from your home?
A: Yes. People "voluntarily" give numerical information to the phone company every time they place a call, so they have no reasonable expectation of privacy in the numbers they dial. *Smith v. Maryland.*

Q: If police question you in violation of your rights, and you tell them where you've hidden an object, then they find your fingerprints on the object, can the fingerprints be used against you?
A: Yes. Failure to Mirandize a suspect does not require exclusion of physical evidence that are fruits of the unwarned statement. *U.S. v. Patane.*

Q: If the police arrest you in your car, can they search the car even if they don't have a warrant or any reason to search?
A: Yes. If the recent occupant of a car is arrested, cops can search inside the car. *Belton v. New York.* A search incident to arrest is okay even if the defendant is cuffed outside car and would not physically be able to reach inside. *Thornton v. U.S.*

Q: Police suspect Julie is growing marijuana in her house. Growing marijuana indoors requires special lamps that give off a lot of heat. From the sidewalk, police use a "thermal imaging device" (a machine that measures heat waves) to look at the heat coming from Julie's house. Are the officers allowed to do this without a warrant?

A: No. Police may not use a device that is not in general public use to see details of a private home that would be unknowable without a physical intrusion. This is a Fourth Amendment search, presumptively unreasonable without a warrant. *Kyllo v. U.S.*

Q: Eva is visiting her son, Bill. While Bill is at the grocery store, an officer knocks on the door. Eva opens it. The officer says he doesn't have a warrant, but wants to look around if it's okay with Eva. "I don't live here," Eva says. "I'm just visiting. But you can come in and take a quick look." The cop enters Bill's house, and looks briefly around each room. Is the cop doing anything illegal?

A: Yes. Third party consent is valid only if police reasonably believe that the consenter had common authority over the premises. *Illinois v. Rodriguez.*

Q: Police search Rhonda's home. They find a letter from Betty to Rhonda, in which Betty admits to selling drugs. Later, a judge decides that the search of Rhonda's house was illegal. Betty is charged with drug sales. Can the letter be used against Betty in trial?

A: Yes. Only a defendant with a reasonable expectation of privacy in the illegally searched property has standing to challenge the search. *Rakas v. Illinois.*

Q: Steve is charged with cruelty to animals, a misdemeanor in his state punishable by either fines or community service. Steve's case goes to trial in front of a jury, and Steve can't afford a lawyer. Does he have a right to have a lawyer provided?

A: No. No right to counsel exists in misdemeanor charges not punishable by jail time. *Argersinger v. Hamlin*; *Scott v. Illinois.*

Q: Larry is arrested. His lawyer, Sue, hears about it and calls the police. The police promise Sue they won't question Larry until Sue gets there. They also promise to tell Larry that Sue called. After hanging up, the police go back to Larry, read him his rights, and question him. They don't tell him about Sue's call. Larry confesses before Sue arrives. Did the police do anything illegal?

A: No. Police deception is generally allowed unless it's so egregious that it makes the confession involuntary; the example does not rise to this level. *Moran v. Burbine.*

Q: Josh and his wife are arrested. The prosecutor offers Josh a deal, saying, "I'll give you a choice. Plead guilty and I'll drop the charges against your wife. Don't plead guilty and I'll charge you *and* your wife with everything I possibly can." Is the prosecutor doing anything illegal?

A: No. Threatening to increase charges isn't unconstitutionally coercive, *Bordenkircher v. Hayes*. Tying a plea to charges against a family member is presumably okay, too. *U.S. v. Pollard.*

APPENDIX B. STUDY 1: CORRECT VERSUS INCORRECT ANSWERS

Question Topic	Correct	Incorrect
Reasonable expectation of privacy in trash	209/365 (57.3%)	156/365 (42.7%)
Legality of pen registries	071/367 (19.3%)	296/367 (80.7%)
Physical fruits of Fifth Amendment violations	165/363 (45.5%)	198/363 (54.5%)
Search incident to arrest in car arrest situation	177/365 (48.5%)	188/365 (51.5%)
Warrantless use of thermal imaging devices	144/364 (39.6%)	220/364 (60.4%)
Third-party consent searches	237/366 (64.8%)	129/366 (35.2%)
Standing to raise Fourth Amendment claims	073/366 (19.9%)	293/366 (80.1%)
Right to counsel in misdemeanor trials	028/365 (7.7%)	337/365 (92.3%)
Police deception, no Fifth Amendment violation	172/363 (47.4%)	191/363 (52.6%)
Threats by prosecutor during plea negotiation	185/366 (50.5%)	181/366 (49.5%)
Total	1461/3650 (40%)	2189/3650 (60%)

BEYOND COURT INTERPRETERS: EXPLORING THE IDEA OF DESIGNATED SPANISH-SPEAKING COURTROOMS TO ADDRESS LANGUAGE BARRIERS TO JUSTICE IN THE UNITED STATES

Kwai Hang Ng

The language barriers experienced among non–English speaking or limited English-speaking citizens of the United States have quietly become a major hindrance to access to justice and a threat to the due process of law. The situation is most acute among the Spanish-speaking minority group, as they make up the overwhelming majority among citizens in need of court interpreters. This article explores whether in practice court interpretation service alone is likely to succeed in overcoming the language barrier. It explains why legislative measures alone (i.e., by guaranteeing litigants the right to a court interpreter) are inadequate to address the needs of a growing population of Spanish-speaking litigants with limited English proficiency. For reasons I will explain below, there are practical challenges to expand the use of court-provided interpreters to ensure access to justice among the group.

Access to Justice
Sociology of Crime, Law and Deviance, Volume 12, 97–118

ISSN: 1521-6136/doi:10.1108/S1521-6136(2009)0000012008

It is my contention that more innovative and effective administrative policies should now be considered to complement the use of court interpreters. By using the Canadian model as a reference, this article suggests that some state courts in acute shortage of qualified interpreters may benefit from adopting the administrative policy of "language matching." Toward the end of the article, I propose the idea of designated Spanish-speaking courtrooms as a possible way to allow the direct use of Spanish within an Anglo-American common law system that upholds English as its language of operation. I will briefly outline the scope and potential benefits of allowing the direct use of Spanish under limited circumstances.

The structure of this article is as follows: I will first describe the problems faced by non–English speaking litigants in their interactions with federal and state courts in the United States. I will then describe how the problem is addressed under the current legislative framework and administrative policies. Next, I move on to consider an alternative model for addressing the problem of language barriers – Canada's model of language rights. The purpose of my comparison, however, is not to suggest that the United States should adopt the "language rights" model; quite the contrary, the purpose of my comparison is to persuade readers that some of the measures adopted by the Canadian courts to cater to the needs of the French-speaking minority group could be decoupled from an official bilingual policy and adopted as *supplementary* solutions to the problem of an expanding population of Spanish-speaking litigants who require court interpretation service.

NON-ENGLISH SPEAKERS AND ACCESS TO JUSTICE

Language use is a highly controversial issue in the United States (Schmidt, 2000). Among all the linguistic access issues (e.g., bilingual education, multilingual ballots), however, the issue of access to justice is probably the least contentious. Most people in the United States seem to agree and appreciate the fact that access to justice premises on the ability of court users to understand the process in which they participate. The integrity of the legal process, particularly for the common law system (like the American legal system), which features an adversarial trial process, would be compromised if litigants were unable to communicate with or understand the judge, witnesses, or opposing parties or counsel. The guiding theory behind the common law is that adversarial trials set up two or more parties to be in conflict with one another in a zero-sum game; it is therefore important for all participating parties to be on equal footing (Thibaut & Walker, 1975).

The increasingly diverse language profile of the country's population, however, is posing a challenge to the availability of equal access to justice for all. Of course, the United States has always been a multilingual country. It is also important to point out that as a nation the United States has never had any official language policy at the federal level, despite "official English" legislation found at the state and local levels (Piatt, 1990; Schmidt, 2000). Yet, census statistics in recent years suggest a rising population of non-English speakers in the country who are very likely to experience difficulty in the court system if unaided by court interpretation services. According to the 2000 Census, 18 per cent of the total population aged 5 and above, or 47 million people, reported that they spoke a language other than English at home (U.S. Census Bureau 2003). This compares to 14 per cent (31.8 million) in the 1990 and 11 per cent (23.1 million) in the 1980 Census. If we use the 18 per cent figure as a parameter, then almost one in five litigants visiting the federal and state court systems in the country require the aid of court interpreters. A more conservative estimate is the number of people who describe their ability to speak and understand English as "less than very well," a standard that many court administrators believe to be "the minimum realistic threshold for meaningful participation in a judicial proceeding" (cf. California Commission on Access to Justice, 2005, p. 9). In the 2000 Census, a total of 21.4 million people, or 8.1 per cent of the total population, reported that they spoke English "less than very well," compared to 4.8 per cent in 1980 and 6.1 per cent in 1990 (U.S. Census Bureau, 2003). The same figure is even higher in some coastal and border states with a higher percentage of new immigrants, particularly in the West. In California, for example, roughly 20 per cent of Californians (almost 7 million people) speak English "less than very well." This evidence suggests that there is a growing population of litigants facing a language barrier in both federal and state courts. How then is the barrier currently addressed in the courts? And is that adequate? This is the topic to which I now turn.

U.S. FEDERAL COURT

I first focus on how the federal court system currently deals with litigants with limited English proficiency. It is sufficient for my purpose to simply point out that in terms of constitutional rights, the United States Supreme Court has never addressed directly the issue of whether a constitutional right to an interpreter in either civil or criminal cases exists, even though the existence of such a right could be argued, and in fact has been argued by some lower courts (most noticeably by the Second Circuit Court of Appeals in *United States ex rel. Negron v. New York*[1]). Many jurists also argue that the right to an interpreter is implied in the Sixth Amendment right to counsel and right to confrontation, as well as in the concept of due process guaranteed by the Fifth and Fourteenth Amendments (see, e.g., Shulman, 1993; Pantoga, 1999; Leighton, 2002). The Supreme Court dealt with the issue of interpreter once in an old case known as *Perovich v. United States* (1907) more than a full century ago. The Court then held that the decision on whether to appoint an interpreter for a non–English speaking defendant or not was within the trial court's discretion.[2]

It is in the area of statutory federal law that the explicit guarantee of equal access to justice by people of limited English proficiency is made. Title VI of the Civil Rights Act of 1964, 42 U.S.C. §2000(d) suggests that no person shall "on the ground of race, color, or national origin, be excluded from participation in, be denied the benefits of, or be subjected to discrimination under any program or activity receiving federal financial assistance." The same act authorizes and directs specified federal agencies "to effectuate the provisions ... by issuing rules, regulations, or orders of general applicability."

In 2000, President Clinton signed Executive Order 13166,[3] which seeks to improve access to services for persons with limited English proficiency. The Order requires all federal agencies, including, of course, federal courts, to meet the same standards in providing *meaningful access* to federally conducted programs for individuals with limited English proficiency. In 2002, the Department of Justice published official guidelines for the implementation of this executive order, which was directed toward Department of Justice recipients (state and local law enforcement agencies and departments of corrections) and also serves as a model for the guidance of other recipient agencies.[4]

So the guarantee in Title VI of the Civil Rights Act makes explicit the legal right to meaningful access to justice. But if we look beyond law in the books, how well does the guarantee translate into practice? In the federal courts, the mandatory use of court interpreters protects access to justice for persons with limited English proficiency. As we know, the term "interpreter" is loosely used in common parlance to describe people of diverse interpretation skills, some of them highly trained, some amateurish.

The Court Interpreters Act which was passed in 1978 requires the use of "certified interpreters" in civil and criminal cases in a United States district court for a defendant or a witness who "speaks only or primarily a language other than the English language" (28 U.S.C. § 1827(d)(1), (2) 1996). Under the Act, the Director of the Administrative Office of the United States Courts must prescribe, determine, and certify the qualifications of persons who may serve as interpreters. The same act stipulates that a certified court interpreter must be used unless one is not "reasonably available." In that case, an "otherwise qualified" interpreter must be appointed.

As a sociologist, the question with which I am concerned is not just the legal guarantee promised but also the extent to which the legal guarantee is carried out in practice. One must acknowledge the fact that though the Court Interpreters Act clearly puts forth qualified interpreters as the standard to which the federal court system must aspire, the Act at the same time acknowledges that it is practically impossible to require the use of qualified interpreters in all circumstances. By allowing for "otherwise qualified" interpreters to be recruited as substitutes in cases when certified interpreters are not reasonably available, in practice it provides federal administrators with an "escape clause." One indicator for gauging how well equal access to justice is implemented in the federal court system is to see how often this escape clause is triggered. Most scholars agree that the performance of "certified" interpreters and "otherwise qualified" interpreters differs. The latter term is indeed a portmanteau category that includes non-certified interpreters who are either "professionally qualified" or "skilled."[5] Surveys of judges and attorneys conducted by the Administrative Office of the U.S. Courts to assess the in-court performance of the interpreters they use consistently show that certified interpreters receive higher marks in their performance against non-certified interpreters (Lowney, 2005). The Federal Court Interpreter Certification Examination (FCICE) is today one of the most demanding active certification programs. The pass rate for the Spanish-English FCICE (which requires a person to pass both a written and oral examination) is reported to be on average only around 4 per cent. Developed as a result of the Court Interpreters Act, the purpose of these tests is to determine whether an interpreter has the appropriate skills to interpret everything that is said accurately and completely (Hewitt, Hannaford, Gill, & Cantrell, 1998, p. 21; McCaffrey, 2000).

As we will see, it is in this area that the federal court system fares palpably better than its state counterparts. In 2004, for example, certified interpreters handled over 88 per cent of proceedings in the federal courts interpreted in Spanish. That figure is, by any standard, a high percentage for the language most commonly spoken among litigants who require court interpretation service. However, a certification program is currently available only for three languages, namely, Spanish, Navajo, and Haitian-Creole, which means that there are no certified interpreters for other minority languages. In cases involving litigants who speak other languages, judges have to rely on the escape clause to appoint an "otherwise qualified" interpreter. Although this situation is not satisfactory, statistically speaking, the impact of the absence of certification programs in other languages might not be as grave as it appears, since Spanish alone accounts for more than 96 per cent of interpreter language needs in the federal courts (Administrative Office of the U.S. Courts, 2007). The remaining 4 per cent are spread over 110 different languages. In fact, the lop-sided presence of Spanish among litigants with limited English proficiency is a phenomenon that has not yet been adequately addressed in the current framing of the problem of language barriers. I will return to this later in the article. In the next section, I discuss how the state courts in the United States cope with the language barrier.

STATE COURTS

Like their federal counterpart, most state courts recognize the right to an interpreter in criminal cases for defendants with limited English proficiency. Some state constitutions, for example, California, New Mexico, Hawaii, explicitly provide that such persons have a right to an interpreter throughout the proceedings. Other states do so by either statute or administrative or judicial regulation (Shulman, 1993).

State courts as a whole, however, appear to lack the kind of implemental clarity that the federal system displays in providing court interpretation service. Legal scholars who write on the topic point out that state court judges are given much greater discretion than federal judges (some would say too great) to decide *when* an interpreter is needed and *who* can be regarded as a qualified interpreter. Regarding the question of when an interpreter is necessary, state statutes are not as explicit as the aforementioned Court Interpreters Act. The Act requires the provision of an interpreter not only in cases in which the defendant does not speak English but also when the defendant *has difficulty understanding the proceedings* without the aid of an interpreter. Legal scholars are doubtful whether trial judges should be left with such broad discretion to determine whether or not a particular defendant requires an interpreter. Most judges are legal experts but not language experts (cf. Pantoga, 1999). Many judges and clerks of court assess a party's language abilities by asking simple "yes/no" questions or by asking whether the person uses English at work or in social settings. These techniques seriously underestimate the level of language skills needed to cope with court proceedings, given the adversarial nature of a common law trial. It is generally agreed among court interpreters and court administrators that "basic conversational skills are not enough to intelligently waive the right to counsel, to understand the implications of a guilty plea, or to undergo cross-examination" (Committee to Improve Interpreting and Translation in the Wisconsin Courts, 2000). Pantoga (1999, p. 632), for example, argues that unless more specific criteria for the appointment of court interpreters are established, miscarriages of justice are bound to continue to occur.

There is even greater concern among scholars on the question of who qualifies as a "qualified interpreter." Most state statutes do not specify clear standards of qualification for court interpreters, which means that in practice it is left to judges or other judicial officials to decide who is qualified and who is not. Furthermore, until recently, only a few states had their own certification programs to certify qualified interpreters. Courtroom misinterpretations, sad to say, are therefore not uncommon in many state courts. Although no systematic interstate study has been conducted to identify the severity of the problem, studies conducted by state court administrators themselves and media investigative reports have identified instances of misinterpretation in cases that involve linguistic minorities.

Here is a rough and ready survey of some of the cases reported. In an informal survey of legal service providers undertaken by the California Commission on Access to Justice, several providers reported the use of children for interpretation. Another reported unwanted interventions in the form of prodding and prompting, that is, encouraging parties to say things that the interpreter thinks the court wants to hear (California Commission on Access to Justice, 2005, p. 24). Other reports also noted similar tendencies among some interpreters to clean up the language of a defendant or refuse to translate obscene language (McCain, 2004; Ewell & Schrieberg, 1989).

The shortage of qualified interpreters is a perennial concern. In a three-year study conducted by the Supreme Court of Pennsylvania that began in 1999, the lack of standards for court interpreters in some county courts was found to pose a threat to the due process of law. The report lists out instances in which judges drafted defendants' relatives and even a court janitor to spontaneously act as interpreters (Cardenas, 2004). Courts go almost anywhere to find someone who can serve as an interpreter, for example, recruiting someone from a local Chinese restaurant to translate Chinese (Ewell & Schrieberg, 1989). Even in some midwestern states that are not traditionally known for having high immigrant populations, there are reportedly shortages of court interpreters. In a report written by the "Committee to Improve Interpreting and Translation in the Wisconsin Courts," for example, the Committee identifies the use of uncertified interpreters, such as "relatives, friends, police officers, social workers, or even fellow prisoners as interpreters" (2000, p. 6), as a serious issue in the state court system. The committee makes the following further criticism:

> [The] state has too many unqualified interpreters, people who really should not be used in court if the goals are accuracy, completeness, and impartiality. Some courts are mistakenly content with whichever interpreter is most easily available. This may be the Spanish teacher from the local high school, a friend or relative of the party, or a local resident who interprets once or twice a year just to help out. Unfortunately, many of these interpreters are woefully underqualified for the job, in ways that are not apparent to a person who does not speak both languages required. While a judge may be able to gauge if an interpreter has a professional demeanor or seems to understand the legal process, a monolingual judge has no way to know whether the substance of the court proceeding is being accurately or completely conveyed (2000, p. 10).

Media reports also expose alleged unprofessional behavior by some state court interpreters. For example, according to an investigative report on a murder case involving Vietnamese-speaking litigants by the *San Jose Mercury News*, the court-appointed interpreter grossly distorted the testimony of the key witness for the prosecution. According to the report, the jury acquitted the accused, a man named Quang Nguyen, because the jury found the prosecution' star witness, a woman named Be whose husband was killed by the accused, to be evasive. The report asserted that Be was not evasive, but rather it was the misinterpretation of the court interpreter – who "omitted words, phrases and whole sentences, mistranslated frequently, and spoke in pidgin English" – that made Be sound evasive (Ewell, 1989; Ewell & Schrieberg, 1989).

As mentioned earlier, the problem can be attributed to the lack (at least until recently) of a system of accreditation or certification for interpreters working in many state courts. Not so long ago, there were only a few states that had their own court interpreter certification programs in place. It was considered by many state courts an unattainable luxury to certify their own interpreters, given their tight budgets. Developing new test instruments and training competent test raters takes time and resources. This problem was partially alleviated by the founding of the Consortium for State

Court Interpreter Certification in 1995. In 1995, four states – Minnesota, New Jersey, Oregon, and Washington – joined together to coordinate test development efforts. The Consortium allowed the pooling together of resources to develop common testing programs and eventually a standardized certification program comparable to the FCICE (Gill & Hewitt, 1996). At the time of writing, a total of 39 states have joined the consortium, with Maine, New Hampshire, and Vermont the latest (in 2007) to join. Still, some member states such as Illinois and Ohio have yet to establish their own certification programs. Furthermore, it is not clear if some of the member states of the consortium have statutes or administrative/judicial rules that stipulate the use of certified interpreters under reasonable circumstances.

In any case, certification is an important step toward securing the service of qualified interpreters. But is this enough? For many state courts, being able to certify their own interpreters does not necessarily mean that they will have the resources to retain their services. State courts often find it hard to compete with the federal court system, which currently pays up to $364 per day for certified and professionally qualified interpreters. It is common knowledge that the private sector pays an even higher rate for quality interpreters. With the possible exception of California, no state pays interpreters for its court system the same rate paid to federally certified interpreters. Yet, even a populous state such as California still has a hard time competing with the federal court and the private sector for qualified court interpreters in various key languages (California has been paying court interpreters at a rate lower than that offered by the federal court system in recent years). Between 1995 and 2005, there has been a significant decrease in the number of certified court interpreters in major minority languages including Spanish, Vietnamese, Cantonese, and Tagalog, whereas the need for interpreters in these languages has continued to increase (California Commission on Access to Justice, 2005).

There is also a discrepancy in standards between criminal and civil proceedings. Simply put, for litigants in civil trials at the state level, there is no guarantee of the right to an interpreter (Berk-Seligson, 1990, pp. 1–9). In criminal proceedings, both federal and state court systems acknowledge the right to have a federal or state-funded interpreter for litigants with limited English proficiency. In civil proceedings, however, the situation is more murky and complex. The federal court recognizes the right of civil litigants to a court interpreter as a result of the Court Interpreters Act. A few states including Idaho, Iowa, Minnesota, and Washington D.C. have similar statutes, which provide litigants with the right to a court-appointed interpreter (Romberger, 2007). But there remain many other states where the supreme courts have held that non–English speaking civil litigants do not have the right to have a court interpreter appointed at public expense, except when a litigant chooses to testify in court as a witness. In most states today, parties involved in civil cases have to pay for their own interpreters. Limited state resources and the dire need for qualified interpreters mean that court interpreters in state courts, particularly in civil trials, are often regarded as a luxury.

So, what are the biggest problems facing state courts today when it comes to providing meaningful access to justice for people with limited English proficiency? For many state courts, the situation can be almost described as playing a game of catch up. The growth of the population of litigants with limited English proficiency, especially in recent years, significantly outpaces the number of new qualified court interpreters that state and even federal certification programs produce, although additional resources have been spent to certify interpreters and retain their services. According to the latest statistics released, in California, for example, $65 million, or 3 per cent of total court expenditures, were spent on the statewide Court Interpreters Program in fiscal year 2003–2004. That might not seem to be an extraordinarily large slice of the budget, but it was an additional $65 million on top of the other recurrent expenditures for the daily operation of the court (Judicial Council of California, 2004). Furthermore, despite recent improvement, there remains much variance in the quality of court interpreters employed by different state courts – bigger states such as California, New Jersey, Washington, and Massachusetts devote resources to developing test and certification programs, and to implementing training programs for interpreters and other judicial personnel on legal interpretation. Most states however lack the necessary expertise and financial resources to determine policy initiatives for strengthening interpretation and translation services in their court systems.

Perhaps the question one should ask is: Is court interpretation service the only way to address the issue of language barriers? In the next section, I am going to look at how Canada deals with the needs of its French-speaking minority in the legal system. Given its official bilingual policy, Canada's solution is obviously very different from the policies adopted by the United States. As I said, it is not my position to suggest that the United States adopt a multilingual policy for its legal system. Quite frankly this is not a question this paper attempts to address. My concern here is purely practical. And my goal here is thereby more modest. I simply want to raise the possibility of going beyond court interpreters to cope with the growing problem of language barriers.

THE CANADIAN MODEL OF OFFICIAL BILINGUALISM

Canada and the United States are both common law systems with their own written constitutions. The two systems adopt similar institutional structures and judicial processes. The roles that judges and counsel play in the mainly adversarial trial processes are also similar.[6] Arguably, the biggest difference between the two is that while Canada has an official bilingual policy, which means English and French enjoy, in principle at least, equal status, the U.S. system uses English as its sole legal language. Canada's official bilingual policy means that the basic model from which Canada approaches the problem of language barriers is very different from the "access to justice" model adopted by the United States. Furthermore, as a jurisdiction that has traditionally used English as its working language, the example of Canada offers us a good case study of a different model for incorporating other languages into the operation of a legal system.

In Canada, the requirement to provide a bilingual interface accessible to litigants is worked out through the idea of *language rights*. What are language rights? What are their meanings and their boundaries? Unfortunately, the scope of language rights has been a matter of contention in Canadian case law. This is in part because the Supreme Court of Canada, as many Canadian jurists suggest, wavered on the issue of where to draw the language rights boundary. For a long time, the court relied on a liberal interpretation of the notion of language rights found in the Canadian constitution. But several important decisions on language rights in the mid-1980s reversed the course.[7] Perhaps the most debated aspect on the question of the boundaries of language rights (and the most interesting point for our comparative purpose) is whether or not the constitution imposes any obligation on the State to require a presiding judge to directly understand the parties in a trial *without* the assistance of an interpreter. Put simply, does the notion of language rights entail not just the right for one to speak in one's own language but also *be understood* in the same language?

The debate was settled for good with the passage of the new *Official Languages Act of Canada* (OLA) (1988). The new act represents the application of the principle of advancement of English and French through legislative means. It mandates the bilingual right by requiring that the person who hears matters (e.g., a judge) be capable of understanding the language(s) of proceedings directly. Section 16 of OLA states that "every litigant has the right to be heard and understood in the official language of his or her choice by a judge or officer without the assistance of an interpreter." In practice, this would mean that if English is the language chosen by the parties for conducting their proceedings, every judge or other officer who hears those proceedings must be able to understand English without the assistance of an interpreter. And if French is the language chosen by the parties for proceedings conducted before them, every judge or other officer who hears those proceedings must be able to understand French without the assistance of an interpreter. In other words, for the French-speaking minority in Canada, language rights mean that they are entitled not just to speak in French, but also to be understood *directly* in French. As the then Deputy Minister of Justice Morris Rosenberg (2004, p. 58) puts it, "a language right is not a right of expression, but rather a right of communication."

The language rights model has far-reaching implications for the language policy adopted by the Canadian court. Its practical consequences are that the Canadian federal court system cannot rely on the use of court interpreters to address the language barrier facing French-speaking litigants; instead, the problem is dealt with in a completely different way, through the implementation of institutional bilingualism. The current arrangement in Canada is that the federal courts have the responsibility to assign cases in such a way that a judge can understand the language of choice (either English or French) without the aid of a court interpreter.

The same act also stipulates that the Canadian government will use the language of the other party in its written and oral pleadings in the proceedings. Section 14 of the same act stipulates that all parties, that is, litigants, counsel, witnesses, judges, and other officers of the court are entitled to use English or French before the federal courts in any pleading and any written or oral submission. Section 18 further stipulates that when the Canadian government or a federal institution is party to civil proceedings before a federal court, the Canadian government shall use, in any oral or written pleadings, the official language chosen by the other parties unless it is established that reasonable notice of the language chosen has not been given. Finally, section 20 requires that all final decisions be issued in both official languages, either simultaneously or at the earliest possible time. Since the enactment of the act, subsequent court cases in the Canadian Supreme Court have further reaffirmed the broad and liberal approach to language rights as stated in OLA.[8] Thus as we can see, the language rights model means the provision of dual language access not just during an open trial, but also in the pre-trial procedures that follow the pleading, as well as in the delivery of oral or written verdicts – basically in every step of the judicial process, from start to finish.

SPANISH-SPEAKING COURTROOMS IN THE UNITED STATES?

Needless to say, the difference between the Canadian model and the U.S. model is obvious. Although the U.S. courts make use of court interpreters to provide access to justice, the Canadian courts try to provide a bilingual environment to the French-speaking minority where no court interpreters are required. In the Canadian case, access to justice is instead achieved, in principle at least, by ensuring that the judicial officials involved know the language of choice, be it English or French, well enough to meaningfully participate in the proceedings without the aid of court interpreters. In an important sense, to say that French is allowed to be used in Canadian courts is an understatement. The official bilingual policy stipulates that the court must protect the language rights of the French-speaking minority – not just the right to speak in French but also the right to be understood in French. In contrast, the U.S. "equal access" model addresses the issue of language barriers by ensuring that all parties are able to express and be understood (either directly or through a court interpreter) in English and only in English.

I am not suggesting that the United States should follow the Canadian "language rights" model. Historically, the idea of "language rights" has not been a popular concept in American jurisprudence. With the exception of a few specific cases (e.g., the Native American Languages Act), there are no positive laws, however symbolic, on preserving language rights in the United States. Quite the contrary, the U.S. courts have historically considered the ability to understand testimonies in a language other than English, especially in the cases of some undiscerning parties such as the jury, a *potential threat* to the administration of justice! This was the rationale behind the well-cited case of *Hernandez v. New York*,[9] when the Supreme Court ruled that it was not a violation of the Equal Protection Clause for prosecutors to use peremptory challenges to disqualify bilingual jurors, citing their hesitation when asked whether they could disregard direct testimony in Spanish and heed only the English translation of the court interpreter. Putting aside the question of whether or not the reason given might be a pretext for what is in fact a race-based preemptory challenge (which if explicitly so framed, would be a blatant violation of the Equal Protection Clause), it is interesting to see how due process is said to be preserved by holding all jurors to the same standard (albeit it is arguable that bilingual jurors supposedly should understand the case better because of their direct access to the evidence before the work of a court interpreter).

What I am suggesting instead is that the "language-matching" policy developed under the "language rights" model could be used in a limited setting to complement court interpreters in order to make available equal access to justice, especially *when there is a clear major minority language for people facing the language barrier*, as in the case of French in Canada, and as I suggest, Spanish in the United States. The underlying rationale is simple. When there is a strong and persistent need for court access among a particular minority language group, a judge or adjudicator who speaks that language can deal with members of the language minority group more efficiently than a court interpreter can (given the one-on-one nature of interpretation and the time-consuming nature of interpretation). One of the problems of the traditional framing of "access to justice" for non–English speaking litigants is that it does not take into consideration the overall demography of these litigants. As mentioned earlier, it is abundantly clear that Spanish alone constitutes most of interpreter language needs in the federal courts. Spanish is far and away the dominant language among litigants who require court interpreters. In California, for example, 160,396 Spanish court interpreter service days were provided by the California state courts during the 2004–2005 fiscal year (Judicial Council of California, 2006). Although the statistics available are not complete, they strongly suggest that in federal courts as well as in state courts in states with high immigrant populations, we are seeing and will continue to see a vast number of litigants who prefer to speak Spanish. There is, sadly, a disjuncture between the supply and demand for Spanish court interpreters. The growth in the number of litigants who prefer to speak Spanish has not been met by a corresponding growth in the number of certified interpreters. Once again, if we use California as an example, 1,536 interpreters were certified by the state certification program in Spanish in 1995, compared with 1,102 at the time of writing (2007) – a near 30 per cent decline![10] Yet, during the same period, the demand for court interpreters continued to rise.

Perhaps it is time to ask whether training more Spanish court interpreters alone can really address the growing number of Spanish-speaking litigants in the country. A policy of language matching seems worth exploring when a particular language minority group has a clear need for court access. And Spanish is by far the most interpreted language and is likely to remain to so for the foreseeable future. It is also noteworthy that in terms of both absolute head counts and relative percentage, Spanish-speaking litigants have a more overwhelming presence among non–English speaking litigants in the United States than French-speaking litigants do among non–English speaking litigants in Canada (see again Table 1).

Table 1. Comparing the United States' and Canada's Judicial Policies to Deal with Language Barriers to Justice.

	United States	Canada
Governing concept regarding the language barrier issue	Access to justice	Language rights
Size of non–English speaking population in respective country	18 per cent of the total population aged 5 and above, or 47 million people, reported they spoke a language other than English at home. Among the group, about 60 per cent speak Spanish at home	66.7 per cent of the population, or 20.8 million, speak English most often at home. 21.4% of the total population, or 6.68 million, speak French most often at home; 3.7 million (11.9%) of the population speak neither English nor French most often at home (Chinese languages are Canada's third most common mother tongue group)
Biggest non–English speaking group among court users	Spanish alone constitutes more than 96 per cent of interpreter language needs in the federal courts; the remaining four per cent are spread over 110 different languages	No directly comparable statistics available; but historically it is the French-speaking minority group. Population of litigants who speak the Chinese languages have increased in recent years
Language policy	No official language policy at the federal level, some states have "English-only" laws	Official bilingual policy (English and French)
Scope of language access policy	Mainly during the open trial process. In some state courts, forms and court documents are available in languages other than English	All parties are entitled to use English or French before the federal courts not just during open trial but in any pleading and any written or oral submission. All final decisions by the court should be issued in both official languages, either simultaneously or at the earliest possible time
Main means to deal with the non-English speaking group	Court interpretation service	Institutional bilingualism

The Canadian model, of course, is a model of institutional bilingualism. It takes tremendous resources to make a legal system bilingual in all its facets; it is an ideal the Canadian courts are still striving to achieve (cf. Canadian Centre for Management Development, 2004). Unlike its rival civil law system (where the Napoleonic Code and some of the later codes have been translated into different languages), the common law remains an "English-language" legal system. Aside from obvious historical reasons, the biggest reason for the predominant use of English has to do with its unique case law system, which continues to play an important role despite the growing role of statutes in most modern legal systems. It is impossible to translate all the precedents from English to another language in any established jurisdiction within a short-time frame. Hence, what I want to point out is that the administrative measure of "language matching" between judges and litigants developed under the Canadian model is not necessarily tied to the idea of legal multilingualism. Legal bilingualism is a much wider concept that goes beyond the concern for equal "access to justice." In other words, French is acknowledged an official language of the Canadian courts not only because of concerns about access to justice for the Canadian French-speaking population, but more importantly, as a means to honor the heritage of French-speaking Canadians. This point is clearly made by the Canadian Supreme Court itself, which acknowledges that honoring language rights has more to do with the history of the country than with protecting the right to a fair trial among French-speaking litigants. In *Beaulac*, Justice Bastarache, writing for the majority, made the following observation:

> "It is also useful to re-affirm here that language rights are a particular kind of right, distinct from the principles of fundamental justice. They have a different purpose and a different origin."[11]

To repeat, the basic premise of my argument is that allowing the limited use of a language other than English in a U.S. court should not be taken as a shift to the "language rights" model. As a supplementary measure, it may help alleviate the ongoing shortage of qualified court interpreters in Spanish. The administrative practice of matching judges and other officials who speak Spanish with litigants who only speak Spanish does not have to be implemented within a full-blown bi- or multilingual legal framework. The program, however, is worth exploring because finding and deploying qualified court interpreters is a costly and often time-consuming exercise. A few Spanish-speaking judges or judicial officers in a designated courtroom can deal with a much bigger group of litigants than one or even a team of court interpreters. The nature of interpretation dictates that a court interpreter can only serve one person at a time. In some state criminal courts, group arraignment can occasionally be seen because of the shortage of interpreters. Such procedural arrangements are a threat to the due process of law (Cooper, 2005). Furthermore, the court time required for the same trial can be shortened because using court interpreters in principle doubles the time needed for to complete the trial (with the exception of so-called dockside interpretation (i.e., simultaneous interpretation)). Delays in resolution of cases due to the lack of interpreters can also be reduced if the policy succeeds in freeing up more court interpreters' time.

Finally, under what circumstances can the use of Spanish be allowed in an English-language legal system? Here I am going to make a tentative proposal to limit the use of Spanish by judges and attorneys to a number of specific occasions in order to preserve the role of English as the legal language of the court. To begin with, Spanish should not be used as an official language of verdicts in state and federal systems that use English as the language of records. There are also administrative issues that make difficult the use of Spanish in pleadings and other written submissions during the pre-trial stage, again because of the role of English as the language of written records. However, Spanish can be used for fact-gathering purposes in trials, particularly trials that take place in more informal formats. I suggest that the direct use of Spanish is most useful during testimonies (and only during testimonies) in some designated courtrooms with Spanish-speaking judges. All parties, that is, judges, counsel, and witnesses who give testimony can communicate directly in Spanish. Under the proposal, these designated courtrooms would be staffed by bilingual judges/judicial officers who can speak and understand Spanish, on top of English. To restrict Spanish to only the "fact-finding stage" means that English would retain its role as the language of choice to address legal issues. It would also mean that court interpreters would still be needed, if necessary, at other stages of such a so-called Spanish-language trial, such as when counsel address the court during opening statements or closing arguments (if made). Allowing Spanish to be used to give testimonies directly however can free up a great amount of court interpreters' time. On average, gathering and examining oral testimonies are by far the most time-consuming stages of an adversarial trial in the Anglo-American system, especially in some lower-tier courts where the legal arguments involved are often described to be straightforward.

The proposal for designated Spanish-speaking courtrooms can best be tried out in the form of a pilot program in a lower-tier state court with limited jurisdiction. It must be an optional scheme. Spanish-speaking litigants can choose to participate in a Spanish-speaking courtroom, or they can participate in a English courtroom aided by court interpreters. Since many state courts do not provide litigants who do not understand English the service of court interpretation in civil trials, the program should first be tested in civil courts. Specifically, if we follow Engel and Steele's (1979) classification of civil cases into three major fields, that is, personal injury, debt collection, and divorce, then for reasons I will elaborate, the pilot program is more suited to the latter two fields. This is particularly true for debt collection cases, the majority of which are processed by small claims courts. Small claims courts appear to be an ideal venue to test out the program. The courts handle civil cases with comparatively small monetary stakes. Its procedures are stripped down because most small claims courts operate under simplified procedural rules with shortened and brief pretrial procedures. Time-consuming depositions and interrogatories are a rarity. In fact, many defendants lose by default because they fail to appear. Trials are held before judges with a higher level of informality (compared with a full-blown civil trial), as parties are generally discouraged from resorting to legal representation. Another reason why small claims courts are a good testing ground is that many small claims courts currently lack the resources to provide qualified court interpreters to claimants. (The small claims court in California, for example, encourages claimants to bring someone who speaks English and ask the judge whether the person can be an interpreter.) Besides small claims courts, family courts, which handle divorce applications and decisions triggered by a divorce (such as property division, child custody, alimony and child support), could be another possible avenue for implementing the pilot scheme. As with the case of small claims courts, cases that appear before a family court typically do not involve a long and protracted trial stage. By contrast, personal injury and other tort cases, given their usually lengthy trial period and the frequent involvement of the jury, are less suited to experiment with the direct use of Spanish in courtrooms.

CONCLUSION

It is perhaps a cliché to say that in a common law system, just results come from the contest of opposing parties on equal footing. As I said, litigants who cannot understand or communicate to the court can hardly be said to be on equal footing with those who speak and understand English as their native language. The problem is particularly acute in some of the financially strapped state court systems in the United States. They are dealing with a growing population of litigants who struggle with the use of English. To overcome the barriers, legal scholars and activists have for a long time called for more comprehensive legal protection of litigants with limited English proficiency. The most common solution suggested is expanding the mandatory use of court-provided interpreters to all civil proceedings. Here, as in other problems relating to access to justice, there is always a gap between principles and actual practices (cf. Rhode, 2004). Attempting to improve the quality of court interpretation and expand the scope of court-provided interpreters in state courts will create substantial practical challenges, for reasons this article has documented. Without the required additional resources, a legal promise, however rosy, brings only false comfort. Statutory requirements in this area are bound to be "soft promises." They, without exception, come in with an escape clause to allow courts to be exempted from the requirement if practical considerations suggest it is necessary to do so. We have seen this to be the case in the federal Court Interpreters Act discussed earlier. Legal measures such as the Court Interpreters Act alone are not sufficient to make court interpreters more readily available. More and better court interpreters can only be produced with greater resources (e.g., by raising the pay rate of certified court interpreters) and with more robust training and testing programs. The situation admittedly is at its worst in some state courts, where resources are often limited. The reality is such that sadly there are simply too many scenarios where certified interpreters are not "reasonably available," and too many state courts have to resort to finding someone who is readily available but not well qualified, let alone certified. Among non–English speaking litigants, Spanish speakers are by far the biggest minority group. Perhaps allowing the use of Spanish in some designated courtrooms with limited jurisdiction can be a way to alleviate the reliance on court interpreters. The pilot program of creating designated Spanish courtrooms should be implemented in state courts where non-certified interpreters are most often used in civil proceedings.

This idea, to allow Spanish-speaking litigants to communicate directly with some Spanish-speaking judges, is inspired by the way the Canadian legal system copes with the problem of access to justice among its French-speaking minority citizens, but in a much more restricted and truncated form (Spanish would be used only during the testifying process in a trial in designated courts). As suggested, a limited "language matching" program is simply a pragmatic measure to help achieve "access to justice" and can be decoupled from the much wider project of legal bilingualism that the

Canadian legal system aspires to achieve. The proposal is not meant to replace competent court interpreters. Quite the contrary, the idea is to free up more competent Spanish court interpreters for their much needed service. Given the tight budgets of many state court systems, retaining the service of quality court interpreter has proved to be a challenge and will likely continue to be so in the foreseeable future.

NOTES

1. 434 F.2d 386 (2d Cir. 1970). The court said: "Negron's incapacity to respond to specific testimony would inevitably hamper the capacity of his counsel to conduct effective cross-examination. Not only for the sake of effective cross-examination, however, but as a matter of simple humanness, Negron deserved more than to sit in total incomprehension as the trial proceeded" (390).

2. 205 U.S. 86 (1907).

3. Executive Order 13166, *Improving Access to Services for Persons with Limited English Proficiency*, 65 Fed. Reg. 50,121 (August 16, 2000).

4. *65 Federal Register 50121* (August 16, 2000).

5. An "otherwise qualified" interpreter is legally defined as someone who is either a professionally qualified interpreter or language-skilled interpreter.

Professionally qualified interpreters are in turn defined as interpreters who have either:

(a) prior employment as an interpreter for the U.S. State Department, the United Nations, or other agencies for which examinations of language proficiency are required or

(b) membership in good standing in a professional interpreters association that requires demonstrated language proficiency as a basis for membership.

Language-skilled interpreters are those interpreters who do not qualify as 'professionally qualified interpreters,' but who can demonstrate to the satisfaction of the court their ability to interpret court proceedings (Hewitt, Hannaford, Gill, & Cantrell, 1998, pp. 6–7).

6. Despite the common law system adopted by both Canada and the United States, Quebec in Canada and Louisiana in the United States are both civil law jurisdictions.

7. For example, *MacDonald v. City of Montreal* [1986] 1 S.C.R. 460 and *Société des Acadiens du Nouveau-Brunswick v. Association of Parents for Fairness in Education* [1986] S.C.R. 549.

8. The most famous case here in this area is *R. v. Beaulac* [1999] S.C.R. 768.

9. 111 S.Ct. 1859 (1991).

10. The 1995 figure is reported in California Commission on Access to Justice (2005). The 2007 figure is retrieved by searching all Spanish court interpreters in the "Master List of Certified Court Interpreters" maintained by the Administrative Office of the Courts, California.

11. *R. v. Beaulac* [1999] S.C.R. 768.

REFERENCES

Administrative Office of the U.S. Courts. (2007). Certifying interpreters a constant two-year cycle for federal courts. October 10. Available at http://www.uscourts.gov/newsroom/interpreterexam.html. Retrieved on December 5, 2007.

Berk-Seligson, S. (1990). *The bilingual courtroom: Court interpreters in the judicial process*. Chicago: University of Chicago Press.

California Commission on Access to Justice. (2005). Language barriers to justice in California: A report of the California Commission on Access to Justice. Available at http://calbar.ca.gov/calbar/pdfs/reports/2005_Language-Barriers_Report.pdf. Retrieved on December 5, 2007.

Canadian Centre for Management Development. (2004). Access to justice in both official languages, English and French before federal courts: Final report. Available at http://www.csps-efpc.gc.ca/research/publications/pdfs/ajbof_e.pdf. Retrieved on December 5, 2007.

Cardenas, J. (2004). Advocates fear justice lost in translation. *The Morning Call*, November 7.

Committee to Improve Interpreting and Translation in the Wisconsin Courts. (2000). Improving interpretation in Wisconsin's courts. October. Available at http://www.wicourts.gov/about/pubs/supreme/docs/interpreterreport.pdf. Retrieved on December 7, 2007.

Cooper, C. (2005). Interpreter shortage leaves courts in a bind. *The Sacramento Bee*, September 8.

Engel, D. M., & Steele, E. H. (1979). Civil cases and society: Process and order in the civil justice system. *American Bar Foundation Research Journal* (Spring), 311–317.

Ewell, M. (1989). What jury heard was not what was said. *San Jose Mercury News (CA)*, December 17.

Ewell, M., & Schrieberg, D. (1989). How court interpreters distort justice incompetence. *San Jose Mercury News*, December 17.

Gill, C., & Hewitt, W. E. (1996). Improving court interpreting services: What the states are doing. *State Court Journal*, *20*(1). Available at http://www.ncsconline.org/wc/publications/Res_CtInte_StateCrtJV20N1WhatStatesAreDoingPub.pdf. Retrieved on December 7, 2007.

Hewitt, W., Hannaford, P., Gill, C., & Cantrell, M. (1998). *Court interpreting services in state and federal courts: Reasons and options for inter-court coordination*. National Center for State Courts.

Judicial Council of California. (2004). A report to the California legislature on the use of interpreters in the California courts. Available at http://www.courtinfo.ca.gov/reference/documents/useinterprept.pdf. Retrieved on December 10, 2007.

Judicial Council of California. (2006). Report to the legislature: 2005 Language need and interpreter use study. Available at http://www.courtinfo.ca.gov/jc/documents/reports/042106ItemB.pdf. Retrieved on December 12, 2007.

Leighton, J. E. (2002). A world of words comes to court. *Trial*, *38*, 20–27.

Lowney, R. (2005). Federal judiciary accomplishments of the last 10 years and the challenges of the future. Speech given at the 26th Annual Meeting of National Association of Judiciary Interpreters and Translators. May 14, pp. 9–11 in *Proteus: Newsletter of the National Association of Judiciary Interpreters and Translators*, 14(3).

McCaffrey, A. (2000). Don't get lost in translation: Teaching law students to work with language interpreters. *Clinical Law Review Spring*, *6*, 347–399.

McCain, M. (2004). Justice lost in translation. *St. Paul Pioneer Press*, June 14.

Pantoga, H. (1999). Injustice in any language: The need for improved standards governing courtroom interpretation in Wisconsin. *Marquette Law Review*, *82*, 601–664.

Piatt, B. (1990). *¿Only English?: Law and language policy in the United States*. Albuquerque: University of New Mexico Press.

Rhode, D. L. (2004). *Access to justice*. New York: Oxford University Press.

Romberger, W. (2007). "Interpreters in civil cases." *Future Trends in State Courts 2007*. National Center for State Courts. Available at http://www.ncsconline.org/WC/Publications/Trends/2007/CtInteTrends2007.pdf. Retrieved on December 10, 2007.

Rosenberg, M. (2004). Closing, pp. 57–59 in *Access to justice in both official languages, English and French before federal courts: Final report*, Canadian Centre for Management Development. Available at http://www.csps-efpc.gc.ca/research/publications/pdfs/ajbof_e.pdf. Retrieved on December 5, 2007.

Schmidt, R. (2000). *Language policy and identity politics in the United States*. Philadelphia, PA: Temple University Press.

Shulman, M. B. (1993). No hablo ingles: Court interpretation as a major obstacle to fairness for non-English speaking defendants. *Vanderbilt Law Review*, *46*, 175–196.

Thibaut, J., & Walker, L. (1975). *Procedural justice: A psychological analysis*. Hillsdale, NJ: Erlbaum.

U.S. Census Bureau. (2003). Language use and English-speaking ability: 2000. Available at http://www.census.gov/prod/2003pubs/c2kbr-29.pdf. Retrieved on December 5, 2007.

ACCESS TO JURIES: SOME PUZZLES REGARDING RACE AND JURY PARTICIPATION

Mary R. Rose

ABSTRACT

Purpose – *This chapter discusses two puzzles emerging from the literature on race and the jury. First, although changes in laws and institutional practices have dramatically expanded jury participation, it is far from clear what additional changes would create more racially representative juries. Second, the push for racial diversity on juries stems, in part, from a belief that composition is related to decision making; nonetheless, empirical research typically fails to link jury composition and case outcomes.*

Methodology/approach – *Through a review of recent research, I identify the bases for these puzzles, and I consider ways to advance the body of work on race and the jury.*

Findings – *Studies on jury representativeness should simultaneously consider both institution-level and individual-level predictors of participation, examining in particular whether and how attitudes toward jury service differ across racial and ethnic groups. The literature would benefit most from longitudinal and multi-jurisdictional studies. Researchers on race and jury decision making should examine the reason* why *racial differences in attitudes and individual verdicts may not have an impact on*

Access to Justice
Sociology of Crime, Law and Deviance, Volume 12, 119–144

ISSN: 1521-6136/doi:10.1108/S1521-6136(2009)0000012009

case outcomes. By studying deliberating groups, scholars should consider whether any racial differences in viewpoints are substantively small, whether differences observed are ultimately irrelevant to group discussions, or whether group dynamics limit the participation and influence of racial minorities on mixed-race juries.

Originality/value – *This chapter advances the literature on race and the jury by considering both questions of representativeness and decision making and by critically examining a number of assumptions and accepted wisdom.*

Few phrases in law are as evocative as "all-white jury." In his concurring opinion in *Georgia v. McCollum* (1992, p. 61, n1), Justice Thomas reported that in a five-year period, this particular descriptor appeared over two hundred times in three major newspapers. This phrase conjures up at least two significant images. One springs from the United States' abysmal history of limiting jury participation to a few highly non-representative groups of people (see Fukurai, Butler, & Krooth, 1993; Van Dyke, 1978), and the phrase evokes the possibility that things have not changed much in the ensuing years. Second, when an "all-white jury" is mentioned in a news account of a case, the tacit suggestion is that the outcome was likely affected by the composition – that is, perhaps a verdict might have been different had a more diverse group heard the same facts. It is perhaps tempting to believe that juries resemble their mostly white counterparts from a half century ago, or to be certain that case outcomes hinge on jury composition. Perhaps high-profile anecdotes in the media further such beliefs. Nevertheless, both suppositions are largely unsupported in the empirical literature on the jury.

In this essay, I consider the racial representativeness on juries, as well as race and jury decision making, by focusing on puzzles that appear in the literatures of each of these domains. I first consider the puzzle presented by the expansion of jury participation that occurred in the late 20th century. In particular, historical trends demonstrate that the actions of courts and legislators dramatically altered the profile of the people who serve on juries. Despite this strong testament to the power of institutional action, the empirical literature does not clearly indicate what more institutions can do now to create more fully representative panels. One problem is the paucity of work in this area, but I also suggest that the literature has given insufficient attention to understanding prospective jurors' own decisions about whether to participate on juries. The literature says little about how people construct the meaning and implications of sitting on a jury, which may not only contribute to differences in participation but may also be challenging for courts or legislation to address.

I next review the puzzle posed by the empirical literature on race and jury decision making. Although people value racially heterogeneous juries (see Ellis & Diamond, 2003), and although there are reasons to believe that white and non-white jurors bring distinctive views to the cases on which they sit, jury composition is only sporadically linked with verdicts, and often there is no link. I consider several reasons why there might be a discrepancy between individual attitudes and group verdicts, including the proposition that minority group members fail to influence fellow jurors.

In the chapter's final section, I discuss some of the current methodological limitations in the existing work on race and the jury, and I also note other potential domains of research that are implicated by the issues that research on race and the jury raises.

It should be noted that this review focuses exclusively on the jury system in the United States. Countries besides the United States use a jury or otherwise incorporate lay people into legal decision making. Although the results of studies discussed below could generalize to these other countries, some of the findings may reflect the particular way that race structures people's experience in the United States. The jury in an international context merits an essay of its own (see Hans, 2008; Kutnjak Ivkovich, 1999; Vidmar, 2000), and I do not attempt to cover this ground here.

1. THE PUZZLE OF JURY COMPOSITION: INSTITUTIONAL ACTIONS MATTER BUT HOW?

Somewhat counter-intuitively, jury service has been expanding in the population during the precise time that trials have been "vanishing" (Galanter, 2004). In a 1999 survey, 24% of respondents said that they had served on a jury, which represents a 50% increase in the 16% rate reported in 1983 (National Center for State Courts, 1999). In 2004, a Harris Interactive poll found that 29% of those contacted had served on a jury (see Mize, Hannaford-Agor, & Waters, 2007). The rise in participation has accompanied substantial institutional efforts to address jury representativeness and to distribute jury service to a wider group of citizens. Specifically, legislation in the late 1960s and early 1970s eliminated many of the non-random methods that jurisdictions used to summon jurors (e.g., through "key-man" systems in which local elites nominated people whom they believed would make good jurors). Jurisdictions were either required (Jury Service and Selection Act, 1968) or encouraged (Uniform Jury Service and Selection Act, 1970, proposing a model law) to use comparatively more representative source lists (e.g., voter registration rolls) and to use random procedures to summon citizens. Landmark court rulings (*Castaneda v. Partida*, 1977; *Taylor v. Louisiana*, 1974) also explicitly prohibited racial and gender discrimination in the process of summoning and qualifying jurors for service. Individual states have also moved to reduce or eliminate several automatic exemptions from service. New York, for example, formerly granted exemptions to members of a diverse range of occupations, including those for whom the specific burden of jury service was not particularly clear (e.g., pharmacists, embalmers, podiatrists, and "Christian Science nurses"); these have all been eliminated (see Continuing Jury Reform in New York State, 2001). In addition, jurisdictions have attempted to make jury conscription less onerous, for instance by increasing juror pay and requiring that people who appear either be selected for a case or conclude their service (so-called one day/one trial forms of service; Kasunic, 1983). Finally, in more recent court cases, the Supreme Court has addressed discrimination in the final phases of jury selection, holding that neither race nor gender can be the basis for attorney decisions about whom to excuse (*Batson v. Kentucky*, 1986; *Edmonson v. Leesville Concrete Co.*, 1991; *Georgia v. McCollum*, 1992; *J.E.B v. Alabama, ex rel T.B.*, 1994; *Powers v. Ohio*, 1991).

Although a broader segment of the population is now tapped for service, the general picture of participation remains similar to the one described 16 years ago by sociologist Hiroshi Fukurai et al. (1993) in their review of jury selection practices: Minorities are under-represented on juries, whereas whites are over-represented, notwithstanding some regional differences. A study of death penalty cases from Philadelphia found that African Americans – especially young African-American males – were vastly under-represented on final juries (Baldus, Woodworth, Zuckerman, Weiner, & Broffitt, 2001). Separate studies of jury selection in large Texas counties (those surrounding Houston, Dallas, and Austin) have also consistently found disparities in who serves, but in these areas Hispanics are under-represented to a greater extent than are African Americans (Hays & Cambron, 1999; Rose & Brinkman, 2008; Walters, Marin, & Curriden, 2005). For example, my colleague and I used census data to estimate the jury-eligible population in Travis County (Austin), Texas and compared that to the profile of jury venires (the group of people assigned to a court to be questioned in a case; Rose & Brinkman, 2008).[1] In a two-month period in

2002, African Americans were roughly 8% of the jury eligible population but 6% of the venire groups, whereas Hispanics were estimated to be 21% of the jury-eligible population but only 12% of all venires.

If previous changes in institutional practices and laws expanded jury service in the population, it seems reasonable to posit that legislatures and courts could now take additional steps to reduce the present racial disparities in jury composition. However, this position assumes that the factors contributing to disparities in racial representativeness are under the control of the courts or law-makers. Courts and legislators have the greatest control over that factors that were the subject of change in recent decades: specifically, how jurors are summoned, qualifications for and permissible exemptions from service, and the how much latitude attorneys enjoy in being able to excuse jurors without providing explanations, that is, their use of peremptory challenges. Do these factors currently contribute substantially to non-representativeness? The available answers are, at best, mixed.

With respect to the last factor – attorneys' use of the peremptory challenge – research on criminal cases consistently shows that prosecutors disproportionately excuse African Americans whereas defense attorneys disproportionately excuse whites (Rose, 1999; Baldus et al., 2001; Clark, Boccaccini, Caillouet, & Chaplin, 2007). Attorney challenges thus provide a salient example of how court actors can shape the composition of particular juries – indeed, Justice Thomas's remark about the significance of jury composition in *Georgia v. McCollum* occurred in a ruling on the peremptory challenge. Peremptory challenges are amenable to change because they are not constitutionally guaranteed (see Hoffman, 1997), and several scholars and judges have suggested that an important way to improve the racial representativeness of juries is to eliminate the peremptory challenge (Hoffman, 1997; Marder, 1995; see also Justice Breyer's concurring opinion in *Miller-el v. Dretke*, 2005).

Interestingly, although peremptory challenges do affect the profile of specific cases (i.e., some people are excused who would have otherwise served), there is some evidence that eliminating them might not dramatically change the aggregate profile of people who serve as jurors. Some studies find that the adversary race-based use of the peremptory produces sets of juries that, on average, reflect the venire composition (Clark et al., 2007; Rose, 1999) – at least in non-capital cases (for a different result in capital cases, see Baldus et al., 2001). An identical pattern – adversarial use of challenges, no net change in the racial representativeness of a set of juries – has also emerged in an analysis of civil cases (Diamond, Perry, Francis, & Dolan, 2008). Furthermore, according to a survey that asked a sample of Texas adults about their jury service histories, on every measure, including race, people who reported that they had made it as far as the questioning phase (but were then dismissed) were statistically indistinguishable from the group of people who have served on at least one jury (Rose, Diamond, & Musick, 2009). In short, to the extent that non-random attrition in the jury selection process remains, the peremptory challenge provides a weak account of why this occurs, and reforms to the peremptory are unlikely to change the aggregate profile of jurors versus non-jurors.

At the earliest phase of the jury selection process, summoning, biases will occur if courts rely on source lists (e.g., voter registration rolls) that do not fully represent the population of interest (see Fukurai et al., 1993). Research suggests that voting does indeed remain a good predictor of jury service. In our study of Texas adults, we showed that having voted in the last five years was one of the strongest means of distinguishing people who reported that they had never been summoned from those who had served on at least one jury (Rose et al., 2009). Voting did not predict attrition at other stages of the selection process. (Net of age and voting, being less educated, unmarried, and less residentially stable also significantly predicted being never-summoned rather than selected for a case. Interestingly, once these factors were accounted for, race did not distinguish those who had never been summoned from those who had served.) Of note, that study examined lifetime jury service, whereas Texas began supplementing jury lists with drivers license records only about ten years preceding the survey. Thus, the results may somewhat overstate the voting-jury service link (Rose et al., 2009). Nonetheless, summoning practices are clearly only as good as the source lists upon which they depend, and to the extent that these lists are biased by race, ethnicity, or any other factor, jury pools will similarly be affected. Additional research can indicate whether courts and legislatures should do more to broaden jury service source lists – an issue over which courts and legislatures have control and can effect changes, if necessary.

Institutional actions and summons response. Even if courts summoned a perfectly random group of people, there would still be attrition because not everyone summoned will be able and available to serve on a case. The rate of summoned people who end up at the courthouse eligible to serve in a case is called the "juror yield," and yield may be under half of all summonses sent (Losh, Wasserman, & Wasserman, 2000); in one recent study of Philadelphia, the overall proportion of jury-eligible people turning out for jury service was just 30% (Taylor, Ratcliffe, Dote, & Lawton, 2007).

Researchers in Pennsylvania have done the most intensive recent work on juror yield, examining yield rates across neighborhoods by geo-coding the areas to which people were sent jury summonses and tracking who appeared at court. One unpublished study of four counties in Pennsylvania found that yield decreased as the percentage of African-Americans and Hispanics in a neighborhood increased (Committee on Racial and Gender Bias, 2003). This effect survived a control for neighborhood residential stability and neighborhood income levels. Taylor and colleagues (2007) looked at these data more intensively, focusing only on results for Philadelphia. For Asian and Hispanic groups, the same linear (and negative) pattern appeared: As the proportion of these groups in a neighborhood increased, yield went down, and this pattern survived additional controls. African Americans exhibited far more contextual effects. In "slightly African-American neighborhoods" (defined as from 0 to 30 percent African-American), average neighborhood yield decreased as the proportion of African Americans increased (from 34% to about 24%). For predominantly African-American neighborhoods (roughly, over 80% African American), yield rates were largely flat, with a slight drop for neighborhoods that were almost entirely African American (ending up at about 28%). Integrated neighborhoods (between 30% and 70–80% African American) were starkly different: yield *increased* as the proportion of African Americans increased. Indeed, after introducing controls for residential stability and neighborhood status, the overall coefficient for African American on yield was positive and significant, which the authors attribute to the effects from integrated neighborhoods.

These studies thus show substantial attrition at the middles stages of selection, and this work also links yield to race and ethnicity, although in complicated ways. What power do courts have to affect this phase of selection? The answer depends on what factor or factors contribute most to lower yield. Yield is affected, in part, by the fact that some summonses go to incorrect addresses. Although estimates of undeliverable summonses vary greatly (cf. Boatright, 1998; Taylor et al., 2007), overall yield rates are higher in neighborhoods that are more stable (Taylor et al., 2007). In our survey of lifetime participation on juries (Rose et al., 2009), residential stability (measured as time in current residence and being a state native) was one of the best predictors of whether people had ever been jurors. To the extent that predominantly minority neighborhoods are also more residentially unstable, courts will have a disproportionately harder time reaching minorities for service.[2] Courts, of course, have little control over how often people move, but greater use of change of address databases may alleviate some of the problem, although this requires courts to pay a fee to the service (see Mize et al., 2007), and people must reliably provide database sources with correct information. Furthermore, as the Taylor et al. study indicates, some race effects survive controls for stability.

Yield is also lower when people summoned are not qualified to serve, or when they seek exemptions. Although jury qualifications vary across jurisdictions (see Rottman, Flango, Cantrell, Hansen, & LaFountain, 2000), some are likely linked with race and ethnicity. Most areas, for example, exclude non-citizens and non-English speakers from serving (but see *State ex rel. Martinez v. Third Judicial District Court*, 2000, which allows for translators), and others, such as Texas, also exclude anyone with a felony record (see Tex. Gov't Code Ann. §62.102). With political support, these qualifications could, in theory, be altered, although the extent to which such changes would impact depressed yield among minority groups has not been established. Similar to the types of efforts that took place in New York State, exemptions could also be tightened, making it more difficult for people to get out of serving when tapped (see Rottman et al., 2000 for state-by-state information on exemptions). There are, however, practical limits on any attempts to become more stringent in response to exemption requests, especially because some excuses reflect clear barriers to serving (e.g., exemptions for being a student, being in the military, or for illness). Rather than restructuring or restricting exemptions, some have suggested that courts need to do far more to make jury service feasible, especially for low income citizens and people with care-giving responsibilities (see Boatright, 1998; Walters & Curriden, 2004). The data are unclear on how much such additional support might alter any racial imbalances in juror yield. The few existing studies suggest that, if anything, whites take more advantage of exemptions than do minorities – at least as indicated by examining the profile of people who formally contact the court to request a waiver from service (Boatright, 1998; Fukurai & Butler, 1991; Losh et al., 2000).

What if the issue is attitudinal? A final factor influencing juror yield is the individual decision to ignore a summons. There are, again, scant data on who fails to respond to a summons, but the few available studies indicate that non-response is higher among minorities than among whites. In particular, among a group of people who appeared at court in response to a summons, minorities were over-represented in the group who had failed to appear previously when summoned (Losh et al., 2000). Boatright (1998) examined people in one county who took a "pre-test" survey of attitudes; this same group was then monitored to observe who responded to a summons and who did not. The author reports that the rate of non-response among whites was 6.3%, whereas for non-whites it was 16.2%. He also notes that on the pre-test, African Americans were more likely to say that they did not have enough knowledge to serve as jurors (27.3%) compared to whites (13.1%). This work suggests that some depressed juror yield among minority groups may stem from explicit decisions they make not to follow up and respond to a summons they have received; it also suggests that the symbolic meaning and conceptions people have about jury service differ by race and ethnicity. Other work supports this proposition.

First, minorities describe themselves as less willing to serve on a jury compared to whites. Rose (2005) surveyed people in North Carolina who had appeared at court and had either been excused from service or had been selected to serve on a jury; people reported their willingness to return in the future. Despite several positive ratings about their current service (e.g., how they were treated during jury selection), none of which correlated with race, African Americans who had been selected rated themselves as less willing to return again. Dote (2007) relied on a survey of 339 Philadelphians and reported that lower willingness to serve among African Americans survived controls for, among other things, how easy it would be to make arrangements to serve, a personal sense of efficacy about jury service, confidence in juries, and sense of community. Notably, like the Taylor et al. study, Dote's data support the idea that some race effects may be bound up in differences in neighborhood subcultures (cf. Sampson & Bartusch, 1998). When her models were reconfigured to predict differences in willingness *within* neighborhoods (rather than across the entire sample), race effects weakened.

Compared to whites, minorities are also less reliably in favor of juries as the best way to solve legal disputes. In a survey of Texas adults, respondents were asked to select a jury or a judge to be the most accurate, if they were accused of crime, if they were plaintiffs in an auto accident lawsuit, or if they were defendants in an auto suit. Whereas whites demonstrated a substantial majority preference for a jury over a judge across scenarios, support among African Americans and some Hispanics[3] was comparably more tempered: Most members of these groups preferred the jury to the judge, but at significantly lower levels than whites. For example, fully 87% of whites selected a jury if they were a criminal defendant; the percentage for Hispanics was 72% and for African Americans, 73%. In imagining themselves as plaintiffs in a civil case, 72% of whites opted for a jury; just 51% of blacks did so (65% of Hispanics favored the jury in this instance, which did not differ significantly from whites).

The notion that minorities may view juries or jury service differently from whites is entirely consistent with findings from other studies on views of the courts and of judges, which find differences in perceptions of the courts across racial lines (see Brooks & Jeon-Slaughter, 2001; de la Garza & DeSipio, 2001; Gibson & Caldeira, 1992; Overby, Brown, Bruce, Smith, & Winkle III, 2005). Furthermore, one small study found that non-response does, to some extent, reflect attitudes – at least according to the self-reports of citizens. Seltzer (1999) interviewed a group of people in Washington, D.C. who had avoided summons; these participants cited not only hardship reasons but also a belief that courts were biased and, furthermore, that they did not like the thought of sitting in judgment of others. (Seltzer's sample of 62 people was small and responses were not reported by race of the respondent, although the District of Columbia has a high proportion of African Americans.) Walters and Curriden (2004) also report on an interview conducted with 800 people who did not show up for jury service; Hispanics who did not respond to a summons stated not only that they could not afford the lost income associated with service but also that they were afraid of serving.

Despite these patterns, the notion that individual juror attitudes might contribute to juror turnout has met with criticism. Fukurai et al. (1993, pp. 18–19), for example, argue that explaining lower juror yield among minority groups in terms of attitudes deflects attention onto the "problems" of individual prospective jurors and away from flaws in court institutional practices. In his report on improving summons response, Boatright (1998) largely dismisses attitudes as a factor that can account for summons non-response among any group. His study found few differences between summons responders and non-responders on beliefs about the jury (e.g., whether it would be interesting to serve) or about courts more generally – a notable exception was that non-responders were somewhat less likely than responders to say that juries represent their communities. According to Boatright, non-response more typically reflects misunderstandings of the jury system (e.g., about whether people facing hardships could get an exemption if they sought one) and a fairly realistic appraisal of costs of serving (e.g., court pay is typically low and courts typically do not cover some hardships, such as childcare in places in which primary caregivers are not automatically exempted). Boatright thus argues that courts could do a better job attending to each of these issues, for example, by engaging in better outreach to explain what jury service entails and by providing better support for jurors who serve.

At the same time, attitudes and institutional behavior are not independent of one another. Some attitudes about juries or the courts may *reflect* the failings of institutions, such as their biases (de la Garza & DeSipio, 2001) or their lack of support for jurors (Boatright, 1998; Walters & Curriden, 2004). In this way, understanding what individuals believe need not be tantamount to ignoring what institutions do. Furthermore, given the need to prioritize responses and reforms, courts clearly need empirical guidance about which factors are most responsible for less than fully representative panels, and, significantly, whether such factors are under the control of courts. If biased lists and wrong addresses best account for lower levels of minority participation – that is, if large numbers of people are simply not being "asked" to serve (Rose et al., 2009) – then court officials can work with legislators to approve better source lists and improved methods for updating these lists. However, institutions' control over representativeness becomes more limited if attrition from service depends on individual attitudes or on an interaction between attitudes and court behaviors. If the arrival of a summons is a harbinger of lost income and unsupervised children, then it makes little sense for courts to invest resources into educating people about service or toughening up summons enforcement so that people are required to give to their communities. The solution in these circumstances is to invest more resources into jury service so that the state demonstrates the same commitment to sacrifice and service that it asks of its citizens. On the contrary, no amount of money devoted to juror pay and better child care will affect summons response if minorities experience more generalized alienation from the courts or a greater aversion to the responsibility that a jury entails. The inability of scholars to tell the courts what factors would make a difference in jury participation represents, in part, the complexity of the issue and the multiple reactions people have to a jury summons. But this review also indicates that the dearth of answers also represents substantial inattention to researching what happens when a summons arrives.

2. RACE AND DECISION MAKING: THE SEEMINGLY MISSING ASSOCIATION BETWEEN COMPOSITION AND VERDICTS

Concerns about a non-representative jury composition stem, in part, from a belief that jurors are not "fungible" with one another – that is, many people reject the notion that any one juror will likely make the same decision as another (see Marder, 2002). With respect to race, attorneys clearly do not see jurors of different races as fungible. As already described, peremptory strikes are strongly patterned on race and indicate that prosecutors assume African Americans will not favor their cases while defense attorneys hold a similar view toward white jurors (Clark et al., 2007; Baldus et al., 2001; Rose, 1999). Experimental data likewise indicate that people who are asked to take on the role of a prosecutor in a criminal case also assume African Americans will be less advantageous to the state's side than a white juror, even when the two jurors otherwise have identical occupational backgrounds and life histories (Sommers & Norton, 2007).

Are such assumptions wholly unwarranted? In general, experimental jury simulations that poll individual jurors' verdicts find that both blacks and whites show an "own-race bias" and are more likely to vote to acquit someone of their own race than an identical cross-race defendant (e.g., Mitchell, Haw, Pfeifer, & Meissner, 2005). Furthermore, on average, African Americans and whites differ in terms of legally relevant attitudes. Compared to whites, African Americans have had more negative interactions with the police and are more likely to assume that police sometimes engage in misconduct (Weitzer & Tuch, 2005), are less supportive of legal institutions (e.g., judges, the courts; Gibson & Caldeira, 1992; Overby et al., 2005), and they show less support for legal policies like the death penalty or drug criminalization (Cochran & Chamlin, 2006; Hagan, Payne, & Shedd, 2005; Meares, 1997). In theory, these factors could affect how individuals respond to a criminal case by creating different perceptions of testimony from the police, by altering standards for reasonable doubt, or these beliefs may structure how people view the legitimacy of using a jury verdict to send a message about the law (i.e., whether to engage in "jury nullification"; see, e.g., Butler, 1995).

Nevertheless, despite these findings, jury composition bears little association with a jury group's final verdict choice (see, e.g., Garvey et al., 2004; Visher, 1987; Vidmar, Beale, Rose, & Donnelly, 1997), especially in routine criminal cases.[4] For example, Eisenberg et al. (2005) studied judge-jury agreement in criminal cases in four jurisdictions (Los Angeles, CA; Maricopa, AZ; Washington, DC; and Bronx, NY). In simple analyses, the data supported the view of black leniency toward criminal defendants: In counties with more African Americans in the population (Bronx, Washington, DC), judge-jury agreement was lower, with disagreement more often occurring when juries acquitted whereas judges privately indicated that they would have convicted. Across jurisdictions, juries that disagreed with judges in this way (jury acquits/judge would have convicted) also had higher than average percentages of African Americans on the jury (37% versus 22% overall). However, there was other evidence that these results may reflect different mixes of case-types across jurisdictions. Upon controlling for strength of evidence, jury composition had no relationship with whether juries and judges voted the same. Indeed, depending on the strength of evidence measure used (the jurors' own ratings, the judges', or a composite of the two), effects were sometimes in the reverse direction, with convictions more likely as the percent of African Americans on the jury increased.[5]

Thus, there is a notable disconnect between the assumption that race should matter for decision making – and the fact that research links race to legally-relevant attitudes – and verdict results in criminal cases. (There has been far fewer studies of civil cases, but studies typically confirm the absence of a relationship between demographics and civil decision making; see Diamond, Saks, & Landsman, 1998; Eisenberg & Wells, 2002.) What might explain this disconnect? There are at least three possibilities.

First, it is conceivable that the "significant" attitudinal differences that jury research scholars, and other scholars of law and public opinion have found, are overblown. That is, although statistically significant, the substantive difference between minorities and whites on a variety of legal attitudes may not be large. Consider the finding of an "own-race bias." In a meta-analysis of jury simulation tasks, Mitchell et al. (2005) found that the effect size for own-race bias on verdicts was $d = 0.09$, a difference of about one-tenth of a standard deviation, or a "small" effect (Cohen, 1992). In this account, there is far more commonality than difference between jurors of different races, even if, on average, the two groups hold somewhat distinctive views.

A second possibility is that the general attitudinal differences between groups are not relevant to the task of jury deliberation. Instead, the specific case facts and the strength of the evidence will likely matter more for jury outcomes than an individual's decontextualized opinions about police behavior or legal policy (e.g., Eisenberg et al., 2005; Visher, 1987). Psychologists reliably find that attitudes are a better predictor of behavior when those attitudes are specific (e.g., how someone feels about a particular type of crime or particular defendant) rather than general (e.g., how people feel about the criminal justice system; see generally Ajzen & Fishbein, 1977; Davidson & Jaccard, 1979). In this view, even if whites and non-whites differ on specific issues, they largely share the goal of wanting guilty people to go to jail and wanting to avoid the conviction of the innocent. They also are likely to be far more affected by specific features of the case facts, rather than a more general worldview.

The above explanations reflect the psychology of decision making and how factors combine to create judgments. Another possible explanation for the disconnect between individual verdict differences by race and group verdicts considers the social dynamics of group decision making. Specifically, diversity on juries will make a difference in case outcomes only to the extent that those taking a different position participate fully in deliberations. That is, even if race strongly predicted individuals' personal leanings in a case, the final verdict would not be associated with differences in composition if the dominant group avoids listening to and deferring to minority positions within the group. In this account, differences between sub-groups of jurors exist and are substantively important, but these differences are lost when the full group decides the outcome. It is well known that when people of different status categories come together in a context like small group decision making, status distinctions affect how group members behave toward one another, with low status people participating less than high status people (see, e.g., Berger, Cohen, & Zelditch, 1972; Correll & Ridgeway, 2003).

Does such status differentiation occur on juries? According to the small body of work on race and jury group dynamics, group participation is lower among minorities than among whites (see Hastie, Penrod, & Pennington, 1983). This same result was confirmed on a highly unusual dataset of the videotaped trials and deliberations of 50 real civil juries (see Diamond, Vidmar, Rose, Ellis, & Murphy, 2003). According to initial analyses of participation, based on word counts measured on transcriptions of deliberations, whites spoke, on average, more words per minute then non-whites (Rose, Diamond, & Murphy, 2006). These results survived controls for several other factors, including income, occupation, gender, education and foreperson status. Results are still being finalized, and our research group is testing different types of models that conceptualize participation in different ways – for example, as a rate of speaking (words per minute of deliberation), as a proportion of total words, or by using deliberation time as a group-level predictor. The word count analysis should also be supplemented with more micro-level coding of how group differences emerge. If the lower rate of talk for minorities is robust, it would be important to know, for example, whether minorities are disproportionately likely to be cut off through interruptions or other dominance behavior, or if low status jurors cede the floor to high status others (see Correll & Ridgeway, 2003).

At the same time, amount of talk is not the same as amount of influence, and other work has questioned the notion that minorities are less influential on juries than whites. York and Cornwell (2006) studied influence directly through a post-trial survey of 62 jurors from 14 cases in two Massachusetts courthouses (all but two were civil cases). Respondents filled in a chart that described the seating positions of each juror during deliberations. Jurors then used this diagram to list those individuals who were "most influential in the decision." Jurors also rated other jurors' level of participation on the jury and were asked to try to recall the race, gender, and class status of each juror; for the latter, jurors were asked to "infer" the juror's occupation and lifestyle. The authors then used participation levels, race, gender, and class status to predict who was likely to be nominated as influential. Race did not predict influence nominations, and neither did gender; however, those of higher social class and higher participation levels were rated as more influential. The study is limited because the authors did not have independent ratings of other jurors' characteristics apart from the reports of those nominating, which introduces the possibility of measurement error. Notably, the race and gender of other jurors are probably less subject to misremembering or misperception than other factors; the same cannot be said of the class and participation effects, as people may have misremembered those whom they regarded as influential as high participators and they may have assumed they were of high social class. The response rate was also low (35%), and other studies have found low levels of consensus among jurors regarding who was influential (Marcus, Lyons, & Guyton, 2000). Nevertheless, if results from this sample of mostly civil cases generalize to criminal juries, it suggests that whites are no more likely to contribute to a final verdict than are non-whites.

Sommers (2006) provides powerful experimental support for the notion that minorities on mixed-race juries are influential – including in ways not previously considered. With the cooperation of a local court, Sommers recruited adults appearing for jury duty into a decision-making study involving an African American defendant charged with sexual assault. He then systematically varied whether white jurors heard and deliberated upon the case with either an all-white jury or with a group that included two African-American jurors (both groups had six members). The differences in the behaviors of whites across the two contexts served as the critical dependent variable. Whites serving on the mixed juries raised more case facts, made fewer factual errors, and were more willing to discuss race-related issues than were those on all-white juries. Mixed-race juries also deliberated for longer than did homogeneous juries. Most intriguingly, despite having been randomly assigned to case type, whites serving on mixed juries were more likely to support an acquittal *before* deliberations began (66.2%) than were whites in homogeneous groups (49.5%). (Most African Americans favored acquittal, 76.8%.)

Sommers' work thus indicates that the effect of the racial composition of the jury changes more than just the types of information and perspectives that may be exchanged during discussion. Greater racial diversity on juries seems also to alter the entire context in which individual jurors hear evidence, think about issues, arrive at their own tentative conclusions, and imagine presenting their opinions to others. Indeed, Sommers conceptualizes his result as supporting the proposition that the race-salience of a trial has a significant impact on the decisions of white jurors because whites want to avoid appearing racist. For example, in other studies of individual decision making (Sommers & Ellsworth, 2000, 2001), an own-race bias among white jurors was eliminated simply by introducing a single fact to enhance the race-salience of a case summary – for example, by noting that a young black (or white) defendant, accused of assaulting a basketball teammate, was one of only two members of that racial group on the team. According to this theory, having blacks on a jury is another way of increasing the racial salience of a case. To avoid appearing racist, whites will tend to behave differently – that is, more carefully and thoroughly – on mixed juries than they will on all-white juries.

The most puzzling aspect of Sommers jury-group study, however, is the absence of any effect for racial composition on *final group verdicts*, and this result raises significant questions about the type of influence minorities in these cases exerted. Because the presence of blacks on the jury increased white jurors' initial support for an acquittal, and because African Americans consistently strongly favored acquittal, then mixed-race juries were more likely than the all-white juries to begin deliberations with groups that were, on average, acquittal-prone. In this circumstance, group polarization effects (in which the initial leaning of the group is exaggerated after deliberation; see Myers & Bishop, 1970; Friedkin, 1999), and common majority-rule decision schemes that groups adopt (e.g., "majority wins"; Davis, 1975) should have generated a disproportionate number of acquittals among mixed-race juries. However, this did not occur. Of the 11 "hung" juries (i.e., no verdict reached after an hour of deliberation), 7 were in the diverse condition, and, in any case, as already noted, final decision (verdicts or no result) did not differ significantly by diversity condition.

This null finding could represent the limits of statistical power (there were 15 mixed groups and 14 all-white groups), as well as the limits of simulations, in which deliberations must be artificially ended (Sommers, 2006). But given the absence of group polarization, it seems plausible that the more thorough deliberations on the mixed juries generated more *uncertainty* among members regarding which verdict to support.

Sommers did not report post-deliberation individual verdicts (and, in a personal communication, recalled that whites and minorities did not differ significantly in post-deliberation verdicts). However, the study raises the possibility that the diversity-exposed jurors felt more uncertainty after deliberations, and the critical question is who may have felt uncertain. If both African American and white jurors responded to the more thorough discussions by seeing what they initially thought was an "obvious" case in more nuanced terms, this suggests that diversity creates precisely the kind of thoroughness and critical evaluation of evidence that one expects to occur on groups with more diverse perspectives. On the contrary, if whites alone became more uncertain, and/or more conviction-prone after interacting with African American jurors on a case involving an African American defendant, then this suggests a very different conclusion. Whites would instead be systematically entertaining more doubts about the innocence of an African American defendant after they have interacted with African American jurors – a highly unintended outcome as we envision goals for more racially representative juries.

It bears repeating that the available evidence from the Sommers study (and from follow-up correspondence with the author) is that race did not predict post-deliberation verdicts. The broader point is that even well-designed and executed work like the Sommers study can point to complicated questions and puzzling results regarding cross-racial interaction and decision making. As I will argue in the next section, to completely understand such complexities, the jury literature needs to move beyond equating individual decision making with group decision making.

3. FINDING ANSWERS TO PUZZLES AND IDENTIFYING OTHER PUZZLES

In this essay, I have offered two examples in which the intersection of race and the jury defies easy description and simple solutions. First, although jury participation has expanded to a wider group of people in the last several decades, race remains a good predictor of who serves and who does not serve, especially if one focuses on the early stages of the jury selection process when courts must assemble people in court for questioning in specific cases. Minorities are less likely than whites to be included in that assembly, and the current literature does not provide a straightforward explanation for why this is the case. Second, despite our strong beliefs that racial composition matters for jury decision making, and despite evidence that minorities and whites hold different attitudes and perspectives about legal issues, the racial composition of a jury has consistently proven to be a poor predictor of final verdicts in most types of cases. Certainly both puzzles call for additional empirical work; however, each area currently faces different types of limitations that need to be overcome. For the puzzle surrounding courts' control over racial representation on juries, the field would benefit from stronger research designs that simultaneously consider predictors about different units of analysis (individual, institutional) and that move beyond cross-sectional analyses. For the puzzles regarding race and decision making, researchers need to ask a broader range of questions in this area.

With respect to racial representativeness, the existing literature on jury participation is limited by being made up of a series of "one-off" studies that identify problems in single jurisdictions. In order to understand the complex interplay between institutional and individual practices, the best study would look across jurisdictions in order to generate wide variation in both units of analysis, the individual and the institutions. Specific questions that demand more information include: What regions have more success than others in increasing juror yield? Are there links between court practices in these areas? How similar or different are the demographic profiles of different regions, and what relationship, if any, do these profiles have with jury participation? Turning to the question of how individual beliefs and attitudes may affect juror participation, the literature could offer substantially more insights into how different racial or ethnic groups may (or may not) construct the meaning of jury service. Does receiving a summons from a court have different significance for groups whose communities are frequently disproportionately affected by the criminal justice system? What interactions do people expect to have with the courts during their time of service? Given that whites are somewhat more likely than minorities to seek exemptions from service, does this represent a different willingness to engage with the courts to seek an exemption, or do people perceive the potential burdens of service differently? What actual limitations do different groups face? What do people imagine the decision-making process will be like? Do minorities concern themselves with whether they might have to decide a case in which a defendant or one of the parties is a minority group member? Does this affect their views of service? How do they imagine interacting with others in a group? Of course, with respect to all of these issues, the important question is ultimately whether and how any of these factors shape people's willingness to serve and how they behave in response to a summons.

Another serious limitation is that nearly all studies of jury participation are cross sectional. The clearest test of whether institutions could do more to change people's response to a summons would instead come from studies of what happens to jury composition before and after a change in institutional behavior. Unfortunately, courts are notoriously reticent about maintaining race information regarding jurors, and this hampers the opportunity to observe how institutional practices affect composition (see Committee on Racial & Gender Bias, 2003, p. 54). However, the value of tracking participation over time cannot be overstated. For example, my colleague and I recently examined the question of whether courts' efforts to make jury participation easier for people – specifically, by impaneling jurors (i.e., assigning people to a jury panel, or "venire") through the Internet – might inadvertently alter the racial composition of jury panels (Rose & Brinkman, 2008). In theory, greater use of the Internet could imperil representativeness by easing the burdens of service more for whites than for minorities, as the latter are less likely to use the Internet. Using a simple before/after analysis, in which we examined the racial composition of jury panels for a few months before the switch to the Internet-based "I-Jury" system (in 2002), and then for several years after, we found no evidence that racial distortions occurred. Indeed, if anything, minority representation slightly *improved* following the county's use of the Internet: whites went from constituting 80% of jury panels in 2002 to 75% in 2006; in the same period, Hispanic representation increased from 12 to 16% (African Americans went from 6 to 7%). Given that we had a short period of pre-Internet observation, we could not be certain that the new system was wholly responsible for the improved representativeness; nonetheless, it was clear that the system had not done harm (see Rose & Brinkman, 2008).

Interestingly, although not the focus of that particular study, there was also a notable *absence* of change in composition following a different jury reform. The post-I-Jury analysis included two years (2005 and 2006), which differed in levels of juror pay. Panel composition was largely identical across these two years, even though pay in Texas went from $12 a day for seated jurors to $40 a day. Possibly, the pay differential had not been in place long enough for people to learn of the change and to alter behavior in response. It is also important to note that Travis County is a distinctive area of Texas – for example, 43% of the county holds a bachelor's degree or higher, compared to 25% statewide. As a state capital, the area also has a number of government workers, who are typically compensated when they serve. Thus, compared to other regions, the decisions of this county's residents regarding how to respond to a jury summons may be less affected by juror pay levels. According to Walters and Curriden (2004), for example, El Paso County in Texas reported that jury participation doubled (from 22 to 46% of those summoned) after the County (acting before the state did) increased both juror pay and summons enforcement. Future work should identify jurisdictions that maintain (or are willing to maintain) records on juror characteristics, including race, and should investigate whether composition changes in light of reforms states have either implemented or are considering (see Mize et al., 2007).

Unlike jury representation studies, the literature on race and decision making does not suffer from a paucity of data. Indeed, the body of literature is sizeable enough to have been subjected to meta-analysis (Mitchell et al., 2005), and studies consist of both well-designed, tightly controlled experimental investigations and multi-jurisdiction field studies. The important question for this literature is *why* studies of the final verdicts of juries largely fail to show a relationship between verdicts and the race of people serving, especially given that racial groups differ in terms of legally significant attitudes. I have suggested at least three possibilities that would explain this disconnect: attitudinal differences may not be as substantial as we assume them to be, attitudinal differences may not ultimately be germane to the jury's decision-making task, or differences of opinion – especially minority opinions – might be ignored, minimized or otherwise lack influence in the decision making process. Although the work I reviewed by Sommers indicates that minority group members are "influential" in surprising ways, that study nonetheless raised additional fascinating questions about what accounts for the null relationship between group composition and outcome.

In the decision-making area, the "black box" for researchers to tackle in decision making is what happens between the time a juror is selected for a case and the time that the group ceases its deliberation and how, if at all, the trajectory of individual and group decision making differs by the race of an individual juror or, as Sommers suggests, by the racial composition of the jury. Final jury verdicts represent more than the sum of individual views, and in understanding the role of race on juries, we need to understand not only individual traits, beliefs, and attitudes but also group processes. This requires careful analysis of the social dynamics that occur in the deliberation room – including questions about who participates in discussion, who is listened to, and under what circumstances participation, influence, or both vary as a function of race, racial composition of the group, or any other factor.

Beyond the questions I have outlined concerning racial representativeness on juries and race and decision making, there are others intersections of race and the jury that merit attention. Despite the rarity of the jury trial in the context of the justice system, juries cast a long "shadow." Jury verdicts can be signals to others about how the justice system is functioning and what to expect for one's own case. Given this, and given the finding that race structures attitudes toward the jury and other legally relevant attitudes, it is conceivable that actual litigants also hold views about the jury that differ by race. No research exists on whether white versus black plaintiffs make different calculations about how the jury will treat their cases. Do views about the jury shape how people think about settlement or the amount they are willing to settle for? How do attorneys communicate to their clients about how juries will likely treat them? Do attorneys make different recommendations to white versus minority plaintiffs? Beyond the courtroom, do any differences in attitudes toward the jury translate into different levels of political support for the institution? Do minorities and whites, for example, vote differently when tort reform items are on a ballot? As scholars begin to tackle these questions, we will have a far richer and broader understanding of the multiple ways in which people respond to, participate in, and shape the jury system.

NOTES

1. We estimated the "jury eligible" population by omitting people described as living in group housing situations (e.g., nursing homes, prisons, dormitories); people who were under 18 or over 70; non-citizens, and we adjusted figures for non-white Hispanics to estimate the number of people between 18 and 70 who were not fluent in English.
2. In their analysis of the under-representation of Hispanics on juries, Walters and Curriden (2004) suggest that this group tends to be more residentially unstable, which the authors attribute to greater social mobility (at least among Hispanics who would otherwise be jury eligible, that, who speak English and are citizens). Other work shows that the relationship between race/ethnicity and residential stability is not straightforward. Small (2007) shows a positive correlation between the proportion of African Americans in a neighborhood and residential stability ($r = 0.34$), but a strongly negative association ($r = -0.74$) between ethnic heterogeneity and stability.
3. Acculturation also shapes support for the jury. In particular, language dominance distinguished different groups of Hispanics. This was indicated by whether the respondent opted to take the survey in Spanish or not. The Hispanics who took the survey in English (all of whom were U.S. citizens) resembled African Americans in terms of jury preferences. By contrast, Spanish-dominant Hispanics

consistently selected a *judge* rather than a jury to decide legal cases. This was true for both citizens and non-citizens (see Rose et al., 2009 for more discussion of these results).

4. Capital cases are an important exception. Bowers, Steiner, and Sandys (2001) studied a set of capital cases and found that verdicts differed according to the race/gender composition of the jury. The probability of death sentence declined if there was at least one African American male on the jury.

5. I have suggested that this result suggests that jurisdictional effects can be explained in terms of differences in cases – that is, once cases are "equated" with one another across jurisdictions, the effects for jury composition on judge-jury agreement are eliminated. Of course, this perspective assumes that a strength of evidence rating in one area is comparable to a strength of evidence rating in another. I know of no data that indicate that people in different jurisdictions – including both jurors and judges – have radically different ideas of what constitutes "strong" versus "weak" evidence. Nonetheless, an ideal study would have a strength of evidence rating for all cases that was independent of the ratings of people who also returned (or, for judges, suggested) verdicts in the case.

ACKNOWLEDGMENT

The author gratefully acknowledges the helpful comments and editorial patience of Rebecca Sandefur.

REFERENCES

Ajzen, I., & Fishbein, M. (1977). Attitude-behavior relations: A theoretical analysis and review of research. *Psychological Bulletin, 84*, 888–918.

Baldus, D. C., Woodworth, G., Zuckerman, D., Weiner, N. A., & Broffitt, B. (2001). The use of peremptory challenges in capital murder trials: A legal and empirical analysis. *University of Pennsylvania Journal of Constitutional Law, 3*, 3–169.

Batson v. Kentucky, 476 U.S. 79 (1986).

Berger, J., Cohen, B. P., & Zelditch, M., Jr. (1972). Status characteristics and social interaction. *American Sociological Review, 37*, 241–255.

Boatright, R. G. (1998). *Improving citizen response to jury summonses. A report with recommendations*. Chicago, IL: American Judicature Society.

Bowers, W. J., Steiner, B. D., & Sandys, M. (2001). Death sentencing in black and white: An empirical analysis of the role of jurors' race and jury racial composition. *University of Pennsylvania Journal of Constitutional Law, 3*, 171–274.

Brooks, R. R. W., & Jeon-Slaughter, H. (2001). Race, income, and perceptions of the U.S. court system. *Behavioral Sciences and the Law, 19*, 249–264.

Butler, P. (1995). Racially based jury nullification: Black power in the criminal justice system. *Yale Law Journal, 105*, 677–725.

Castaneda v. Partida 430 U.S. 482. (1977).

Clark, J., Boccaccini, M. T., Caillouet, B., & Chaplin, W. F. (2007). Five factor model personality traits, jury selection, and case outcomes in criminal and civil cases. *Criminal Justice and Behavior, 34*, 641–660.

Cochran, J. K., & Chamlin, M. B. (2006). The enduring racial divide in death penalty support. *Journal of Criminal Justice, 34*, 85–99.

Cohen, J. (1992). A power primer. *Psychological Bulletin, 112*, 155–159.

Committee on Racial and Gender Bias. (2003). *Final report of the Pennsylvania Supreme Court committee on racial and gender bias in the justice system,* Administrative Office of the Courts, Philadelphia, PA. Available at http://www.courts.state.pa.us/Index/Supreme/biasreport.htm

Continuing jury reform in New York state: January 2001 report. New York State Unified Court System, New York, NY.

Correll, S. J., & Ridgeway, C. L. (2003). Expectations states theory. In: J. Delamater (Ed.), *Handbook of Social Psychology* (pp. 29–52). New York, NY: Kluwer Academic/Plenum Publishers.

Davidson, A. R., & Jaccard, J. (1979). Variables that moderate the attitude-behavior relation: Results of a longitudinal study. *Journal of Personality and Social Psychology, 37*, 1364–1376.

Davis, J. H. (1975). The decision processes of 6- and 12-person mock juries assigned to unanimous and two-thirds majority rules. *Journal of Personality and Social Psychology, 32*, 1–14.

de la Garza, R. O., & DeSipio, L. (2001). A satisfied clientele seeking more diverse services: Latinos and the courts. *Behavioral Sciences and the Law, 19*, 237–248.

Diamond, S. S., Perry, D., Francis, F. J., & Dolan, E. (2008). The effects of voir dire and jury size on the composition of the jury, Paper presented to the Law and Society Meeting, Montreal, Canada, May 31.

Diamond, S. S., Saks, M. J., & Landsman, S. (1998). Juror judgments about liability and damages: Sources of variability and ways to increase consistency. *DePaul Law Review, 48*, 301–325.

Diamond, S. S., Vidmar, N., Rose, M. R., Ellis, L., & Murphy, B. (2003). Juror discussions in civil trials: Studying an Arizona innovation. *Arizona Law Review, 45*, 1–81.

Dote, L. (2007). *Citizen willingness to serve: Explaining attitudes toward jury service in Philadelphia (Pennsylvania)*. Unpublished doctoral dissertation, Temple University, Philadelphia, PA.

Edmonson v Leesville Concrete Co., 500 U.S. 614 (1991).

Eisenberg, T., Hannaford-Agor, P. L., Hans, V. P., Waters, N. L., Munsterman, G. T., Schwab, S. J., & Wells, M. (2005). Judge-jury agreement in criminal cases: A partial replication of Kalven and Zeisel's *The American Jury*. *Journal of Empirical Legal Studies, 2*, 171–206.

Eisenberg, T., & Wells, M. T. (2002). Trial outcomes and demographics: Is there a Bronx effect? *Texas Law Review, 80*, 1839–1875.

Ellis, L., & Diamond, S. S. (2003). Race, diversity, and jury composition. *Chicago-Kent Law Review, 78*, 1033–1058.

Friedkin, N. E. (1999). Choice shift and group polarization. *American Sociological Review, 64*, 856–875.

Fukurai, H., & Butler, E. W. (1991). Organization, labor force, and jury representation: Economic excuses and jury participation. *Jurimetrics, 32*, 49–69.

Fukurai, H., Butler, E. W., & Krooth, R. (1993). *Race and the jury: Racial disenfranchisement and the search for justice*. New York, NY: Plenum.

Galanter, M. (2004). The vanishing trial: An examination of trials and related matters in federal and state courts. *Journal of Empirical Legal Studies, 1*, 459–570.

Garvey, S. P., Hannaford-Agor, P., Hans, V. P., Mott, N. L., Munsterman, G. T., & Wells, M. T. (2004). Juror first votes in criminal trials. *Journal of Empirical Legal Studies, 1*, 371–398.

Georgia v. McCollum, 505 U.S. 42 (1992).

Gibson, J. L., & Caldeira, G. A. (1992). Blacks and the United States supreme court: Models of diffuse support. *Journal of Politics, 54*, 1120–1155.

Hagan, J., Payne, M. R., & Shedd, C. (2005). Race, ethnicity, and youth perceptions of criminal injustice. *American Sociological Review, 70*, 381–407.

Hans, V. (2008). Juries systems around the world. *Annual Review of Law and Social Science*, (in press).

Hastie, R., Penrod, S. D., & Pennington, N. (1983). *Inside the jury*. Cambridge, MA: Harvard University Press.

Hays, J. R., & Cambron, S. (1999). Courtroom observation of ethnic representation among jurors in Harris County, Texas. *Psychological Reports, 85*, 1218–1220.

Hoffman, M. B. (1997). Peremptory challenges should be abolished: A trial judge's perspective. *University of Chicago Law Review, 64*, 809–871.

J.E.B. v. Alabama, ex rel. T.B., 511 U.S. 127 (1994).

Kasunic, D. E. (1983). One day/one trial: A major improvement in the jury system. *Judicature, 67*, 78–86.

Kutnjak Ivkovich, S. (1999). *Lay participation in criminal trials: The case of Croatia*. Lanham, MD: Austin and Winfield Publishers.

Losh, S. C., Wasserman, A. W., & Wasserman, M. A. (2000). 'Reluctant jurors:' What summons responses reveal about jury duty attitudes. *Judicature, 83*, 304–310.

Marcus, D. K., Lyons, P. M., & Guyton, M. R. (2000). Studying perceptions of juror influence *in vivo*: A social relations analysis. *Law and Human Behavior, 24*, 173–186.

Marder, N. (2002). Juries, justice, and multiculturalism. *Southern California Law Review, 75*, 659–725.

Marder, N. S. (1995). Beyond gender: Peremptory challenges and the roles of the jury. *Texas Law Review, 73*, 1041–1138.

Meares, T. (1997). Rethinking federal law: Charting race and class differences in attitudes toward drug legalization and law enforcement: Lessons for federal criminal law. *Buffalo Criminal Law Review, 1*, 137–174.

Miller-el v. Dretke 545 U.S. 231 (2005).

Mitchell, T. L., Haw, R. M., Pfeifer, J. E., & Meissner, C. A. (2005). Racial bias in mock juror decision-making: A meta-analytic review of defendant treatment. *Law and Human Behavior, 29*, 629–637.

Mize, G., Hannaford-Agor, P., & Waters, N. L. (2007). *The state-of-the-states survey of jury improvement efforts: A compendium report*, National Center for State Courts, Charlottesville, VA. Available at http://www.ncsconline.org/D_Research/cjs/pdf/SOS-CompendiumFinal.pdf

Myers, D. G., & Bishop, G. D. (1970). Discussion effects on racial attitudes. *Science, 169*, 778–789.

National Center for State Courts. (1999). *How the public views the state courts: A 1999 national survey*. Report presented at The National Conference on Public Trust and Confidence in the Justice System. May 14, Washington, D.C.

Overby, L. M., Brown, R. D., Bruce, J. M., Smith, C. E., Jr., & Winkle, J. W., III. (2005). Race, political empowerment, and minority perceptions of judicial fairness. *Social Science Quarterly*, *86*, 444–462.

Powers v. Ohio 499 U.S. 400 (1991).

Rose, M. R. (1999). The peremptory challenge accused of race or gender discrimination? Some data from one county. *Law and Human Behavior*, *23*, 695–702.

Rose, M. R. (2005). A dutiful voice: Justice in the distribution of jury service. *Law and Society Review*, *39*, 601–634.

Rose, M. R., & Brinkman, M. (2008). Crossing the digital divide: Using the Internet to impanel jurors in Travis County, Texas. *Journal of Court Innovation*, *1*, 5–32.

Rose, M. R., Diamond, S. S., & Murphy, B. (2006). He said/she said: An analysis of gender and participation in real jury deliberations. Paper presented to the Annual Meeting of the American Sociological Association. Montreal, Canada, August 14.

Rose, M. R., Diamond, S. S., & Musick, M. A. (2009). *Selected to serve: An analysis of lifetime jury participation*. Manuscript submitted for publication.

Rottman, D. B., Flango, C. R., Cantrell, M. T., Hansen, R., & LaFountain, N. (2000). *State Court Organization*, Bureau of Justice Statistics Report, Washington, DC (NCJ 178932). (Available at http://www.ojp.usdoj.gov/bjs/pub/pdf/sco98.pdf).

Sampson, R. J., & Bartusch, D. J. (1998). Legal cynicism and (subcultural?) tolerance of deviance: The neighborhood context of racial differences. *Law and Society Review*, *32*, 777–804.

Seltzer, R. (1999). The vanishing juror: Why are there not enough available jurors? *The Justice System Journal*, *20*, 203–218.

Small, M. L. (2007). Racial differences in networks: Do neighborhood conditions matter? *Social Science Quarterly*, *88*, 320–343.

Sommers, S. A., & Norton, M. I. (2007). Race-based judgments, race-neutral justifications: Experimental examination of peremptory use and the *Batson* challenge procedure. *Law and Human Behavior*, *31*, 261–273.

Sommers, S. R. (2006). On racial diversity and group decision making: Identifying multiple effects of racial composition of jury deliberations. *Journal of Personality and Social Psychology*, *90*, 597–612.

Sommers, S. R., & Ellsworth, P. C. (2000). Race in the courtroom: Perceptions of guilt and dispositional attributions. *Personality and Social Psychology Bulletin*, *26*, 1367–1379.

Sommers, S. R., & Ellsworth, P. C. (2001). White juror bias: An investigation of prejudice against Black defendants in the American courtroom. *Psychology, Public Policy, and Law*, *7*, 201–229.

State ex rel. Martinez v. Third Judicial District Court, Vol. 39, No. 7 SBB 12 (N.M. 2000).

Taylor v. Louisiana 419 U.S. 522 (1974).

Taylor, R. B., Ratcliffe, J. H., Dote, L., & Lawton, B. A. (2007). Roles of neighborhood race and status in the middle stages of juror selection. *Journal of Criminal Justice*, *35*, 391–403.

Van Dyke, J. (1978). *Jury selection procedures: Our uncertain commitment to representative panels*. Cambridge, MA: Ballinger.

Vidmar, N. (2000). *World jury systems*. New York, NY: Oxford University Press.

Vidmar, N., Beale, S. S., Rose, M. R., & Donnelly, L. F. (1997). Should we be rushing to reform the criminal jury? Consider conviction rate data. *Judicature*, *80*, 286–290.

Visher, C. A. (1987). Juror decision making: The importance of evidence. *Law and Human Behavior*, *11*, 1–17.

Walters, R., & Curriden, M. (2004). A jury of one's peers? Investigating underrepresentation on jury venires. *Judges' Journal*, *43*(Fall), 17–21.

Walters, R., Marin, M., & Curriden, M. (2005). Are we getting a jury of our peers? *Texas Bar Journal*, *68*, 144–146.

Weitzer, R., & Tuch, S. A. (2005). Racially biased policing: Determinants of citizen perceptions. *Social Forces*, *83*, 1009–1030.

York, E., & Cornwell, B. (2006). Status on trial: Social characteristics and influence in the jury room. *Social Forces*, *85*, 455–477.

LEGAL SERVICES FOR THE POOR: ACCESS, SELF-INTEREST, AND PRO BONO

Stephen Daniels and Joanne Martin

ABSTRACT

Purpose – *Decreasing governmental support means access to legal services for the poor depends upon the interests of private actors controlling the needed resources. Law firms are a major source of resources for non-profit entities providing those services. This chapter examines the nature of that support.*

Design/methodology/approach – *Law firms are guided by self-interest. How this influences their pro bono activities supporting legal services to the poor is explored through a case study of the legal services market in Cook County, IL and Chicago. It draws from: documentary research on over 50 private legal service providers in Cook County; interviews with 31 lawyers participating in the market for legal services in Cook County; and a focus group with 10 lawyers participating in that market.*

Findings – *The interests driving law firm support for legal services do not match the demonstrated areas of greatest legal need or the stated purposes of the non-profit entities receiving that support. Instead, they reflect reasonable firm self-interest in such goals as lawyer training and*

Access to Justice
Sociology of Crime, Law and Deviance, Volume 12, 145–166

ISSN: 1521-6136/doi:10.1108/S1521-6136(2009)0000012010

marketing. Consequently, non-profit entities receiving support must accommodate those goals.

Research limitations/implications – *This study points to the need for more empirical research into the consequences of the privatization of legal services.*

Originality/value – *Privatization means that some crucial legal needs will never be met, and this study provides an empirical context for the debate over "civil Gideon" – whether there should be a constitutional right to legal representation in civil matters akin to the constitutional right in criminal matters.*

INTRODUCTION

Published in 1977, Barbara Curran's seminal study *The Legal Needs of the Public* (Curran, 1977) documented a staggering amount of unmet legal need for people of limited means.[1] Over 80% of that need across the nation was unmet. Recent studies show that little has changed (Rhode, 2001, pp. 1787–1790; 2003, pp. 47–48). A 2005 study of legal needs in Illinois (the focus of our research) found that "low-income households had legal assistance for only one out of every six (16.4%) legal problems encountered in 2003 … the most common response (65.8%) to a legal problem was to attempt to resolve it without legal assistance … Many of these problems were complex matters with potentially serious consequences" (Chicago Bar Association et al., 2005, pp. 1–2). Though scant, the available empirical research demonstrates that having a lawyer can make a difference in outcomes for poor people in legal proceedings (Seron, Frankel, & Van Ryzin, 2001).

Given that there is no constitutional right to counsel for the indigent in civil matters as there is in criminal matters (see *Lassiter v. Dept. of Social Services*, 1981), the seemingly intractable problem is how to respond to a situation in which demand will always outstrip supply.[2] While there is public funding available for legal services, almost all commentators agree that it is woefully inadequate to meet the need. Since the 1970s, the trend has been one of decreasing financial support by government coupled with increasing limitations on the public funds (both federal and state) available (see Houseman, 1999; Rhode, 2004, pp. 102–108; Cummings, 2004, pp. 7–33). The gaps left by governmental retrenchment are filled, if they are filled at all, by private resources – private sources of financial support, private legal service providers, and especially the pro bono services of lawyers. One commentator has gone so far as to claim that voluntary pro bono has become "the dominant model of delivering free legal services" (Cummings, 2004, p. 5).

In short, the key has been privatization along with what Scott Cummings calls the "institutionalization of pro bono" (Cummings, 2004). In his words, pro bono and privatized legal services are "distributed through an elaborate organizational structure embedded in and cutting across professional associations, law firms, state-sponsored legal service programs, and non-profit public interest groups" (Cummings, 2004, p. 6). Cummings' work shows this to be an ad hoc structure made up of multiple actors and its character may vary from place to place and time to time. It works, to varying degrees, in matching demand and supply by trying to promote collaboration among the various players and providing connections or conduits between those needing legal services and those providing them. It is only partially successful because there are multiple actors each with their own and even competing goals and interests.

Underlying the ad hoc institutionalization of legal services, in other words, is self-interest, and this is a necessary consequence of the privatization of legal services for the poor. Those providing the resources have their own goals and interests in supporting such services, some of which go beyond simply serving the needs of the poor – and they will often take priority. As Rebecca Sandefur observes, "The substantial reliance of American-style civil legal assistance on pro bono implies that those factors influencing it may also affect the availability of legal aid. In particular, both the amount and the type of available civil legal assistance may be affected by conditions in the markets for legal services" (Sandefur, 2007, p. 85). Given this, it may be unrealistic to expect the foci of existing supply (both in terms of lawyer resources and financial resources) to actually match the demonstrated areas of demand for legal services.

Our interest is in the private (non-governmental) supply side of legal services – mapping its contours and exploring how the goals and interests of the private actors controlling the resources help shape the nature of the market for legal services for the poor. This focus is important because, as a practical matter, individuals have only the legal rights of which they are aware and which they can hope to enforce or use. Access to legal services, in turn, is usually the avenue to meaningful legal rights, and for people of limited means access may depend heavily on the interests of those who control the supply of legal services. Given Cummings observations on the ad hoc structure and organization of privatized legal services, one useful approach to exploring how the goals and interests of private organizational actors interact to shape the market for those services is to look in some detail at the delivery of legal services for the poor in a single locale. This is what we have chosen to do and our research site is Cook County, Illinois and the city of Chicago.

In this, a report on the early parts of our study of the delivery of legal services in Cook County, we examine the private supply side with a focus on pro bono in large law firms. We do so because it reveals in interesting and important ways how self-interest shapes the market for legal services for the poor. We draw from our documentary research on over 50 private legal service providers we identified in Cook County, in-depth interviews (one to one and one-half hours each) with 31 lawyers involved in the local market for legal services, and a two and one-half hour focus group involving 10 lawyers.[3] The interviewees were chosen so that they would provide a cross-section of lawyers who play a major role in legal services. We targeted lawyers employed by private legal service providers as directors or managing attorneys as well as lawyers who serve on the boards of such agencies. We targeted lawyers working in Chicago-area law school clinics, and we included interviewees from each local law school. Also included are lawyers in key positions in organizations that fund legal services, along with lawyers who are large law firm pro bono partners/coordinators.

Sixteen of the interviewees are important for our purposes not only because of their current positions, but because they are lawyers who have at least 10 or more years of experience (often in more than one role) in the Chicago-area legal services market. This includes some who have been associated with one or more of the major private funders of legal service activities in Cook County. As a result, these lawyers can provide a broader and longer-term picture of the delivery of legal services to the persons of limited means in Chicago. The focus group included 10 lawyers, chosen because of their involvement in the local legal services arena. They included the key people in large law firms in Chicago, a lawyer from a major corporate counsel's office in Chicago, and a lawyer from a major service provider organization. Unless otherwise noted, all quoted lawyer comments are from the interviews or the focus group. Because of promises to keep the lawyers' identities confidential, no individual, firm, or provider names are used.

SELF-INTEREST AND THE AVAILABILITY OF SERVICES FOR THE POOR

The scarce private resources available are not free, nor are they purely charitable in nature. There is still a market based on some exchange that distributes these resources. Demand does not drive the market; rather, it is the interests and priorities of those providing the resources. They expect certain things from the recipients (here meaning both the service providers and even the individuals ultimately benefiting from the service) in exchange for the resources invested, and continued support is dependent on the recipients upholding their end of the bargain. Because resources are limited, there will be competition among the non-profit service providers vying for support as well as competition regarding which specific areas of legal need will be addressed. This competition itself may even be institutionalized. Funders and resource providers establish programs that embody their priorities along with formal application and review processes to determine the groups in which resources will be invested. Those seeking resources will compete to show how their activities best serve the interests and priorities of the funders or resource providers.

This model of philanthropy is not, by any means, limited to the legal services arena. Any non-profit arena heavily dependent on philanthropy for resources will have to respond to the interests of those providing these resources. Philanthropy is consciously goal-driven and non-profit entities, in a sense, become the delivery mechanisms for funders' interests. Again, this is not charity and there is little philanthropy today that does not come with strings, conditions, and expectations attached. One simply cannot understand the real world of the current, privatized situation for the delivery of legal services to the poor without considering this kind of market-oriented approach.[4]

Most obviously, the interests of those with the resources will evidence themselves in the specific legal needs chosen for attention, but those interests can go much deeper – to the actual structuring of the delivery of legal services in a given locale. No single funder can literally impose a structure on this market, but those with resources will try to shape it in ways they believe will better serve their goals. This, of course, may mean that the price a service provider pays for resources is a certain loss of autonomy. For instance, one of the major funding agencies in Chicago is a foundation. This foundation makes grants of varying sizes to as many as 40 or more legal service providers in the Chicago area each year, so that legal services can be made available to at least some persons of limited means. But as a resource provider it has other goals as well. It also wants to influence the way in which legal services are provided – by promoting less overlap and competition among service providers within the community. In short, it wants to encourage what it sees as a more rational allocation of legal services. The comments of a lawyer who served on this foundation's board are very revealing in this regard:

> In that role [board member] I worried about the overlapping legal service providers. And like every other funder, one of our secondary missions was to try to give our money in ways which would help these agencies define their missions and not overlap each other, or better, saying it affirmatively, trying to give money in a way which would cause them to cooperate with each other rather than compete.

A service provider with a steady and diversified set of funding sources may be able to escape this kind of external control, but few are in this position.

The interests of resource providers can go still deeper. A resource provider may want to promote more efficiency and rationality not only among service providers, but also within a provider group it supports so that the most benefit, in the funder's estimation, can be derived from the available resources. An interviewee who sits on another funding agency board noted, "we have a limited amount of money to give away ... we're looking for organizations with a track record, capable staff, real lawyers. We want to make sure the money's being put to the best use." And, on occasion a service provider will lose its support from a funding agency for not upholding its end of the bargain. One head of a service provider told of "being busted down by them [a funding agency] the first year I was here ... we went from $68,000 to $40,000, which was just devastating ... They didn't like our staff turnover."

Those dispensing resources are likely to be interested in supporting particular areas of legal need and not just legal needs in general. Here, too, service providers may lose some autonomy, but it is something with which those agencies must live. They know there is an exchange with expectations, and sometimes this may mean altering what they do in order to get or keep resources. While service providers may have their own priorities, like any organization their first challenge is keeping their doors open. Doing so may take them away, to some degree, from what they see as their primary mission.

For example, one service provider did not like the idea of doing large, single-issue projects, preferring to focus resources on representing individuals with a range of the day-to-day legal problems that fit within the top three areas of legal need as demonstrated by the 2005 Illinois legal needs survey.[5] When faced with a request to take on a special, funded project involving children, the agency only did so reluctantly. It was not in a position to turn the opportunity away. However, once the agency started the project, they discovered, as a key person in the agency exclaimed, "There's money in kids!" The project grew as law firms and other funders saw the project as attractive and consistent with their goals. Now this agency has an ongoing, very well-funded single-issue project. While this does take the agency away from its own priorities to some degree, the funds do cover much of their overhead and staff costs thereby helping the agency in pursuing its own goals.

THE IMPORTANCE OF LARGE LAW FIRMS

Perhaps the most important contemporary source of resources for the delivery of legal services to the poor, in terms of both money and people, is large law firms. Cummings' model of institutionalized and privatized legal services gives a prominent place to large law firms. He argues that in many respects they constitute the keystone of this structure. He says "(p)ro bono's institutionalization has depended critically on the rise of the big corporate law firm. Although small-scale practitioners have been important actors in the pro bono system, it has been big firms that have provided the resources and prestige ..." (Cummings, 2004, p. 33). This is certainly the case in Chicago where a number of the largest firms are deeply involved in pro bono activities, providing money and people for the work being done by service providers.

Although the largest firms may represent only a small stratum of the local legal community, the influence of these firms on the delivery and nature of legal services can be quite substantial. Members of these firms hold leadership positions in local professional organizations and serve on the boards of both funding/resource provider entities and service providers. For the 20 legal service provider agencies in Cook County for which we have full lists of board members, the top 10 law firms in Chicago by number of lawyers (*Crain's Chicago Business*, 2007, p. 31)[6] held 107 of the total 696 board seats for these agencies. At the low end, two of the top 10 firms held seven seats each and at the high-end one firm held 17 seats. Overall, 110 different law firms had at least one of the 696 board seats and 70 of those firms had only one seat. With this kind involvement by most firms, a small number of large firms with numerous board seats can exert a substantial influence.

Such involvement allows firms to shape the nature and delivery of legal services consistent with their own goals and interests, and to protect their investment while doing so. The largest firms are a major source of financial resources for service providers. Monetary contributions for a single firm can be as a high as $1 million per year, and combined personnel and monetary contributions can total millions of dollars per year. One pro bono coordinator said that his firm donated "a little over $900,000" last year alone. He estimated that the firm's signature pro bono project used "22,900 hours over the past five years." Another lawyer reported that his firm's own charitable foundation gives "probably in the seven figures annually." This kind of activity is, of course, a characteristic of only the largest firms. Smaller firms simply lack the financial wherewithal to play a major role in pro bono activities.

The importance of large law firms goes beyond the resources they provide. They want to protect their investment. Like many other philanthropies, the large firms exert a substantial influence on the service providers with whom they work because they expect a meaningful return on their investment. At the extreme, a firm may withdraw from a working relationship with a service provider because of concerns over the way in which the agency operates. Less drastic and more typical, a pro bono partner in a major firm said:

> I went over to a staff meeting of the ABC Legal Clinic and I explained to them the operation of our pro bono program. I said, "Look, here's why we really don't take many cases from you and here's why you take cases from us and this is why we, in turn, give you money [over $25,000/year]. And now what we have to do is come up with solutions and help you think outside the box."

The problem in this instance was that the clinic was not providing the kinds of cases or pro bono opportunities the law firm wanted to see. However, it is possible that service providers respond all too well to funder interests in this environment – favoring the largest benefactors with the best opportunities. Said a pro bono partner in a major firm, "I wonder what's the relationship between contributions and the provision of pro bono work. I suspect that if you give that mightily, you might get the better cases."

Despite the potential drawbacks, most service providers actively court the large law firms for support, often finding themselves in competition with other service providers for a firm's resources. Some may have little choice given the importance of law firms as perhaps the main source of private resources. This reliance provides an additional reason for focusing on large law firms and their approach to pro bono as a way to explore the ways in which the interests of resource providers shape the availability of legal services. To probe more deeply, the next section draws from our research in Cook County to address four basic questions about large firms and pro bono: why do large firms invest in pro bono (and by implication, why smaller ones do not or cannot); how do large firms structure and manage pro bono within the firm itself in light of their own interests; how do firms make choices as to the particular pro bono activities in which they will participate; and how do they handle the conflicts of interest involved in undertaking pro bono activities.

LARGE LAW FIRMS AND PRO BONO

Why Invest in Pro Bono: "The Pro Bono Business is Good Business"

The simplest answer to the question of why firms invest in pro bono came from a lawyer with over 30 years experience with large law firms and with pro bono activities. He said with emphasis, "Self-interest of the law firms!" Law firms look at their investment in pro bono very pragmatically. Certainly, concerns about professional responsibility and ideas of equal justice (of doing "God's work") are important considerations, but these interests are clearly secondary for firms as business entities. Of course, this does not mean that the interests of the individual lawyers who actually do the pro bono work are equally mercenary, but they too may have a mix of goals.

The lawyers we interviewed, as well as the focus group participants, consistently mentioned two primary areas of organizational interest. One area is more internal to the firm and centers on the recruitment, retention, and training of lawyers. The other is more external and focuses on marketing, image, and client relations. One large firm lawyer's candid remarks summarize what we heard from everyone else:

> Those of us who manage law firms know that the pro bono business is good business for large law firms. It's the value that it has to the law firms in terms of training young lawyers, improving the quality of life at the law firms, enhancing our institutional reputation in the communities where we practice law, and network with the clients and judges. There's tremendous value there that far outweighs any short-term costs ... We're not running a charity here. This is good business and its essential business for large law firms.

In short, pro bono activity can be an integral part of a firm's larger business plan.

At the heart of every law firm and its success are personnel – the legal talent. Among the top firms there is a sense of intense competition in attracting the best law school graduates and lateral hires, and then there is the challenge of keeping that top talent once hired. A lawyer from a major Chicago firm was recently quoted in the *New York Times* saying, "We're in a war for talent ... and we have to do everything we can to attract and retain that talent" (Browning, 2007, p. C1). Pro bono opportunities are valuable because of the feeling that many, if not most, of the lawyers these firms want to hire expect to participate in certain kinds of causes or professional opportunities. Said a pro bono partner about his firm, "I'm sure there's an ongoing competition for the best and the brightest and there's a recognition that if you want the best people out of law school, if you want to get the best laterals, many of those people want to do pro bono. And so you'd better have an opportunity for them to do pro bono."

Such opportunities may also be valuable in attracting potential hires whose interests are more practical and who are looking for immediate opportunities for skill development. For instance, one firm recruits young lawyers who want to do appellate work and it makes pro bono opportunities involving federal appellate work available. The firm's pro bono coordinator said that their approach to a highly attractive potential hire might emphasize the firm's appellate litigation pro bono project – a project intended to serve both recruitment and training interests. He said the approach might be, "come to us ... If you went to another firm, by the time you get to the XX Court, you'd probably have to be a partner, five to seven years out ... we can get you an XX Court appeal within a week of your arrival." In a similar vein, a lawyer from another firm said, "Many of the new lawyers are most interested in getting experience and building a resume in their practice area ... Many of our new litigators are anxious to get experience with depositions, arbitrations, court appearances." Pro bono work provides the opportunity for these and other kinds of experience for new associates.

Pro bono is especially important if cost-conscious clients do not want to pay for training opportunities for new associates. Still another pro bono coordinator provided the following example from his firm:

> The intellectual property area leadership came to me and said that our clients will not pay for our first year associates to be involved in cases. Their [the clients'] attitude is, "First year associates can't really help us. They're only along so that they can learn how to be lawyers. If you want to staff them on our projects, that's fine, but we won't pay for

> them." Consequently, the first year associates in IP weren't learning how to talk to people. They didn't know how to deal with clients. So the IP leadership said, "Could you find us a source of pro bono cases?"

Without pro bono there would be fewer training opportunities and this would mean a longer time before associates become a profitable part of the firm. One pro bono coordinator said his position was created "basically because mentoring had broken down and I was brought in to help bridge the gap." He went on to say, "even though I have no formal responsibilities for recruitment and retention, it was obvious to me that a silent subtext of my job is how to get them, how to keep them, how to train them."

In addition to these interests, pro bono also serves more externally oriented interests such as firm marketing, image, and client relations. Perhaps the most interesting remarks we heard in this regard came not from someone at a large firm, but from the head of a well-respected legal service provider. He said:

> I try to have people from major law firms on my board ... you have to understand that law firms give away money. It's not charity; it's marketing. They don't say, "Here it is. This is it. Our firm would like to give $5000. Please just make it anonymous." ... They want their name out. They want their name affiliated with it ... you're making a client happy or you're trying to improve the firm's overall image. And the idea of gee, my heart bleeds for you doesn't work. There's just too much on the table.

Image and marketing that image are especially important in what is an intensely competitive environment in terms of attracting and retaining clients as well as attracting and retaining legal talent. In the estimation of everyone we interviewed and of all who participated in the focus group, being visibly active in pro bono activities says something positive about a firm, but equally important not being visibly active says something negative.

In both situations the emphasis is on "*visibly*," and the reason for this is illustrated by one lawyer's recounting of a conversation with a recent elite law school graduate who was working for a public interest group for the summer. As the lawyer told the story:

> ... and so I said [to the recent law school graduate], just kind of half-kidding, "So, do you care about pro bono? Do you really care?" He said, "Absolutely." I said, "Why?" He said, "Well, you know, some people care because they really want to do pro bono. Other people care because it gives them a shorthand way of evaluating a law firm. If the firm says nothing about pro bono, has nothing on their website, doesn't care, that's a firm I'm not interested in, even if I don't want to do it [pro bono]. It tells you something in a shorthand way."

One can easily see how potential clients as well as potential hires could use this "shorthand."

While not mentioned in the lawyer's story earlier, one of the more interesting "shorthands" for evaluating the large firms with regard to pro bono is the *American Lawyer* rankings of law firms, which include a score for each firm based on the level of pro bono activity (Hallman, 2008).[7] Despite complaints about the nature and validity of these rankings, law firms prize high rankings and fear low ones. For some firms the rankings are a driving force behind their pro bono efforts. An interviewee with many years of experience in pro bono and large firms said, "I think the firms [with low scores on the pro bono ranking] are embarrassed. They feel like hell if they can't match up." One pro bono partner noted that his position was created after the firm's leadership came to the conclusion that the firm's reputation might be threatened if the firm was not among the top pro bono firms in the rankings. More than one interviewee mentioned the rankings as a key incentive for an increased investment in pro bono, and they told the story of a Chicago law firm that made a very visible increase in its pro bono activity (including the hiring of a pro bono partner) after being excoriated in the *American Lawyer* for its meager investment in pro bono in light of its very substantial profits.

Equally important as a factor in driving some firms to invest more in pro bono, and not unrelated to rankings, are clients. In the view of some firms, their clients expect pro bono activity, and some firms are even partnering with major clients in pro bono activities. An experienced pro bono activist in a large firm said:

> In this town, Exxon, Abbott Laboratories, Sears, probably others that I'm not aware of, all partner with their outside legal service providers on pro bono projects. They might partner in staffing a clinic. They might partner in a particular type of case or a particular project. Inside counsel at the corporate law department would reach out to one of their outside law firms and say, here's a project we'd like to work with you on.

A corporate general counsel provided the perspective from the client or potential client side:

> It's a big deal for me when law firms are publicly and civically minded and committed. We have an enormous number of wonderful law firms out there that are trying to get our business, and it makes a big difference to me whether they do pro bono work or not and whether they're really committed to it. I don't know if it's that way for everybody, but I think it can't hurt ... particularly if you couple it with opportunities to train our lawyers and to partner with our lawyers so that we can make our internal lawyers happy. It can be a significant advantage in trying to get work.

However, it appears that not all firms feel the same need to work with clients or that a commitment to pro bono helps to get clients. A key person at one major firm told us. "Few, if any, clients have come to us and said, 'We want to do this with you.' Our experience so far has been us going to them, with mixed success."

How Large Firms Structure and Manage Pro Bono: "Just Like Paid Work"

Large firms invest heavily in pro bono. How they internally structure and manage it provides additional insight into how self-interest helps to shape the legal services available to people of limited means. If firms want specific kinds of returns from their investment in pro bono efforts they may want to find ways to make pro bono an integrated part of the firm's overall organizational structure and business plan. One pro bono partner summarized this idea as follows:

> I honestly believe the driving factor internally behind my being hired was the fact that when the leadership of the firm sat down and thought about what they want pro bono to look like they said what everybody else says, "We want it be handled just like paid work." They really looked at it from a business perspective and said, "No, we really want it to be handled just like paid work" ... So we are very worried that we would have more and more people who are clearly expressing interest in doing this but running off and doing a project on their own, without peer supervision, and that would be bad. And I think that sort of focus on excellence ... we are so big that even the smallest mistake can put the entire firm at risk. And that's not to mention the public risk of being seen as a law firm that did a bad job ... I think quality control is what might have brought us along.

As another pro bono partner simply put it, his firm's leadership wanted more pro bono activity and "wanted somebody to focus that effort and have day-to-day responsibility."

Hiring a pro bono coordinator/partner or establishing a formal pro bono committee is the most visible ways of institutionalizing pro bono. Of the 10 largest Chicago law firms by number of lawyers, eight have a pro bono partner or pro bono coordinator with primary responsibility for the pro bono program. The other two firms have vigorous pro bono programs, but operate without a formal pro bono partner or coordinator. Instead, they both have a pro bono committee. Of the 15 firms ranked 11–25, eight have pro bono partners or coordinators and another two operate with a committee. The remaining five firms have less formal arrangements.

Firms will also create rules and procedures – for the amount of time that can be spent on pro bono, for the kinds of pro bono projects that will be acceptable, for the amount of money that can be spent, etc. There may be incentives to encourage pro bono activity within those rules and procedures. For instance, firms may count some number of pro bono hours towards a lawyer's annual requirements for billable hours (e.g., 200 h of pro bono will count towards a 2,000 h annual requirement) or factor pro bono hours into bonus considerations. To encourage participation and coordination, firms also seek out or develop certain kinds of pro bono opportunities for its lawyers rather than just allowing firm members to independently seek out their own opportunities.

Structuring and managing pro bono allows for direction, planning, budgeting, and especially accountability. There are many variations among firms in the formal ways in which they structure and manage pro bono efforts, but one practical concern stands out – the centralized coordination of interests, needs, and opportunities. Coordination means, first, finding the right kinds of opportunities for the firm. Earlier, we mentioned a pro bono coordinator who was asked by his firm's intellectual property leadership to find appropriate pro bono opportunities to provide training and experience for first-year associates since the clients refused to pay for first-year associate time. He was able to do so by turning directly to a service provider agency he knew that could provide such opportunities.

Second, coordination means developing opportunities and working with service providers so that they know what the firm wants and expects of them. Part of this is bureaucratic, as one lawyer explained:

> One of the issues [in working with service providers] is that some of the legal service providers are ... better at accommodating the needs and preferences of law firm pro bono programs than others. What we want from a legal services provider is a regular stream of opportunities ... [communication] that accurately describes what's involved in each matter, particularly in terms of time and effort. We want institutional backup, because if they're doing work in an area and we don't have anybody in our firm who knows that subject area, we need co-counsel ... Every pro bono matter that comes from one of these organizations should have one person from the organization assigned to it and one person from the law firm ... The most frustrating organizations to deal with are those that just hand you a file and say, go do it.

Another part of this is substantive, as another lawyer explained with regard to one of his firm's signature pro bono projects: "The only way we gain an edge [in terms of cost effectiveness] is for me to work with someone at the XX Court and say, 'No, that's not interesting. No, I don't want to do that.' Or, 'yes, yes, that's truly good, we'll take it.' We try to be efficient because we're training, we're teaching skills."

Developing pro bono opportunities also involves responding to service providers that appeal to the firm for support and creating ongoing relationships with them. Service providers, of course, know that large law firms often are *the* major source of private resources and service providers are always anxious for the opportunity to sell their cause. Large law firms occasionally hold "dog and pony shows" (as a number of people described them) in which five or six different service providers will come in and make presentations in the hope of getting support. The more successful ones will make a case that appeals to the firm's pragmatic interests in pro bono, like training or the need for opportunities for transactional lawyers. As a key person at one of the more successful service providers put it, "You've got to sell . . . and you ain't going to sell them by saying its God's work because there's too much competition that is frankly just as deserving as whoever you are." His appeal is that his agency provides opportunities that utilize the skills of transactional lawyers.

Third, coordination involves sorting through and dealing with ideas or proposals coming from within the firm itself. One lawyer said:

> We spend a lot of time vetting through projects, vetting opinions from individuals in the different offices on what is important to them. Is it children? Is it human rights? Is it death penalty work? Is it predatory lending? Is it transactional? Making sure that we're doing things that are appealing to our transactional folks as well as our people who are willing to litigate.

Finally, it also involves actually getting lawyers involved in pro bono. As one pro bono partner put it, "much of my time is spent on what I call matchmaking, which is identifying pro bono opportunities that are out there, identifying individual attorneys' pro bono interests, and hooking them up." Another pro bono partner noted, "Well, it's a sale job. You've got a whole bunch of very, very busy lawyers trying to make their billable hours . . . and it's not always an easy sell." This is why he emphasizes the pragmatic reasons for doing pro bono – training, experience, etc. "That they might become better human beings – I'll get to that towards the end of the pitch," he said.

How Firms Choose the Pro Bono Opportunities to Support: "You Ain't Going to Sell Them by Saying its God's Work"

Many service providers and firm lawyers agree with the provider agency lawyer quoted earlier that "you ain't going to sell them by saying its God's work." Even when there is a pro bono interest within the firm beyond purely pragmatic concerns, it is unlikely to be focused on one of the most pressing areas of demonstrated legal need. Other substantive areas, for various reasons, are far more attractive to firms and their lawyers. A pro bono partner illustrates:

> To some extent it does depend upon what kinds of work the lawyers want to do. Now there's an inexhaustible supply of work representing poor people in the difficult situations that they face in life, and some lawyers will do that for a while but not extensively so. I'm always looking for things that they're interested in. Asylum right now is hot. If they're interested in doing asylum work because it's challenging and makes you feel good and you can learn something about litigation, I can sell it. But let's say for eviction court, I try to sell that all the time and I don't make many sales. Maybe once in a while, but not often enough.

In the recent Illinois legal needs survey, housing-related issues were the second highest category of problems for the poor (17.8% of all problems), while immigration matters of any kind were the 11th highest (1.6% of all problems) and the last area of need on the list (Chicago Bar Association et al., 2005, p. 17).

Firms will take on legal issues in which there is substantial need only if it serves one of the firm's practical needs like recruitment or training – assuming, of course, there are no conflict of interest issues. The top three areas of legal need in Illinois, according to the 2005 survey, are consumer, housing, and family (Chicago Bar Association et al., 2005, p. 17). These areas involve the nitty-gritty matters of everyday life and they may not be interesting or challenging enough or provide the kinds of opportunities needed to meet the firms' practical needs. According to one lawyer, "my job is to decide if among the [potential] project cases there are things that are unusual, that make a difference and that would fit in with a number of models. So no, we don't do consumer fraud cases or divorce." These areas of need may not be attractive to individual lawyers either. The problem, as one pro bono partner put it, is that "everybody says, give me something exciting and challenging, something that really tests me. Well, sometimes there are those matters and sometimes there are just people that need representation."

Family matters present a special problem because no one seems to be interested in handling them – they are too nasty and stressful and the clients may be unsympathetic. As a key person in a major service provider said, "it's a huge, and it's a legitimate, area of need. But it also sucks the life out of pro bono programs." He went on to say that volunteers "can't handle really hard, nasty divorces all the time. You can't do that to your volunteers … demand is always going to exceed supply because they're hard cases and the lawyers will take one, but won't come back for a second one a lot of times."

Individual lawyers' decisions are not particularly likely to follow demonstrated legal need either. One pro bono partner said that he found the following in regard to lawyers' decisions:

> There are four or five reasons why people pick up pro bono cases. Some of it is a true sense of "I have to do something about the world." Some of it is skills development, some of it professional development. Some of it is boredom. I mean, some of it is, "I've been doing this and this isn't what I thought it was going to be and I wonder how long I can do this. Maybe this will titillate me." And the fifth category I would add here is this idea of business development, because we have gotten into this client partnering, doing things with some of our biggest clients.

Lawyers' interests are important because they will be a key part of the mix in combination with the firm's practical interests that will determine what opportunities the firm will encourage and support.

Lawyers' individual interests can be important in deciding where a firm's often substantial monetary contributions will go. As one pro bono partner very directly put it, "Our money follows our people." For very understandable practical reasons firms are especially interested in supporting those agencies on whose boards their lawyers serve. He continued:

> We try to make the priority that the money follows the people. And that means people sitting on boards … we try to make sure that we are supporting with a charitable donation the organizations that we're creating partnerships with … to think about stronger partnerships, making possibilities for our associates to do all kinds of different work, so that the ones that want skill development are getting it, but the ones that just want to go out and save the world are getting that.

Another pro bono partner said his firm gives money to support "our lawyers who have leadership positions in public interest organizations. If you're on a board and make a contribution, we match it at least … We're a law firm; we're not a general foundation. So we're principally supporting legal-related agencies." With that said, the attorney added that the firm also gives money for another reason – because major clients request donations to particular charities.

There is a certain efficiency in having the money follow the people. It helps the firm know how the service provider is doing – if it is worthy of continued support – and to help ensure an appropriate return on the investment. Said one lawyer: "It's always been our philosophy that we are more willing to give money to an organization that we give time to because we know them better. We're working with them; we know the quality of the lawyers we're working with and so forth." Similarly, a lawyer at another firm said:

> I expect from our firm member that they tell me how that organization is doing. Are they running efficiently? Are they running well? And then to honor the board member – the lawyer from the firm – then I will contribute some money. In return I expect ... that they will do a good job of screening cases and that they will give us interesting cases.

The idea of money following people is not lost on service providers. As we earlier quoted the head of a provider agency, "I try to have people from major law firms on my board. You have to understand that law firms give away money."

Conflicts of Interest: "Pro Bono Loses"

If pro bono work is institutionalized as an integrated part of the firm's overall organizational structure and business plan, then just like paid work it must face conflict of interest scrutiny. This means consideration of both actual conflicts involving existing clients and positional conflicts involving the firm's more general business interests. This is where the firm's interests become powerfully evident. All interviewees from firms indicate that pro bono work at their firms is indeed treated like paid work and it receives a full conflicts review. "We treat the pro bono opportunities no differently than other client opportunities." More than one described it as the "bane of their existence." A lawyer said, "It's terribly difficult ... It's particularly a problem for pro bono ... many of these conflicts get resolved on the basis of which is the more lucrative client. Well, on that analysis, pro bono always loses."

Actual conflicts of interest are a straightforward matter for pro bono work. Firms either avoid such cases explicitly or they get waivers from their clients. It is the general positional (or business) conflicts that are more revealing of how self-interest shapes pro bono activities. Large firms worry about appearing in a negative light in the industries or business sectors in which they frequently work or want to work. While said lightheartedly, this lawyer was deadly serious in reporting:

> I was joking once with our managing partner and said, 'Now, let me see. We can't sue banks because we represent banks. We can't sue any local governments because we do bond work. We can't do any employment discrimination because we defend employment

> discrimination cases. I mean, pretty soon, the only people we're going to be able to represent are poor against other poor people.'

More directly another lawyer said:

> I've been talking with [a service provider] and ... they've got some cases that are plaintiffs who have lost their jobs and need representation for those who have been discriminated against. And this firm, and I think many firms, say we won't handle claims cases because it's a positional conflict with a number of our clients. We represent big corporations. If we take a case and we win, they won't be happy. So, despite the fact that I used to be a plaintiffs' lawyer in employment discrimination, that's the policy and we live with it.

Such positional conflicts mean that firms do not entertain certain broad categories of cases – they're simply out of the picture. "Our mainstream clientele is corporate America and there are a lot of individuals suing corporate America. We try to provide pro bono services in areas where legal services are not readily available. Anybody with an employment dispute with their employer ... can watch TV or open a newspaper and get a lawyer. We're not in the business of providing pro bono services to those types of parties."

Related to such positional conflicts are the problems raised by controversial cases. Firms are concerned that such cases may offend an important client or potential client, or offend some key subset of partners within the firm. More than one lawyer noted that while most pro bono cases generally are not controversial, there are some that simply cannot be done. One pro bono partner tied a reluctance to take on controversial issues to changes in the "law industry." In particular, he pointed to an increased competition for big clients and less secure relationships with existing clients. He also noted what he called a "lack of loyalty" to the firm among some partners who may have a substantial book of business and threaten to leave.

Finally, there is the issue of politics and whether pro bono by nature has a "liberal tilt" and whether conservative issues, conservative partners, and conservative associates can comfortably be incorporated into pro bono activities. This too raises the potential for controversy. Pro bono partners and coordinators admit that much available pro bono work has not included what might be seen as "conservative issues" or attracted conservative lawyers in their firms. "I have not successfully gotten a lot of our most conservative-leaning attorneys involved in projects so far," said a pro bono partner at a large firm. Another pro bono partner agreed and said:

> We haven't had a lot of requests from organizations that are more toward the right of the spectrum. And we wouldn't say no – especially if there were a partner that said,

> "I think we ought to do this." The Pro Bono Institute defines pro bono as legal assistance to those of limited means and they're the ones driving this, I think. And so that's going to put you on the left of the spectrum. You know, you're representing poor people.

This pro bono partner said that if a pro bono opportunity involving the conservative side of the abortion issue arose "I'm sure there'd be a big battle on that one because we have been on the other side of that." This, of course, adds a whole new dimension to the idea of positional conflicts of interest.

CONCLUSION

As a practical matter, individuals have only the legal rights of which they are aware and which they can hope to enforce or use. Access to legal services is usually the avenue to meaningful legal rights. For people of limited means access is problematic because of its cost, and this is especially so when the need may involve something as basic as housing or something that absolutely requires legal action such as divorce and related family matters. Such people must rely upon whatever free or at greatly reduced cost legal services are available, and increasingly these services have become dependent on private resources. Ultimately, this means that at least for some people access to legal services will depend heavily on the goals and interests of those who control the supply of legal services.

This is not intended as a criticism of those, like the large firms, who invest heavily in legal services and do so with certain goals and interests in mind. It is a consequence of the increasing privatization of legal services for the poor and the reliance on philanthropy for the needed resources (both in terms of money and people). As our case study of one locale indicates, the self-interests of those providing the resources – easily understandable and clearly rational ones for the resource providers – can have a powerful influence on what services will be available, who will provide them, and how they will be provided. Those interests do not necessarily match the demonstrated areas of greatest legal need and likely never will. One pro bono partner's comments represent the views of many of his peers. He said:

> I'm becoming convinced that many of the low level day-to-day legal problems of the poor cannot be met by the legal system. There's simply not enough interest in some of those low level problems which bring people into the courts in large numbers ... one of the most interesting developments now is the recognition that we might not be able to satisfy everyone's legal needs.

In other words, access will remain problematic for some people – an intractable systemic problem.

Some have looked at this problem and argued for what is called "civil Gideon" – a constitutional right to legal representation in civil matters akin to the constitutional right in criminal matters (Bindra & Ben-Cohen, 2003; Sweet, 1998). This would mean, as one recent article argued, that "government must establish some form of civil public defenders office. Just as the state is required to supply counsel for those indigent criminal defendants brought before a court, it must also do the same for indigent civil defendants" (Bindra & Ben-Cohen, 2003, p. 2). However, few advocates for legal aid go this far because the costs would be prohibitive. Even prominent advocates like Deborah Rhode stop short of such a bold stance believing – regardless of what they would ideally like to see – that establishing such a right is practically impossible at this time. Given current realities, rather than arguing for a constitutional right Rhode argues, instead, for changes that would allow for adequate, if not equal, access for poor people (Rhode, 2004, pp. 1815–1819).

NOTES

1. The situation in earlier years was no different (see Brownell, 1951, pp. 1–24).
2. Some recent legal commentators have argued that there should be such a constitutional right (see Bindra & Ben-Cohen, 2003; Sweet, 1998).
3. The interviews were conducted in 2006–2007 and the focus group in 2006. In addition to the 10 lawyers participating in the focus group, six scholars who study the legal profession also participated.
4. For a brief general discussion of the differences between a market-oriented approach to pro bono and its main rival – a classical professionalism approach – see Sandefur (2007, pp. 85–89).
5. Those areas are consumer problems, housing, and family law (Chicago Bar Association et al., 2005, p. 17, Tables 1 and 2).
6. *Crain's Chicago Business* is a weekly business journal and it annually ranks local law firms by size (number of attorneys in the Chicago office).
7. The 2008 "A-List," as the *American Lawyer* labels its pro bono rankings, is the sixth annual ranking.

REFERENCES

Bindra, S., & Ben-Cohen, P. (2003). Public civil defenders: A right to counsel for indigent civil defendants. *Georgetown Journal on Poverty Law and Policy, 10*, 1–36.

Brownell, E. (1951). *Legal aid in the United States: A study of the availability of lawyers' services for persons unable to pay*. Rochester, NY: Lawyers Cooperative Publishing Co.

Browning, L. (2007). For lawyers, perks to fit the lifestyle. *New York Times*, November 22, p. C1.

Chicago Bar Association et al. (2005). *The legal safety net: A report on the legal needs of low-income Illinoisans*. Chicago: Chicago Bar Association.

Crain's Chicago Business. (2007). Crain's list: Chicago's largest law firms. *Crain's Chicago Business*, Vol. 30, No. 14, April 2, p. 31.

Cummings, S. (2004). The politics of pro bono. *UCLA Law Review*, *52*, 1–149.

Curran, B. (1977). *The legal needs of the public: The final report of a national survey*. Chicago: American Bar Foundation.

Hallman, B. (2008). A-list 2008: Rarefied air. American lawyer. Available at http://www.law.com/jsp/tal/PubArticleTAL.jsp?id = 1202422444403. Accessed on July.

Houseman, A. (1999). Restrictions by funders and the ethical practice of law. *Fordham Law Review*, *67*, 2187–2240.

Lassiter v. Social Services. (1981). 452 U.S. 18.

Rhode, D. (2001). Access to justice. *Fordham Law Review*, *69*, 1785–1819.

Rhode, D. (2003). Access to justice: The social responsibility of lawyers, equal justice under law, connecting principle to practice. *Washington University Journal of Law and Policy*, *12*, 47–62.

Rhode, D. (2004). *Access to justice*. New York: Oxford University Press.

Sandefur, R. (2007). Lawyers' pro bono service and American-style civil legal assistance. *Law and Society Review*, *41*, 79–112.

Seron, C., Frankel, M., & Van Ryzin, G. (2001). The impact of legal counsel on outcomes for poor tenants in New York city's housing court: Results of a randomized experiment. *Law and Society Review*, *35*, 419–434.

Sweet, R. (1998). Civil Gideon and confidence in a just society. *Yale Law and Policy Review*, *17*, 503–506.

EXPANDING ACCESS TO LAWYERS: THE ROLE OF LEGAL ADVICE CENTERS

Masayuki Murayama

ABSTRACT

Purpose – *To find major determinants of access to legal services and consider an effective way of expanding access to lawyers.*

Methodology – *(1) A survey of Japanese individuals between 20 and 70 years of age, conducted in 2005; (2) A survey of visitors at legal advice centers of Bar Associations, conducted in 2007 and (3) A survey of visitors at law offices, also conducted in 2007.*

Finding – *The use of a lawyer for legal services is not affected by income or a general knowledge of the law, but by the past experience of using a lawyer and personal connections with a legal professional. Both lawyers and people have anxieties about each other. Thus, a lawyer wants to accept a client who is introduced by someone that the lawyer knows personally. People who seek legal advice also worry about the cost and the unapproachabilility of lawyers. Direct or indirect personal connections help to reduce such anxieties. This traditional pattern of legal access is found among visitors at law offices. However, visitors at legal advice centers do not have such experience or connections. Legal advice centers, rather than to law offices, could expand access to lawyers more*

Access to Justice
Sociology of Crime, Law and Deviance, Volume 12, 167–201

ISSN: 1521-6136/doi:10.1108/S1521-6136(2009)0000012011

effectively, because the former is easier for people without personal connections to get access to legal advice.

Research limitations – *The response rate of the office survey is very small.*

Value of chapter – *It contributes to a current debate on what affects the use of a lawyer and suggests a policy for expanding access to lawyers in Japan.*

1. INTRODUCTION

It is well known that among economically developed countries Japan has a small population of lawyers. This is a result of the recruiting policy that has restricted the number of bar examination passers for more than 20 years to only 500 persons per year.[1] The number of bar examination passers began to increase gradually from the early 1990s. The Judicial Reform Council, established in 1999, recommended in its final report in 2001 the creation of law schools for professional teaching at the graduate level to increase the number of bar examination passers. Based on this recommendation, new law schools were established in 2004 and law school graduates began to take a new bar examination in 2006.[2] Under the new bar examination system, the number of passers increased to 1,851 in 2007 and it is expected that the increase in bar examination passers will continue, though the nature of the bar examination as a competitive examination has not been changed.[3]

However, despite the recent increase in bar examination passers, the number of lawyers in Japan is still very small: there were 5,518 people per private attorney in 2007, as against 1,363 people per private attorney in France in 2005.[4] The difference between Japan and the United States is much larger, as there were only 285 people per private attorney in the United States in 2005 (Nihon Bengoshi Rengokai, 2007, p. 90).

Whereas the number of lawyers has not increased rapidly, the national economy has grown and expanded significantly since the 1960s. Concomitant industrial urbanization has profoundly changed the social structure of Japanese society. The rise in service industries and the deregulation of the labor market resulted in the proliferation of individual labor disputes. Changing ideas of family and marriage have led to an increase in divorce. Neighborly disputes are not rare among urban residents. Now people face various problems as employees, consumers, car drivers, property owners, etc. A large number of people experience legal problems in their everyday life (Murayama, 2007, pp. 4–8). The image of Japanese society as dispute-free is simply a myth.

It is apparent that the small number of lawyers cannot provide enough legal services to cope with increasing legal problems and disputes. As a result, persons other than legal professionals tend to provide "legal advice" and services for dispute resolution (Rokumoto, 1971, pp. 219–220).[5] Insurance agencies are the major advisors for traffic accidents, and administrative agencies, rather than lawyers, are much more often relied upon for advice and information regarding various problems (Murayama, 2007, pp. 16–17).

However, given the expected increase in the number of lawyers in the near future, it is crucial to understand the present structure of the legal service market and explore the way in which we can expand the market to facilitate access to lawyers. In this chapter, drawing upon findings of the three recent surveys, I will consider what affects the public use of lawyers and how access to lawyers can be improved.

2. RESEARCH AND DATA

In this chapter we rely on findings of the following three recent surveys.

2.1. The Disputing Behavior Survey

The Disputing Behavior Survey was conducted in 2005 as a part of a larger research project, the Civil Justice Research Project in Japan. The sample was 25,014 individuals randomly chosen from among Japanese citizens between 20 and 70 years of age. 12,408 individuals completed both a face-to-face interview and a self-administered questionnaire; thus the response rate was 49.6% (Murayama, 2007, pp. 1–4).[6]

2.2. The Legal Advice Center Survey

Legal Advice Center Survey (hereinafter, the Center Survey) was designed by the Legal Consultation Research Group[7] and carried out by the Japan Federation of Bar Associations (hereinafter, JFBA)[8] in 2007. There are 52 Bar Associations nationwide, each of which is located in a prefecture, except in Tokyo and Hokkaido.[9] The JFBA is the national organization of the

52 Bar Associations.[10] Each Bar Association manages at least one Legal Advice Center in its jurisdiction. In addition, JFBA manages the Traffic Accident Consultation Centers nationwide, each of which is also located in a prefecture.

The sample of the Center Survey was 1,500 individuals: 1,386 individuals who visited the Bar Association Legal Advice Centers and 114 individuals who visited the JFBA Traffic Accident Consultation Centers.[11] Questionnaires were distributed to the 50 general and 20 specialized consultation centers all over Japan. Visitors at the centers were asked to fill out a questionnaire after consultation. The survey was conducted from the end of June to the end of August 2007. We obtained 1,287 responses (92.9%) from the Bar Association Consultation Centers and 92 responses (80.7%) from the JFBA Traffic Accident Consultation Centers. In total, there were 1,379 responses, the overall response rate being 91.9%.[12]

2.3. The Legal Advice at Law Office Survey

The Legal Advice at Law Office Survey (hereinafter, Office Survey) was also designed by the Legal Consultation Research Group and carried out by the JFBA in 2007.[13] As we expected that the response rate would be very low, we did not do any sampling, but rather sent out a questionnaire to all the lawyers registered with the JFBA.[14] We asked lawyers to hand out questionnaires to their clients who visited their offices seeking legal advice *for the first time*. As we expected, we obtained only 282 responses, with the response rate being less than 1.5% during the period from the end of June to the end of September 2007.[15] There seems to be several reasons for this extremely low response rate. First, there might not be many clients who visited law offices to seek advice; clients often come to law offices to retain lawyers for their problems. Secondly, clients of law offices tend not to be seeking advice for the first time; they have usually sought advice from that law office before. Therefore, it is probable that the number of first-time visitors for advice may not be very large. Third, the lawyers may have been fed up with the questionnaires and might have thrown them away without reading them.[16] Fourth, but not least, our questionnaire included questions concerning customer satisfaction. In these questions, we asked visitors to "evaluate" lawyers and their performance. In the Center Survey, administrative staff handed out questionnaires to visitors, but in the Office Survey, lawyers could decide whether to hand out questionnaires to visitors. It is possible that the lawyers declined to hand out questionnaires to first-time visitors.

Because of the extremely low response rate, the results of the Office Survey should be treated very carefully. We will use the data of the Office Survey only to get a contrasting picture between the legal advice center and the law office.

3. PECULIARITIES OF THE JAPANESE LEGAL SERVICES MARKET: HEAVY RELIANCE ON PERSONAL CONNECTIONS

In a developed country, it is more or less assumed that money can buy legal services provided by a lawyer. As the rich have property and are likely to have property problems, not only do they often need lawyers they can also afford their services. However, we now know that the indigent as well as middle-income earners often have legal problems, even if not the same kind as the rich have, and, therefore, need lawyers to handle their problems.[17] This is why it is necessary to develop a legal aid system under which the indigent are not denied opportunities for asserting their rights.

When we consider the improvement of access to justice by expanding legal aid, we usually assume that the lack of financial resources and insufficient information could deter access to a lawyer. In other words, we tend to assume that one can get access to a lawyer, if one knows where to find a lawyer and can pay for the service by her/himself or through legal aid.[18] Previous studies indicate that people who have knowledge about lawyers and the court are in a better position to know how to use the legal system and tend to use lawyers and the courts.[19]

However, in Japan, financial resources and legal knowledge themselves do not seem to be relevant to whether a person chooses access to the service of a lawyer. Even level of education seems to be irrelevant to access a lawyer. Because the population of lawyers has been small, lawyers do not compete to obtain clients,[20] but rather develop personal networks through which they obtain clients. Personal connections with lawyers would help people to get access to legal services anywhere, but what is peculiar in Japan is that connections with lawyers are tightly interlocked with the traditional practice of how lawyers obtain clients.[21]

We do not know how the practice developed, but Japanese lawyers usually expect their clients to seek their advice after introduction by a person or an organization that they know directly or indirectly.[22] They are reluctant to take cases for clients who are referred by their bar associations, because such referral indicates that the clients do not know any persons who could introduce them to lawyers.

According to lawyers,[23] they are cautious of visitors: first, visitors might tell false stories to manipulate lawyers for their dubious purposes; second, clients might make excessive demands, asking more than what lawyers can do and third, lawyers might have disputes with clients. When clients come with personal introductions, (1) lawyers are more or less assured that they would not tell false stories; (2) clients do not generally insist on an impossible outcome and (3) introducers would intervene if disputes occur between lawyers and clients. Because of these reasons, introduction was firmly rooted in the routine practice of lawyers.[24] According to a survey of lawyers, most of the first clients visited lawyers with some kind of introduction and only 5.1% of them came without any introduction (Nihon Bengoshi Rengokai, 2002, p. 77).[25]

We also find that connections with lawyers significantly increase the possibility that people who have legal problems seek advice from lawyers. Table 1 indicates that the stronger the connections with a legal professional, the more probable it is the person will consult with a lawyer.[26]

Similarly, as Table 2 shows that the past experience of using a lawyer greatly increases the possibility of consulting with a lawyer in the future; 40% of those who had used a lawyer before consulted with a lawyer this

Table 1. The Correlation between Connections with a Legal Professional and Consultation with a Lawyer (Disputing Behavior Survey, 2005).

Connections with a Legal Professional[a]	Consulted with a Lawyer[b]		Total (%)	*N*
	Yes (%)	No (%)		
None	7.8	92.2	100.0	1,477
Can be introduced	11.4	88.6	100.0	342
Can consult with	24.9	75.1	100.0	413
Total	11.5	88.5	100.0	2,232

Note: χ^2 sig. < .001.
[a]Private attorney, judge, prosecutor, notary and law professor.
[b]Private attorney, notary, tax lawyer, judicial scrivener, etc.

Table 2. The Correlation between the Prior Use of a Lawyer and Consultation with a Lawyer (Disputing Behavior Survey, 2005).

Used a Lawyer in the Past	Consulted with a Lawyer[a]		Total (%)	*N*
	Yes (%)	No (%)		
Yes	40.4	59.6	100.0	277
No	7.4	92.6	100.0	1,967
Total	11.5	88.5	100.0	2,244

[a]Private attorney, notary, tax lawyer, judicial scrivener, etc.

time again, while only 7% of those who had not used a lawyer before consulted with a lawyer this time.[27]

The significant effects of connections with and the prior use of a lawyer does not disappear in the logistic regression analysis. As has been pointed out in previous studies, problem type is a significant variable that has an almost decisive effect upon advice-seeking behavior (Miller & Sarat, 1980–1981, pp. 544–546; Kritzer, Bogart, & Vidmar, 1991; Genn, 1999, pp. 135, 280). Table 3A shows that Japan is not an exception: compared with those who have consumer problems, those who have problems related to family, money/credit, land/house, neighborhood and rented apartments significantly tend to consult with lawyers. However, curiously, socio-economic variables, such as income and education, do not have significant effects upon consultation with a lawyer. In contrast, prior use of a lawyer and that of the court are significant predictors of legal consultation.

Table 3B shows results of a logistic regression analysis which includes experience of learning the law, exposure to the law through work and personal connections with a legal professional as well as all the independent variables listed in Table 3A. As Table 3B illustrates, personal connections with a legal professional significantly increase the likelihood of seeking legal consultation, but experience of learning the law and exposure to the law through work does not have any significant effect upon legal consultation. Problem type, the prior use of a lawyer and that of the court are still significant predictors of legal consultation. It seems that a general knowledge of the law does not increase the probability of legal consultation, but personal experience and connections do. In this second model, socio-economic variables, such as income and education, do not have significant effects on legal consultation.

Table 3A. Logistic Regression Analysis of "Consultation with a Lawyer" – Model I (Disputing Behavior Survey, 2005).

Variable	Consultation with a Lawyer		
	B	*p*-value	Odds ratio
Problem type (RC = Consumer problem)		0.000	
Purchase of land/house	1.565	0.001	4.783
Rent of apartment	1.258	0.026	3.519
Employment	0.177	0.721	1.194
Family	3.080	0.000	21.766
Accident	0.335	0.453	1.398
Neighbor	1.338	0.002	3.813
Money/credit	1.727	0.000	5.622
Private insurance	0.358	0.664	1.431
Tax/pension/public insurance	0.636	0.354	1.889
Gender (RC = Male)	0.170	0.465	1.185
Age (RC = 20–39 years old)		0.007	
40–59 years old	0.046	0.838	1.047
60–70 years old	−0.788	0.014	0.455
Living in the same area (RC = Less than 10 years)		0.056	
10–19 years	−0.152	0.546	0.859
20–29 years	−0.157	0.554	0.854
30–39 years	−0.109	0.722	0.897
40 and more years	0.657	0.030	1.928
Urban–rural (RC = Designated 14 cities)		0.135	
Cities with population greater than or equal to 200,000	−0.525	0.032	0.591
Other cities	−0.244	0.288	0.783
Towns and villages	−0.496	0.083	0.609
Individual annual income (RC = Less than JP¥4 million)		0.242	
Less than JP¥8 million	0.431	0.093	1.538
JP¥8 million or more	0.235	0.541	1.265
Job (RC = Managerial)		0.059	
Fulltime employee	−0.854	0.025	0.426
Part-time/temporary/side work	−0.190	0.662	0.827
Self-employed	−0.158	0.695	0.853
House wife/house husband/family worker	−0.183	0.679	0.833
No job/student	−0.269	0.566	0.764
Education (RC = junior high)		0.857	
Senior high	−0.135	0.671	0.874
College/university/graduate	−0.049	0.880	0.952
Connections with quasi-legal professionals (RC = None)		0.113	
Can be introduced	0.123	0.673	1.131
Can consult with	0.447	0.039	1.563
Connections with insurance agent (RC = None)		0.824	
Can be introduced	−0.057	0.859	0.944
Can consult with	−0.126	0.534	0.881

Table 3A. *(Continued)*

Variable	Consultation with a Lawyer		
	B	*p*-value	Odds ratio
Connections with court officials/conciliators (RC = None)		0.839	
Can be introduced	−0.280	0.556	0.756
Can consult with	−0.047	0.922	0.954
Connections with police officer		0.119	
Can be introduced	−0.625	0.068	0.535
Can consult with	−0.317	0.173	0.728
Used a lawyer in the past (RC = No)	1.848	0.000	6.345
Used the court in the past (RC = No)	0.629	0.018	1.875
Type of main opponent (RC = Individual) [Organization]	−0.186	0.501	0.830
Constant	−2.885	0.000	0.056

Notes: $n = 1{,}884$; $-2\text{LL} = 973.238$; $\chi^2 = 368.650$ (d.f. = 39, $p < .001$). Hosmer & Lemeshow $p = .898$; Nagelkerke $R^2 = .349$.

Legal advice is given by a lawyer at various places, such as a municipal office, a legal advice center of a bar association, a legal aid office, as well as an office of a private attorney. Cost of consultation with a lawyer also varies: free legal advice is given at a municipal office and a legal aid office. Legal advice at other places is not free of charge, but usually not very expensive, JP¥5,000 (US$50) for half an hour.

However, retaining a lawyer is a more serious decision for an ordinary citizen to make, because it costs much more than simple consultation. For instance, in an ordinary divorce case, one probably has to pay JP¥500,000–600,000 (US$5,000–6,000), excluding expenses, for retaining a lawyer.[28]

Connections with a legal professional and the prior use of a lawyer affect retention of a lawyer more significantly. As Table 4 illustrates, only 3% of those who had not had any connections with a legal professional retained a lawyer, whereas 22% of those who had had a legal professional to consult with retained a lawyer to resolve their problems.[29] Also, Table 5 shows that only 2% of those who had not used a lawyer before retained a lawyer, whereas 37% of those who had used a lawyer before did so this time.[30]

Both connections with a legal professional and the prior use of a lawyer remain significant predictors for retaining a lawyer. Table 6A shows that problem type and the prior use of a lawyer significantly affect the likelihood of retaining a lawyer, but individual income, job and level of education do not have any significant effects upon retention of a lawyer. Table 6B shows the results of a logistic regression analysis based on the second model, which

Table 3B. Logistic Regression Analysis of "Consultation with a Lawyer" – Model II (Disputing Behavior Survey, 2005).

Variable	Consultation with a Lawyer		
	B	*p*-value	Odds ratio
Problem type (RC = Consumer problem)		0.000	
Purchase of land/house	1.625	0.001	5.081
Rent of apartment	1.314	0.020	3.720
Employment	0.221	0.659	1.248
Family	3.147	0.000	23.272
Accident	0.342	0.450	1.407
Neighbor	1.331	0.003	3.786
Money/credit	1.765	0.000	5.841
Private insurance	0.418	0.611	1.519
Tax/pension/public insurance	0.739	0.280	2.094
Gender (RC = Male)	0.174	0.460	1.190
Age (RC = 20–39 years old)		0.003	
40–59 years old	−0.014	0.951	0.986
60–70 years old	−0.917	0.004	0.400
Living in the same area (RC = Less than 10 years)		0.023	
10–19 years	−0.189	0.463	0.828
20–29 years	−0.176	0.512	0.838
30–39 years	−0.026	0.933	0.974
40 and more years	0.750	0.014	2.118
Urban–rural (RC = Designated 14 cities)		0.179	
Cities with population greater than or equal to 200,000	−0.455	0.067	0.635
Other cities	−0.117	0.618	0.890
Towns and villages	−0.454	0.118	0.635
Individual annual income (RC = Less than JP¥4 million)		0.276	
Less than JP¥8 million	0.403	0.121	1.496
JP¥8 million or more	0.103	0.795	1.109
Job (RC = Managerial)		0.092	
Fulltime employee	−0.772	0.045	0.462
Part-time/temporary/side work	−0.099	0.821	0.905
Self-employed	−0.124	0.761	0.883
Housewife/house Husband/family worker	−0.111	0.804	0.895
No job/student	−0.159	0.738	0.853
Education (RC = Junior high)		0.949	
Senior high	−0.103	0.748	0.902
College/university/graduate	−0.080	0.810	0.923
Legal education (RC = No)	0.044	0.847	1.045
Law on the job (RC = No)	−0.084	0.768	0.919
Connections with legal professionals (RC = None)		0.000	
Can be introduced	0.494	0.070	1.640
Can consult with	1.059	0.000	2.883

Table 3B. (*Continued*)

Variable	Consultation with a Lawyer		
	B	*p*-value	Odds ratio
Connections with quasi-legal professionals (RC = None)		0.698	
Can be introduced	−0.036	0.905	0.965
Can consult with	0.170	0.459	1.186
Connections with insurance agent (RC = None)		0.535	
Can be introduced	−0.169	0.612	0.845
Can consult with	−0.229	0.269	0.796
Connections with court officials/conciliators (RC = None)		0.616	
Can be introduced	−0.433	0.367	0.649
Can consult with	−0.222	0.647	0.801
Connections with police officer		0.056	
Can be introduced	−0.708	0.041	0.493
Can consult with	−0.410	0.085	0.664
Used a lawyer in the past (RC = No)	1.632	0.000	5.113
Used the court in the past (RC = No)	0.546	0.040	1.727
Type of main opponent (RC = Individual) [Organization]	−0.200	0.475	0.819
Constant	−3.227	0.000	0.040

Notes: $n = 1{,}884$; $-2LL = 953.743$; $\chi^2 = 388.146$ (d.f. = 43, $p < .001$). Hosmer & Lemeshow $p = .657$; Nagelkerke $R^2 = .365$.

Table 4. The Correlation between Connections with a Legal Professional and Retention of a Lawyer (Disputing Behavior Survey, 2005).

Connections with a Legal Professional[a]	Retained a Lawyer		Total (%)	*N*
	Yes (%)	No (%)		
None	2.6	97.4	100.0	1,039
Can be introduced	8.4	91.6	100.0	263
Can consult with	21.6	78.4	100.0	329
Total	7.4	92.6	100.0	1,631

Note: χ^2 sig. $< .001$.

[a]Private attorney, judge, prosecutor, notary and law professor.

includes the experience of learning the law, prior exposure to the law through work and personal connections with a legal professional as well as all the independent variables used in the first model. In the second model, the prior use of a lawyer, that of court procedure and connections with

Table 5. The Correlation between the Prior Use of a Lawyer and Retention of a Lawyer (Disputing Behavior Survey, 2005).

Used a Lawyer in the Past	Retained a Lawyer		Total (%)	*N*
	Yes (%)	No (%)		
Yes	37.0	63.0	100.0	235
No	2.4	97.6	100.0	1,404
Total	7.3	92.7	100.0	1,639

a legal professional appear to be more significantly related to the retention of a lawyer than legal consultation. However, in the second model, socio-economic variables do not appear to be significant. It is interesting to note that strong connections with an insurance agency significantly decrease the possibility of retaining a lawyer. This finding seems to support the hypothesis that insurance agencies play the role of a pseudo-lawyer in settling disputes, particularly in traffic accident cases (Rokumoto, 1978, p. 41).[31]

If legal service is a commodity readily available in a market, wealthy people buy it more often than the poor, as the services of a lawyer is not inexpensive. However, in Japan, higher income itself does not facilitate legal consultation or retention of a lawyer. Legal education and contact with the law on the job also do not facilitate retention of a lawyer. Rather, personal experience of having used a lawyer and personal connections with a legal professional significantly facilitate the retention of a lawyer. These findings indicate that the Japanese legal service market is deeply rooted in personal networks between lawyers and people with whom the lawyers have connections, and is not widely open to the general public.

4. DIFFERENTIATION OF ADVICE SEEKERS BETWEEN LAW OFFICE AND LEGAL ADVICE CENTER

As we have seen, legal advice is given at various places, such as a law office, municipal office, legal advice center and legal aid office. To what extent these places are visited for legal advice is shown in Table 7. Among people who have legal problems, there are not many people who seek legal advice to resolve their problems. Among the legal advice seekers, the law office is most often

Table 6A. Logistic Regression Analysis of "Retaining a Lawyer" – Model I (Disputing Behavior Survey, 2005).

Variable	Retain a Lawyer		
	B	*p*-value	Odds ratio
Problem type (RC = Consumer problem)		0.001	
Purchase of land/house	2.029	0.009	7.604
Rent of apartment	1.112	0.262	3.040
Employment	0.877	0.278	2.405
Family	2.317	0.003	10.146
Accident	0.752	0.323	2.121
Neighbor	0.899	0.247	2.456
Money/credit	2.053	0.007	7.792
Private insurance	0.929	0.464	2.531
Tax/pension/public insurance	−17.973	0.998	0.000
Gender (RC = Male)	0.112	0.740	1.119
Age (RC = 20–39 years old)		0.147	
40–59 years old	0.286	0.422	1.332
60–70 years old	−0.480	0.339	0.619
Living in the same area (RC = Less than 10 years)		0.780	
10–19 years	0.179	0.639	1.197
20–29 years	0.510	0.194	1.665
30–39 years	0.320	0.500	1.377
40 and more years	0.297	0.548	1.346
Urban–Rural (RC = Designated 14 cities)		0.076	
Cities with 200,000 or more population	−0.699	0.053	0.497
Other cities	−0.938	0.012	0.391
Towns and villages	−0.560	0.172	0.571
Individual annual income (RC = Less than JP¥4 million)		0.820	
Less than JP¥8 million	−0.009	0.981	0.991
JP¥8 million or more	0.299	0.576	1.349
Job (RC = Managerial)		0.684	
Fulltime employee	−0.916	0.094	0.400
Part-time/temporal/side work	−0.921	0.157	0.398
Self-employed	−0.810	0.172	0.445
Housewife/househusband/family worker	−0.741	0.266	0.477
No job/student	−0.606	0.363	0.546
Education (RC = Junior high)		0.813	
Senior high	−0.106	0.832	0.899
College/university/graduate	−0.267	0.609	0.766
Connections with quasi-legal professionals (RC = None)		0.570	
Can be introduced	0.039	0.931	1.040
Can consult with	0.332	0.312	1.394
Connections with insurance agent (RC = None)		0.019	
Can be introduced	0.815	0.066	2.260
Can consult with	−0.449	0.168	0.638

Table 6A. (*Continued*)

Variable	Retain a Lawyer		
	B	*p*-value	Odds ratio
Connections with court officials/conciliators (RC = None)		0.451	
Can be introduced	0.582	0.307	1.790
Can consult with	0.487	0.414	1.628
Connections with police officer		0.788	
Can be introduced	−0.321	0.520	0.725
Can consult with	−0.141	0.683	0.869
Used a lawyer in the past (RC = No)	3.047	0.000	21.058
Used the court in the past (RC = No)	0.567	0.108	1.763
Type of main opponent (RC = Individual) [Organization]	−0.510	0.267	0.600
Constant	−3.699	0.001	0.025

Notes: $n = 1{,}402$; $-2LL = 442.306$; $\chi^2 = 273.339$ (d.f. = 39, $p < .001$). Hosmer & Lemeshow $p = .051$; Nagelkerke $R^2 = .443$.

visited, followed by the legal consultation bureau at a municipal office, legal advice center at a bar association and legal advice bureau at a legal aid office.[32]

These agencies give legal advice in different ways. A lawyer usually charges JP¥5,000–10,000 for a half-an-hour to one-hour consultation. Consultation fees at a law office may cost more, but sometimes a visitor may not pay anything, if s/he is introduced by a person who has a close relationship with the lawyer.

A municipal government usually provides various kinds of consultation services free of charge to local residents and commuters. A legal consultation bureau is one of them. In most cases, half an hour of legal advice is given by a lawyer who is paid for the work by the municipal government. Because most municipal governments prohibit lawyers from being retained by visitors,[33] and because of the short period of consultation, i.e., half an hour, users' negative evaluation of legal consultation at a municipal office is the highest among the four.[34] Although a legal consultation bureau is often the busiest bureau for consultation, it is inconceivable that municipal governments would expand this service in the near future, as the budgets of municipal governments tend to get tighter.

The bar association has legal advice centers where lawyers give legal advice. Consultation lasts for half an hour and, in principle, cannot be extended.[35] They charge JP¥5,000 for half an hour's consultation with some exceptions.[36] Lawyers used to be prohibited from acquiring clients from those consulting at a legal advice center, but are now allowed to do so in most bar association

Table 6B. Logistic Regression Analysis of "Retaining a Lawyer" – Model II (Disputing Behavior Survey, 2005).

Variable	Retain a Lawyer		
	B	*p*-value	Odds ratio
Problem type (RC = Consumer problem)		0.039	
Purchase of land/house	2.414	0.006	11.175
Rent of apartment	1.295	0.254	3.651
Employment	0.875	0.329	2.398
Family	1.525	0.088	4.594
Accident	0.775	0.360	2.171
Neighbor	0.555	0.524	1.742
Money/credit	1.916	0.024	6.794
Private insurance	1.099	0.400	3.000
Tax/pension/public insurance	−17.072	0.998	0.000
Gender (RC = Male)	−0.111	0.766	0.895
Age (RC = 20–39 years old)		0.027	
40–59 years old	0.395	0.345	1.485
60–70 years old	−0.767	0.167	0.464
Living in the same area (RC = Less than 10 years)		0.275	
10–19 years	0.280	0.511	1.323
20–29 years	0.724	0.097	2.063
30–39 years	1.030	0.043	2.800
40 and more years	0.581	0.279	1.788
Urban–Rural (RC = Designated 14 cities)		0.411	
Cities with 200,000 or more population	−0.604	0.125	0.547
Other cities	−0.472	0.244	0.624
Towns and villages	−0.609	0.190	0.544
Individual annual income (RC = Less than JP¥4 million)		0.776	
Less than JP¥8 million	−0.289	0.477	0.749
JP¥8 million or more	−0.162	0.795	0.850
Job (RC = Managerial)		0.600	
Fulltime employee	−0.632	0.275	0.531
Part-time/temporal/side work	−0.930	0.183	0.395
Self-employed	−0.590	0.348	0.554
Housewife/Househusband/family worker	−0.504	0.471	0.604
No job/student	0.006	0.994	1.006
Education (RC = Junior high)		0.650	
Senior high	0.225	0.674	1.252
College/university/graduate	−0.076	0.895	0.927
Legal education (RC = No)	0.481	0.213	1.618
Law on the job (RC = No)	0.550	0.235	1.733
Connections with legal professionals (RC = None)		0.000	
Can be introduced	1.595	0.000	4.926
Can consult with	2.238	0.000	9.376

Table 6B. (*Continued*)

Variable	Retain a Lawyer		
	B	*p*-value	Odds ratio
Connections with quasi-legal professionals (RC = None)		0.959	
Can be introduced	−0.130	0.793	0.878
Can consult with	0.003	0.994	1.003
Connections with insurance agent (RC = None)		0.024	
Can be introduced	0.438	0.379	1.550
Can consult with	−0.751	0.039	0.472
Connections with court officials/conciliators (RC = None)		0.705	
Can be introduced	0.508	0.404	1.662
Can consult with	0.077	0.907	1.080
Connections with police officer		0.434	
Can be introduced	−0.684	0.236	0.505
Can consult with	−0.300	0.429	0.741
Used a lawyer in the past (RC = No)	2.829	0.000	16.935
Used the court in the past (RC = No)	2.445	0.000	11.534
Type of main opponent (RC = Individual) [Organization]	−0.604	0.232	0.546
Constant	−5.903	0.000	0.003

Notes: $n = 1{,}402$; $-2LL = 368.365$; $\chi^2 = 347.279$ (d.f. = 43, $p < .001$). Hosmer & Lemeshow $p = .091$; Nagelkerke $R^2 = .549$.

Table 7. Percentage of People Who Sought Legal Advice by Type of Consultation Place (Multiple Answer) (Disputing Behavior Survey, 2005).

Type of Place for Legal Advice	*N*	%
Law office	128	9.3
Municipal office	77	5.6
Legal advice center	39	2.8
Legal aid office	4	0.3
Total[a]	1,376	100.0

Note: The number of respondents who experienced at least one problem is 2,244.
[a]The number of respondents who consulted with someone or some agency.

legal advice centers. In large urban centers, bar associations provide specialized legal consultation concerning credit/loan, employment, consumer and family matters. The JFBA also provides specialized legal consultation for traffic accident cases, which again takes place at bar association legal advice centers.[37]

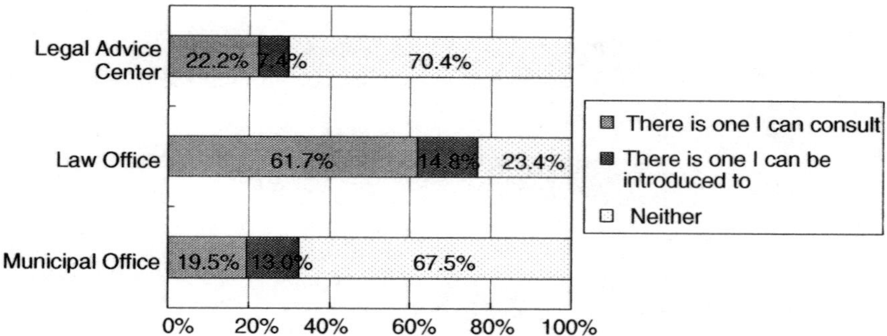

Fig. 1. Place of Legal Advice and Connections with a Legal Professional. *Source:* Disputing Behavior Survey (2005).

The legal aid bureau also gave free legal advice to the indigent, but the number of clients for free advice was small. Free legal advice is now given by a new organization, the Japan Judicial Support Center, but the number is still not very large, though it is increasing,[38] and provided only to the indigent under the poverty line.

Legal advice centers and municipal offices tend to attract different kinds of people from the types of people who are attracted to law offices. Fig. 1 shows that people who have connections with a legal professional tend to visit law offices for consultation, whereas those who do not have any such connections tend to go to legal advice centers or legal consultation bureaus in municipal governments.

Fig. 2 also shows a similar differentiation of visitors. Almost 70% of the law office visitors had prior experience of using a lawyer. In contrast, more than 60% of those who visited legal advice centers or municipal legal consultation bureaus did not use a lawyer before visiting there.

In Section 3, we saw that access to lawyers is heavily influenced by connections and prior experience. Such a pattern of access to lawyers is clearly seen among visitors at law offices. Lawyers usually work at their offices, where they meet former clients or people who have some introduction or connection, which assures them of their clients credibility. In contrast, lawyers do not work exclusively at legal advice centers or at municipal offices: they give advice at those places for supplementary work. But those places are precisely where people who do not have any connections or have not used lawyers previously, visit to seek help from lawyers.

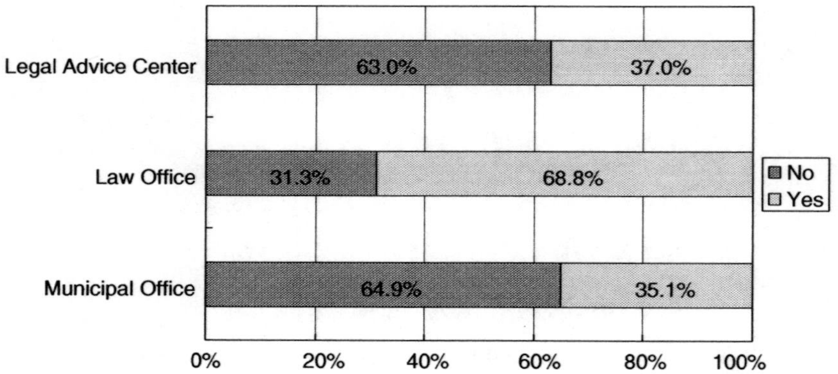

Fig. 2. Place of Legal Advice and the Prior Use of a Lawyer. *Source:* Disputing Behavior Survey (2005).

5. REFERRAL VERSUS INTRODUCTION: DIFFERENT PATHS TO THE ADVICE CENTER AND THE LAW OFFICE

If legal advice centers attract people without any connections to a legal professional, while the traditional pattern of access to lawyers is embedded in the legal practice centering on law offices, the manner in which people come to legal advice centers and law offices differ.

In this section, we will show differences and similarities in behavior and concerns between visitors at legal advice centers and those at law offices, drawing upon the findings of the Center Survey and the Office Survey (hereinafter jointly referred to as the Legal Advice Surveys).

Despite the fact that most municipal offices provide legal consultation services and the number of municipal offices is very large nationwide, in the Legal Advice Surveys, we did not include legal consultation at municipal offices for several reasons. Firstly, because the period of legal consultation at a municipal office is brief, and lawyers tend to give general information about the law rather than specific advice. Moreover, since lawyers are prohibited to take on cases they have been consulted about, there is little possibility that visitors will come to law offices later to entrust their cases to these lawyers.[39] Secondly, given that budgets of municipal governments are mostly very tight, it is highly unlikely that municipal offices will expand legal consultation services in future, although legal consultation seems to be used to capacity at many municipal offices.[40] Therefore, we concluded that legal consultation at municipal offices would not play a large role in expanding the legal service market in the future. Thirdly, the number of legal consultation bureaus at municipal offices is huge, though the capacity of each bureau in terms of visitors is small. As we had to obtain agreement from each municipality in order to conduct a survey, we considered the transaction cost unbearable. For these reasons, we conducted surveys only on legal advice centers and law offices.

As we saw in Section 3, the response rate to the Office Survey was extremely small. Therefore, we will only look at large differences in findings between the Center Survey and the Office Survey.

In the Legal Advice Surveys, we asked whether visitors had consulted with someone or an agency before coming to these particular places to seek advice. The percentage of prior consultation is very similar between advice center visitors (67%) and law office visitors (66%). However, to whom or to which agencies the visitors consulted prior to that particular visit tended to differ, as is shown in Fig. 3. Visitors at legal advice centers tended to seek free legal advice or consulted with family/relatives, friends/acquaintances, municipal offices and police more often than law office visitors. It is characteristic that all these instances of advice and consultations were free of charge.[41]

However, the sources of information about the places where they visited to seek legal advice differ significantly between law office visitors and legal advice center visitors. As Fig. 4 shows, more than 50% of the law office visitors obtained information about the lawyers from their family members, relatives or friends. The corresponding percentage for legal advice center visitors is only 14%. In contrast, legal advice center visitors tended to obtain information about the centers through the Internet (22%), municipal legal consultation (14%) and the telephone directory (11%). Although legal advice center visitors consulted their relatives and friends more often than law office visitors, as shown in Fig. 3, their relatives and friends apparently did not know lawyers, and the visitors had to rely on impersonal sources of information.

Although law office visitors rely on personal connections to find lawyers, this does not always mean that they did not hesitate before visiting law offices. Thirty nine percent of the law office visitors ("office visitors") felt hesitation before their visit, whereas it was 44% for legal advice center visitors ("center visitors"). It is interesting to see that both legal advice center visitors and law office visitors seem to share their concerns, as illustrated in Fig. 5. More than 60% of the advice center visitors and law office visitors worried how much it would cost to consult with lawyers. Also a quarter of the center visitors and more than a third of office visitors hesitated to attend, considering that the fees were expensive. For both center

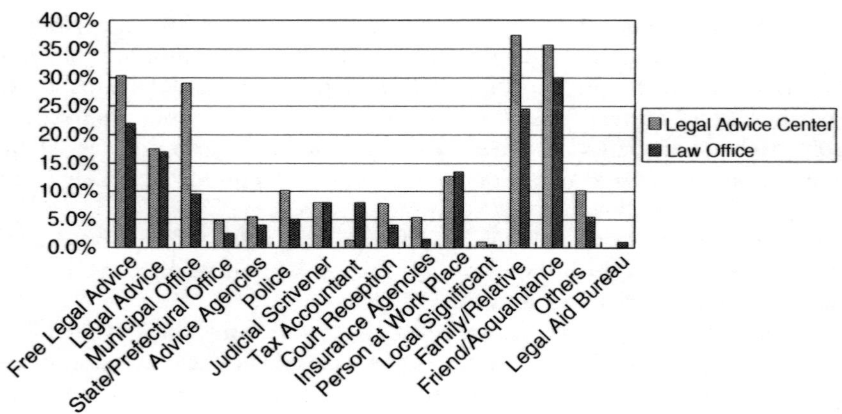

Prior Consultation	Legal Advice Center	Law Office
Free Legal Advice	30.3%	22.0%
Legal Advice	17.5%	17.0%
Municipal Office	29.0%	9.5%
State/Prefecture Office	4.9%	2.5%
Advice Agencies	5.5%	4.0%
Police	10.2%	5.0%
Judicial Scrivener	8.0%	8.0%
Tax Accountant	1.3%	8.0%
Court Reception	7.8%	4.0%
Insurance Agencies	5.3%	1.5%
Person at Work Place	12.7%	13.5%
Local Significant*	1.1%	0.5%
Family/Relative	37.3%	24.5%
Friend/Acquaintance	35.7%	30.0%
Others	10.1%	5.5%
Legal Aid Bureau	-	1.0%
N of Respondents	745	158

* A person who has some influence in a local district, such as a head of a neighborhood association.

Fig. 3. Persons/Agencies for Prior Consultation (Multiple Answers). *Source:* Legal Advice Surveys (2007).

visitors and office visitors, how much they had to pay the lawyers was the largest concern.

Center visitors and office visitors also shared another concern. More than 40% of both visitors worried about the difficulty of approaching lawyers and about 20% of both groups felt it difficult to talk to lawyers. These

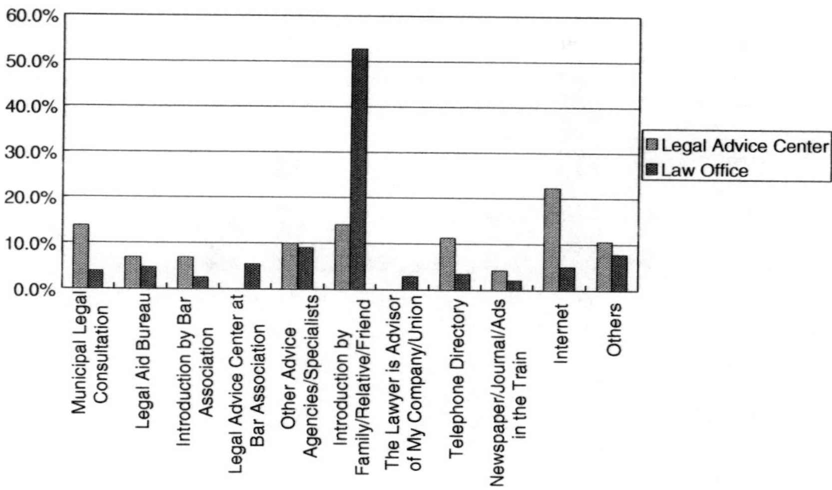

How Did You Get Information about This Place?	Legal Advice Center	Law Office
Municipal Legal Consultation	13.7%	4.0%
Legal Aid Bureau	6.9%	4.7%
Introduction by Bar Association	6.8%	2.5%
Legal Advice Center at Bar Association	-	5.4%
Other Advice Agencies/Specialists	10.0%	9.0%
Introduction by Family/Relative/Friend	14.2%	52.7%
The Lawyer is Advisor of My Company/Union	-	2.9%
Telephone Directory	11.3%	3.6%
Newspaper/Journal/Ads in the Train	4.3%	2.2%
Internet	22.4%	5.1%
Others	10.5%	7.9%
Total	100.0%	100.0%
N of Respondents	1,287	282

Fig. 4. The Source of Information about Legal Advice Center/Law Office. *Source:* Legal Advice Surveys (2007).

results indicate that people tend to consider lawyers as "distant" elites with "foreign" special skills and languages.

These two concerns, lawyer's cost and social distance, symbolize major obstacles which most people have to overcome before visiting lawyers. This also explains why legal education and exposure to law at work themselves do not facilitate legal consultation or retention of a lawyer. By learning the law or using law in one's work, people can learn what the law is in their

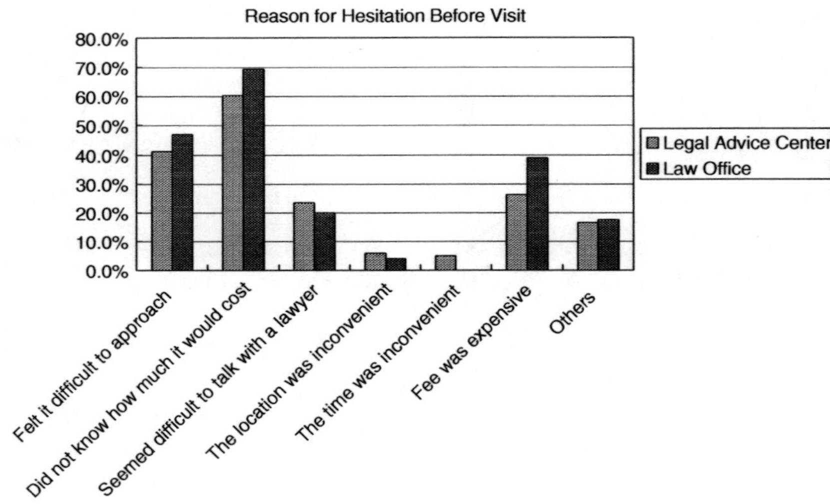

Reason for Hesitation	Legal Advice Center	Law Office
Felt it difficult to approach	41.1%	47.1%
Did not know how much it would cost	60.5%	69.4%
Seemed difficult to talk with a lawyer	23.4%	19.8%
The location was inconvenient	5.8%	4.1%
The time was inconvenient	5.0%	
Fee was expensive	26.1%	38.8%
Others	16.6%	17.4%
N of Respondents	555	99

Fig. 5. Reasons for Hesitation Felt Before Their Visit (Multiple Answers). *Source:* Legal Advice Surveys (2007).

favor or how it works. However, when people consider whether or not to consult a lawyer, their concern is not only expense, but also rather the ambiguity surrounding the amount of fee that they have to pay. They are also concerned about the social distance from lawyers. How much would "this" lawyer ask me to pay? what kind of attitude would "that" lawyer have toward me? or is "this" lawyer willing to listen to my story? – people have these "concrete" concerns before going to meet lawyers. Legal education or exposure to law at work cannot give such information. Only people who know lawyers personally can give such information and assure future visitors of the competence and trustworthiness of lawyers.[42]

Fig. 6 illustrates how visitors overcame obstacles before coming to legal advice centers or law offices. Conspicuously, half of the law office visitors

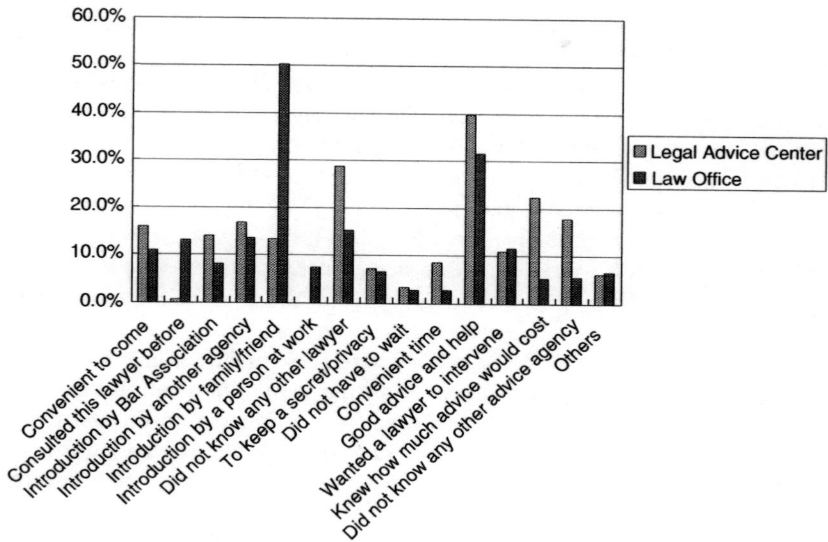

Reason for Visiting Here	Legal Advice Center	Law Office
Convenient to come	16.0%	11.0%
Consulted this lawyer before	0.7%	13.1%
Introduction by Bar Association	14.0%	8.2%
Introduction by another agency	16.8%	13.5%
Introduction by family/friend	13.4%	50.4%
Introduction by a person at work	0.0%	7.4%
Did not know any other lawyer	28.7%	15.2%
To keep a secret/privacy	7.3%	6.7%
Did not have to wait	3.5%	2.8%
Convenient time	8.6%	2.8%
Good advice and help	39.8%	31.6%
Wanted a lawyer to intervene	10.9%	11.7%
Knew how much advice would cost	22.3%	5.3%
Did not know any other advice agency	17.8%	5.7%
Others	6.3%	6.7%
N of Respondents	1,287	282

Fig. 6. Reasons for Visiting Legal Advice Center/Law Office (Multiple Answers).
Source: Legal Advice Surveys (2007).

went to meet lawyers because family members or friends introduced them to the lawyers. Apparently, a family member or a friend gave information about how much "this" lawyer would cost and what kind of person s/he was, which must have helped reduce their sense of distance and uncertainty with the lawyer and the amount of fees payable.

In contrast, the responses of the advice center visitors clearly show that they did not have such personal information. Twenty nine percent of them visited advice centers, because they did not know any other lawyer. Again 18% of them came to advice centers because they did not know any other advice agency. For both combined, 47% of them visited advice centers because they knew only advice centers for legal advice.

The major concern of people who wanted to consult a lawyer was that they were often not sure how much it would cost. The legal advice center was a solution for them, since the fee was fixed and listed on the website. As shown in Fig. 6, 22% of the visitors said that they came to legal advice centers, because they had known how much it would cost to obtain advice there.

Findings in this section clearly indicate that legal advice centers provide advice to the people who do not have any connections with lawyers, whereas law offices tend to obtain clients through personal introductions. Insofar as access to lawyers is embedded in personal networks, it is difficult to expand the legal service market effectively. It is the provision of legal services by a legal advice center that has the potential for effective expansion of the legal service market in future.

6. OUTCOMES OF LEGAL CONSULTATION: ANOTHER DIFFERENTIATION BETWEEN LEGAL ADVICE CENTER AND LAW OFFICE

In the same way that people come to seek advice from legal advice centers and law offices by different paths, their actions following the receipt of the advice differ depending on whether the advice was obtained from an advice center or a law office. Among the law office visitors, 59% of them entrusted the resolution of their problems to lawyers. In contrast, only 11% of those who visited legal advice centers entrusted the resolution to lawyers. The JFBA Working Group estimated that visitors who decided further to consult with the same lawyer will entrust the resolution of their problems to that lawyer sooner or later. Twenty three percent of the office visitors and

19% of the center visitors decided to consult with the same lawyers. Combining the percentages of these two categories, we can estimate that 82% of office visitors will retain lawyers, while 30% of the center visitors will do so (Fig. 7).

However, the results of consultation at legal advice centers tend to be ambiguous. Thirty one percent of the center visitors answered that they would resolve their problems by themselves. Again 19% of them answered that they had not decided what to do even after consultation. Fourteen percent of them said that they would come back to get legal advice again, indicating that they could not find a proper solution at that time.

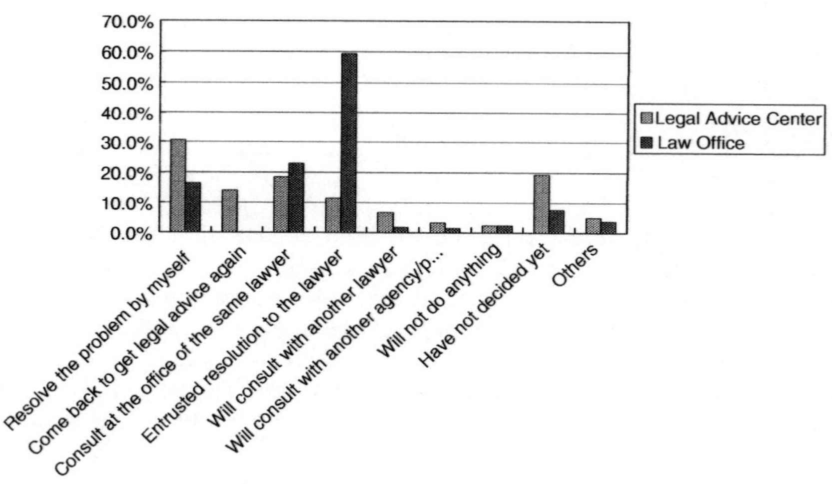

What Will You Do, Based On Advice?	Legal Advice Center	Law Office
Resolve the problem by myself	30.8%	16.7%
Come back to get legal advice again	14.2%	0.0%
Consult at the office of the same lawyer	18.7%	23.0%
Entrusted resolution to the lawyer	11.5%	59.2%
Will consult with another lawyer	6.8%	1.8%
Will consult with another agency/person	3.2%	1.4%
Will not do anything	2.5%	2.5%
Have not decided yet	19.4%	7.8%
Others	5.1%	3.9%
N of Respondents	1,287	282

Fig. 7. What will be Done After Consultation (Multiple Answers). *Source:* Legal Advice Surveys (2007).

Table 8. Types of Problems Brought to Advice Centers and Law Offices (Legal Advice Surveys, 2007).

Problem Type	Place of Consultation	
	Center	Office
Consumer	3.9%	2.5%
Credit/debt	24.7%	29.4%
Real estate	6.7%	10.3%
Employment	5.1%	3.2%
Family	26.1%	29.4%
Accident	14.5%	8.2%
Neighbor	2.3%	1.8%
Criminal	2.0%	1.1%
Others	4.9%	7.1%
N.A.	2.4%	1.4%
Unable to classify	7.2%	5.7%
Total	99.8*%	100.1*%
N	1,379	282

*Rounding errors.

When we compare the outcomes of legal consultation between advice centers and law offices, a clear difference appears: most law office visitors tend to retain lawyers, while most advice center visitors do not.

One might ask why the percentage of retention is so different between office visitors and center visitors. One possible reason is that center visitors and office visitors bring different kinds of problems. The percentages of the types of problems brought to advice centers and law offices are shown in Table 8. Purchase of land/house, credit/debt and family-type problems have a high rate of retention of lawyers,[43] which in turn are higher at law offices than at advice centers. However, the differences do not seem large enough to explain the difference in the retention rate.

It might also be possible that problems concerning payment of money or seeking damages were brought to law offices much more often than advice centers. If this be the case, the retention rate could be higher at law offices than at advice centers, because such “money problems” are more easily resolved by legal proceedings. Table 9 shows that the percentage of problems whose amounts at stake were unknown is larger at advice centers than at law offices. The percentage of problems which were not concerned with money is almost identical between advice centers and law offices.

Another possibility is the difference in the amount of money at stake. As Table 10 shows, the amount at stake tends to be smaller at advice centers

Table 9. What is at Stake (Legal Advice Surveys, 2007).

Place of Consultation	What is at Stake				Total (%)	*N*
	Amount known (%)	Amount unknown[a] (%)	Not referable to money (%)	N.A. (%)		
Advice center	51.0	30.9	12.7	5.4	100.0	1,379
Law office	58.5	25.9	12.8	2.8	100.0	282

[a]"Amount Unknown" includes "Amount Unknown" and "Amount Not Remembered."

Table 10. Amount of What is at Stake (Legal Advice Surveys, 2007).

Place of Consultation	Amount at Stake (JP¥) [JP¥100 = US$1]				Total (%)	Average (Unit = 10,000)	*N*
	Up to 2,000,000 (%)	More than 2,000,000–5,000,000 (%)	More than 5,000,000–10,000,000 (%)	More than 10,000,000 (%)			
Advice center	40.5	28.4	15.8	15.3	100.0	909	701
Law office	28.8	27.6	19.6	23.9	100.0	1,941	163

than at law offices. At advice centers the average amount at stake is about JP¥9 million, whereas at law offices it is about JP¥19 million. In particular, the percentage of problems whose amounts at stake are JP¥2 million or less is 41% at advice centers, while it is 29% at law offices.

This might indicate that lawyers are reluctant to take cases where the amounts at stake are low. Table 11 seems to show that this is the case, as the smaller the amount at stake, the lower the retention rate on average. Yet, there is also a consistent tendency that the retention rate is higher at law offices than at advice centers for each category of the amount at stake. Lawyers at law offices might take cases which are brought with introduction, even if the work might be not profitable. Or, most visitors at law offices might decide to retain lawyers, when they meet lawyers by way of introduction.[44] In contrast, when visitors meet lawyers at advice centers, they might not be able to decide upon retaining lawyers, because they do not have "concrete" information about the lawyers to overcome their concerns. Lawyers at advice centers might also feel uneasy about the visitors without introduction. We speculate that the retention rates result partly from

Table 11. Retention Rate[a] by Amount at Stake (Legal Advice Surveys, 2007).

Place of Consultation	Amount at Stake (JP¥) [JP¥100 = US$1]			
	Up to 2,000,000 (%)	More than 2,000,000–5,000,000 (%)	More than 5,000,000–10,000,000 (%)	More than 10,000,000 (%)
Advice center	26.4	49.2	41.4	33.6
Law office	70.2	77.8	90.6	89.7

[a]"Retention Rate" includes "Entrusted Resolution to the Lawyer" and "Consult at the Office of this Lawyer."

personal introductions, and also partly from cost-benefit considerations both by visitors and lawyers.

7. CONCLUSION

We saw that the Japanese legal service market is deeply embedded in the social network of connections. Given their small population , lawyers do not face much competition and obtain clients through introductions. Introduction assures a lawyer of the trustworthiness of a visitor, while for a visitor it also helps to reduce the uncertainty of the lawyer's fee and the uneasiness which a visitor often feels before going to meet a lawyer.

This traditional practice of obtaining clients is rooted in the work of lawyers at law offices. People rarely visit a law office without introduction and most clients have connections with a legal professional or have used a lawyer in the past. Insofar as lawyers rely on this kind of personal connection to obtain new clients, it would be difficult to expand the traditional legal service market effectively.

In contrast, legal advice centers are places where people without connections may contact lawyers. As bar associations manage legal advice centers, it would not be very difficult to expand the capacity to provide legal services, given that the number of bar examination passers continues to increase. Legal advice centers seem to be open windows of the otherwise closed market of legal services.

Lawyers and their services are foreign and mysterious to most people. Legal advice centers with a fixed fee system could function to allay people's discomfort about meeting a lawyer and their uncertainty about lawyer's fees. Legal advice centers seem to present opportunities for expanding the legal services market in Japan.

NOTES

1. The number of the bar examination passers was only 265, when the post-war bar examination started in 1949. It took almost a decade for the number to increase to more than 300 in 1958. It reached 508 in 1964, but since then, until 1991 the number had not increased beyond 560 (Homusho Daijin Kanbo Jinjika, 2008).

2. 68 law schools were created in 2004 and 6 in 2005, totaling 74 nationwide. As only law school graduates are allowed to take the new bar examination, the passing rate drastically increased from about 3% for the old bar examination to more than 40% for the new bar examination, though the passing rate is expected to decrease for the new bar examination with the increase in law school graduates.

3. Although the bar examination seems to be a qualifying examination, it has never been conducted as such. Every year, the number of passers is more or less pre-determined by the Supreme Court, the Ministry of Justice and the Japanese Federation of the Bar Associations, though how they determine the number is not well known. Insofar as the bar exam is not conducted as a qualifying examination, the number of passers is subjected to a political decision negotiated among the controlling organizations. The group of new law schools, and/or the Ministry of Education and Sciences representing their interests, is the fourth group interested in this process, but to what extent they may influence the former three groups is not known.

4. France has a small number of lawyers among Western European countries. The Judicial Reform Council recommended an increase in the number of lawyers in Japan to that of France.

5. As early as in the late 1960s it was found that quasi-legal specialists, such as insurance agencies and employees of a taxi company in charge of traffic accidents, played the role that a lawyer would have played, if available.

6. Disputing Behavior Survey was conducted by the Grant-in-Aid for Scientific Research on Priority Areas (607).

7. The Members of the Legal Consultation Research Group are Masayuki Murayama (Meiji University), Akira Moriya (Kansai Gakuin University), Tomohiko Maeda (Meijo University), Tsuneo Niki (Osaka University) and Rie Ono (Chiba University). The research on legal advice was supported by Grant-in-Aid for Scientific Research (A) (17203008).

8. The Legal Consultation Research Group worked with the Working Group on Citizens' Legal Needs in the Project Team on Legal Needs and Lawyers' Population, JFBA. The members of the Working Group are Maki Kanekawa (Tokyo Bar Association), Takashi Iida (Daini Tokyo Bar Association), Ryoko Ozeki (Yokohama Bar Association), Junko Yatsugake (Tokyo Bar Association) and Kosuke Ikuta (Tokyo Bar Association).

9. There are three Bar Associations in Tokyo for historical reasons and four in Hokkaido for geographical reasons.

10. A lawyer has to register with both a local Bar Association and the JFBA in order to practise as a private attorney.

11. Though a Bar Association could have legal advice centers both at its headquarters and branch offices, we implemented the survey at the headquarters of the Bar Associations. The number of individuals whom we asked to fill out the questionnaire at the headquarters of a Bar Association was decided based on the number of clients who visited legal advice centers of a Bar Association in 2005. At nine Bar Associations whose jurisdictions include large urban centers, such as Tokyo, Osaka, Nagoya, specialized legal advice for certain types of problems, such as consumer credit and loan, family and employment problems, was provided separately. As the number of consumer credit and loan cases was very large both at the specialized advice centers and at the general legal advice centers, we did not assign the proportional number to the specialized advice center for consumer credit and loan cases so that those cases would not dominate the total number of cases.

12. We are very grateful to the respondents who cooperated in our research.

13. The Legal Consultation Research Group and the JFBA Working Group on Citizens' Legal Needs also worked together to conduct the Law Office Survey.

14. The response rate of a well-known survey on lawyers' work conducted by JFBA in 2001 was only 17% (Nihon Bengoshi Rengokai, 2002, p. 11).

15. We are grateful for the cooperation of lawyers and their clients, without which we could not have made any comparison between legal advice centers and law offices.

16. According to lawyers in Tokyo, they receive questionnaires so frequently that they are tired of answering them and throw them away.

17. Already in the 1960s, legal needs across social strata were recognized (Mayhew & Reiss, 1969, p. 309). The ubiquitous nature of legal problems has become a common ground on which access to justice is discussed. In later years, it began to be noticed that legal problems tended to be experienced more frequently by the socially disadvantaged (Pleasence et al., 2004, pp. 10–13).

18. In fact, those earning higher incomes and lower incomes are more likely to obtain legal advice from solicitors than those earning middle incomes because of the legal aid provision in England and Wales (Genn, 1999, p. 86).

19. Knowledge itself has been considered important in using the machinery of law. For instance, knowledge of law and the legal machinery was considered to be an element of "legal competence" (Carlin, Howard, & Messinger, 1966, p. 70). "Repeat players" have the advantage of a "one-shotter," partly because "repeat players" have advance intelligence (Galanter, 1974, p. 98). In England and Wales, not only income but also education had significant correlations with seeking advice (Genn, 1999, pp. 279–280).

20. According to the JFBA survey in 2001, 43% of respondents answered that they were rarely conscious of competition with other lawyers, and 41% answered that they were sometimes conscious of competition. Those who were conscious of competition on a daily basis totaled only 15%. Even in Tokyo, 40% were rarely conscious of competition (Nihon Bengoshi Rengokai, 2002, pp. 188–189).

21. Having connections or personal connections with a lawyer means that one knows a lawyer as a person or that one can be introduced by a person who knows a lawyer as a person. The reason why one knows a lawyer as a person can be various: a former classmate, a former or present legal advisor of one's company, a lawyer who

represented her/himself or the other party, etc. It does not mean that one knows the name of a lawyer or where a law office is located.

22. A lawyer's relative, friend or former client might introduce a new client, or a visitor might be an employee of a company or a member of a labor union for which the lawyer works (Nihon Bengoshi Rengokai, 2002, p. 77).

23. In previous research, I asked lawyers why they were reluctant to take cases of clients who visited their offices without introduction. The research was about criminal defense in the broader context of a lawyer's work, and I asked lawyers how they managed their offices, including how clients came to attend the lawyer's office (Murayama, 2002, pp. 42, 55).

24. Introduction seems much more important for lawyers in Tokyo than for those in rural areas. This may sound ironical, but in a rural area, a lawyer can get some idea of what kind of person a potential client is by obtaining information on where s/he lives. This is impossible in urban centers.

25. The percentage was 2.3% in Tokyo, whereas it was 9.0% in rural cities (Nihon Bengoshi Rengokai, 2002, p. 78).

26. To measure "connections with a legal professional," we asked the following question: "Among lawyers, judges, prosecutors, notaries and law professors, is there anyone you can consult with when you have a problem? If not, do you think that you could be introduced to one of those legal professionals?" We asked this question to all the respondents, whether they reported that they had experienced a problem or not. In cases where a respondent answered that s/he had experienced a problem in the previous five years, the interviewer was instructed to tell the respondent, "Please ignore people with whom you have become acquainted in connection with that problem." "Consultation with a lawyer" includes seeking legal advice at a legal advice bureau in a municipal office, a law office, a legal advice center of a Bar Association and a legal aid association (Murayama, 2007, pp. 16–17, 58).

27. Concerning the past experience of using a lawyer, we asked all the respondents the following questions, "Have you ever used a lawyer or experienced a court procedure, such as a conciliation or litigation? Please choose all that applies, including your experience in conciliation or litigation that was filed against you.

1. I have used a lawyer (asked to answer, yes or no).
2. I have experienced conciliation (asked to answer, yes or no).
3. I have experienced litigation (asked to answer, yes or no)."

In case a respondent answered that s/he had experienced one or more problems in the previous five years, they were asked to chose the most serious problem, and the interviewer was instructed to tell the respondent, "please answer with respect to your experience before you had the problem on which we inquired in detail" (Murayama, 2007, p. 59).

28. A client has to pay fees and expenses when retaining a lawyer. Fees include starting fee and success fee: the former has to be paid when a client retains a lawyer, the latter to the extent that the client is successful. The success fee is different from a contingent fee in the United States, which is not allowed in Japan. Expenses include

all the expenses which a lawyer incurs for the work: postage, copies, transportation, telephone calls, accommodation, etc. Lawyers might also request the payment of day to day expenses as an additional general payment. There is no official standard for a lawyer's fee. According to a survey conducted by the JFBA in 2005, for a hypothetical conciliation case of a divorce where a wife with a 3-year-old child obtained JP¥2 million (US$20,000) for divorce triggered by domestic violence and JP¥30,000 (US$300) for monthly child support, lawyers answered that they would request payment of the following amounts as starting fee and success fee (Sample size was 4,005 lawyers and 1,567 responded).

Amount Requested	Start Fee		Success Fee	
	N	%	*N*	%
About JP¥200,000	446	43.9	314	30.9
About JP¥300,000	436	42.9	435	42.9
About JP¥400,000	78	7.7	139	13.7
About JP¥500,000	30	3.0	85	8.4
About JP¥600,000	4	0.4	14	1.4
Others	22	2.2	28	2.8
Total	1,016	100.1*	1,015	100.1*

JP¥100 = US$1.
*Rounding errors.

The JFBA published the survey results in a booklet for the public. The editor of the booklet warns readers that, because a lawyer considers the amount of fee as the total of the starting fee and the success fee, the starting fee range may not correspond to the success fee range (Nihon Bengoshi Rengokai, 2006, pp. 1–2, 18).

In a divorce case where both spouses agree on divorce and its conditions, they usually do not use lawyers, because spouses can divorce by mutual agreement without any legal or judicial intervention in Japan (Murayama, 2009). Spouses are only required to submit a document to the office of the Family Register. They divorce when the document is accepted. 90% of divorces are made in this way annually. Therefore, lawyers are usually consulted or retained when spouses expect or face conflicts between them. In such a case, if a spouse retains a lawyer to negotiate an agreement, the amount of success fee would be similar to what is requested to pay for representation for conciliation shown earlier. However, spouses sometimes ask lawyers to write a contract for divorce by mutual agreement. This is similar to writing a notarial deed.

29. As for details of the question about personal connections with a legal professional, see note 26. We phrased the question of retention in the following way: "Did you entrust the resolution of the problem to a lawyer? 'Entrust' means asking a lawyer to handle the problem, rather than a simple consultation." We asked this question to the respondents who had contacted the other party in some way, with regard to their problems.

30. For the past experience of using a lawyer, see note 27. For retention of a lawyer see note 29.

31. It is also pointed out that insurance adjusters play a significant role in settling disputes in traffic accident cases in the United States (Ross, 1980). Yet, the litigation rate of traffic cases was much larger in the United States than in Japan. Given that both parties are represented by lawyers in litigation in the United States, the larger litigation rate indicates the larger role of lawyers in traffic accidents cases in the United States.

32. The national system of legal aid was subsequently changed. A new nationwide system, the Japan Judicial Support Center, was established in 2006 to provide multiple services for civil legal problems: free referral service by telephone and free legal advice and representation. Free referral service is given to anybody, but free legal advice and representation is given only to the indigent.

33. This prohibition is a long-time tradition. One has to speculate why. A municipal government prohibits lawyers from acquiring clients from legal consultation, probably because they are afraid that the lawyers might "create" legal problems unnecessarily in order to retain the clients. Or they might consider it improper for a public government to promote the "private business" of lawyers. Whatever be the reason, this prohibition may discourage lawyers from working hard during consultation at a municipal office.

34. The percentage of users who answered that legal consultation was not helpful was 38% for legal consultation at a municipal office, 23% for the legal advice center, 17% for law office and none for the legal aid office.

35. Consultation for family matters, including divorce, is exceptional and can be extended to one hour.

36. Consultation about consumer loans is given for free of charge. However, in family cases, when time of consultation is extended to one hour, JP¥10,000 is charged.

37. Specialized consultation provided by the JFBA Traffic Accident Consultation Center is free of charge, as the services are subsidized by the state.

38. The Japan Judicial Support Center provided free legal advice for 147,430 cases in 2007, which was 37% more than the number in 2006 (Nihon Shiho Shien Senta, 2008, p. 14). The numbers of cases for which legal advice was given by Bar Associations in 2006 and 2007 are not available yet, but, in 2005, legal advice was given in 88,513 cases on legal aid, while ordinary (not free) legal advice was given in 215,556 cases (Nihon Bengoshi Rengokai, 2007, p. 201).

39. Municipal offices might give the names of lawyers to visitors, if visitors asked after consultation. But this is not a common practice and the prohibition is still the rule.

40. For instance, the Tokyo Prefecture Government stopped providing free legal consultation, because free legal advice was also provided by almost all wards, cities and towns in the prefecture. Another rationale for the abolition was that public offices did not have to provide services which private agencies did. In this case, everybody can buy legal services and there is legal aid for the indigent.

41. Where "free legal advice" in Fig. 3 was provided is not very clear. Respondents answered in this way, when they remembered that advice was free but did not know how the consultation was provided. It could be free legal consultation provided by municipal governments, bar associations in cooperation with municipal governments, or judicial scriveners.

42. In this sense, the introducers function as intermediaries to assure both lawyers and their clients of their mutual trustworthiness.

43. In comparison with consumer problems, the odds ratio of Purchase of Land/House is 11.175 ($p = 0.006$), Money/Credit 6.794 ($p = 0.024$) and Family 4.594 ($p = 0.088$). See, Table 6B.

44. The JFBA Working Group speculated that the amount at stake did not affect the decision to retain a lawyer, because that decision was already made before going to meet the lawyer at the law office (Nihon Bengoshi Rengokai, 2008, pp. 63–64).

ACKNOWLEDGMENTS

I thank Rebecca Sandefur for helping me to clarify arguments and Susan Reid for helping me to improve the English.

REFERENCES

Carlin, J. E., Howard, J., & Messinger, S. L. (1966). Civil justice and the poor: Issues for sociological research. *Law and Society Review*, *1*(1), 9–89.

Galanter, M. (1974). Why the 'Haves' come out ahead: Speculations on the limits of legal change. *Law and Society Review*, *9*(1), 95–160.

Genn, H. (1999). *Paths to justice: What people do and think about going to law*. Portland, OR: Hart Publishing.

Homusho Daijin Kanbo Jinjika [Ministry of Justice, Minister's Secretariat, Personnel Section] (2008). "Kyu Shiho Shiken Dainiji Shiken Shutsuganshasu/Gokakushasu nado no Suii [Annual Changes of the Number of Applicants and Passers of the Old Second Bar Examination]," Available at http://www.moj.go.jp/PRESS/071004-1/19syutu-gou2.html. Accessed on July 31, 2008.

Kritzer, M. H., Bogart, W. A., & Vidmar, N. (1991). Context, context, context: A cross-problem, cross-cultural comparison of compensation seeking behaviour. A paper prepared for the Joint Meeting of Law and Society Association and Research Committee on Sociology of Law, Amsterdam.

Mayhew, L., & Reiss, A. J., Jr. (1969). The social organization of legal contacts. *American Sociological Review*, *34*(3), 309–318.

Miller, R. E., & Sarat, A. (1980–1981). Grievances, claims, and disputes: Assessing the adversary culture. *Law and Society Review*, *15*(3–4), 525–566.

Murayama, M. (2002). The role of the defense lawyer in the Japanese criminal process. In: M. Feeley & S. Miyazawa (Eds), *The Japanese adversary system in context: Controversies and comparisons*. Basingstoke, Hampshire: Palgrave Macmillan.

Murayama, M. (2007). Experiences of problems and disputing behaviour in Japan. *Meiji Law Journal*, *14*, 1–59.

Murayama, M. (2009). Convergence from the opposite directions? Characteristics of Japanese divorce law in a comparative perspective. In: H. N. Scheiber & L. Mayali (Eds), *Japanese family law in comparative perspectives*. UC Berkeley, Berkeley, CA: The Robbins Collection, School of Law.

Nihon Bengoshi Rengokai [JFBA]. (2002). Nihon no Horitsu Jimusho 2000 – Bengoshi Gyomu no Keizaiteki Kiban ni kansuru Jittaichosa Hokokusho [Law Offices in Japan in 2000 – Research Report on the Economic Basis of Lawyers' Work]," Jiyu to Seigi (Liberty & Justice), Vol. 53, No. 13 (special issue).

Nihon Bengoshi Rengokai [JFBA]. (2006). Anketo Kekka ni motozuku Shimin no tameno Bengoshi Hoshu no Meyasu – 2005 Nen Anketo Kekka Ban [Tentative Criteria of Attorney's Fees for the Citizens Based on the Results of Survey – 2005 Survey Result Edition]. Tokyo: Nihon Bengoshi Rengokai.

Nihon Bengoshi Rengokai [JFBA]. (2007). *Bengoshi Hakusho [White Paper of Lawyers]*. Tokyo: Nihon Bengoshi Rengokai.

Nihon Bengoshi Rengokai [JFBA]. (2008). *Shimin no Hoteki Nizu Chosa Hokokusho [Research Report on Legal Needs of Citizens]*. Tokyo: Nihon Bengoshi Rengokai.

Nihon Shiho Shien Senta [Japan Judicial Support Center]. (2008). *Heisei 19 Nendo Gyomu Jisseki Hokokusho [Fiscal Year 2007 Report of Provided Services]*. Tokyo: Nihon Shiho Shien Senta.

Pleasence, P., Buck, A., Balmer, N., O'Grady, A., Genn, H., & Smith, M. (2004). *Causes of action: Civil law and social justice*. London: The Stationery Office.

Rokumoto, K. (1971). *Minji Hunso no Hoteki Kaiketsu [Legal Resolution of Civil Disputes]*. Tokyo: Iwanami Shoten.

Rokumoto, K. (1978). "Higaishagawa Tojisha no Ho Kodo [Legal Behavior on the Side of Victims]," in Kawashima, T. and Hirano, R. [Eds.], Jidosha Jiko wo Meguru Hunso Shori to Ho [Dispute Resolution and the Law Concerning Traffic Accidents], pp. 33–82.

Ross, L. H. (1980). *Settled out of court: The social process of insurance claims adjustments*. New York, NY: Aldine De Gruyter.

PERSONAL RESPONSIBILITY V. CORPORATE LIABILITY: HOW PERSONAL INJURY LAWYERS SCREEN CASES IN AN ERA OF TORT REFORM

Mary Nell Trautner

ABSTRACT

Who is ultimately responsible for the harms that befall us? Corporations who make dangerous products, or the consumers who use them? The answer to this question has a profound impact on how personal injury lawyers screen products liability cases. In this chapter, I analyze results from an experimental vignette study in which 83 lawyers were asked to evaluate a hypothetical products liability case. Half of the lawyers practice in states considered to be difficult jurisdictions for the practice of personal injury law due to tort reform and conservative political climates (Texas and Colorado), while the other half work in states that have been relatively unaffected by tort reform and are considered to be more "plaintiff friendly" (Pennsylvania and Massachusetts). While lawyers in reform states and non-reform states were equally likely to accept the hypothetical case with which they were presented, they approached the case in different ways, used different theories, and made different

Access to Justice
Sociology of Crime, Law and Deviance, Volume 12, 203–230

ISSN: 1521-6136/doi:10.1108/S1521-6136(2009)0000012012

arguments in order to justify their acceptance of the case. Lawyers in states with tort reform were most likely to accept the case when they focused on the issue of corporate social responsibility – that is, what the defendant did wrong, how they violated the rules, and how they could have prevented the injury in question. Lawyers in non-reform states, however, were most likely to accept the case when they believed that jurors would feel sorry for the injured child and not find their client at fault for the injury.

Who is ultimately responsible for the harms that befall us? Corporations that make dangerous products, or the consumers who use them? The answer to this question has a profound impact on how personal injury lawyers screen products liability cases. Contrary to popular public opinion, personal injury lawyers are highly selective about the cases they pursue, often accepting only a small percentage of cases with which they are presented. And while individuals who have suffered a compensable injury do occasionally pursue cases on their own with success, lawyers are generally thought to be a necessary, but not sufficient, condition for obtaining compensation through the civil justice system (Kritzer, 1996, 1997, 2004; Martin & Daniels, 1997; Michelson, 2006). In this way, plaintiffs' lawyers act as gatekeepers to justice.

In addition, most scholars of torts[1] have argued that the tort compensation system has a number of positive functions. The most obvious is that people suffering from injuries receive monetary compensation, which aids in the recovery and/or caretaking process. This compensation is designed to make the plaintiff "whole" again in the aftermath of an injury, by replacing lost wages, providing for lost earning capacity, and reimbursing past medical expenses as well as those the plaintiff may incur in the future. Tortfeasors are also often asked to compensate for a plaintiff's pain and suffering, emotional anguish, disfigurement, or loss of enjoyment.[2] But the benefits extend beyond paying damages to individuals. Through lawsuits, civil litigants and plaintiffs' lawyers also expose dangers and risks that have otherwise gone unnoticed by regulators, and the criminal side of law, for example, the dangers posed by exposure to asbestos, silicone breast implants, or the bad batch of Firestone tires. As a result, personal injury litigation benefits the public interest by punishing and guarding against such things as unsafe products, workplace hazards, unfair employment practices, and preventable medical errors (Koenig & Rustad, 2001). Personal injury litigation, in other words, acts not only as a deterrent to "bad" behavior, encouraging self-regulation (Bogus, 2001) but also directly impacts public policy (Burke, 2002). Many of the safety laws we now take for granted (e.g., seatbelts, drug tests, warning labels, machine guards) initially arose from personal injury lawsuits.

Since the mid-1980s, tort law has come under attack a number of times by corporate and business interests seeking to restrict their legal liability and responsibility for financial compensation (Haltom & McCann, 2004). Most states have since passed some type of tort reform. Some have capped the amount of money a plaintiff may receive for his/her injuries, generally agreed to be the most severe change to tort law. Others placed restrictions on joint and several liability. Until reform, all wrongdoers could bear equal financial responsibility for an injury under joint and several liability, regardless of comparative fault. For example, if Doctor A was 10 percent responsible for a patient's death, and Doctor B was 90 percent responsible, but lacked insurance, a plaintiff could collect all monetary damages from Doctor A. Other reforms have added requirements for expert witnesses (such as having particular credentials or filing particular reports at a designated time), or restricting the venue or jurisdiction in which a lawsuit may be filed.

Some researchers argue that tort reform depresses the number of personal injury lawsuits filed by lawyers (Daniels & Martin, 2000; Finley, 1997; Kessler & McClellan, 1996; Sharkey, 2005). Studies suggest that because some tort reforms impact the monetary values of cases, lawyers screen cases more carefully than they would without such reforms (Daniels & Martin, 2000, 2001). However, few empirical studies test anecdotal accounts of more careful lawyer screening by comparing the screening process pre- and post-reform, or comparing screening patterns of lawyers in states affected by tort reform with lawyers who practice in states without tort reform. How does tort reform impact the process by which lawyers evaluate cases? If lawyers do indeed screen cases differently under tort reform, what are the broader social implications of those screening methods and processes?

Knowing how lawyers screen cases also represents an important addition to understanding the trajectory of disputes. Socio-legal scholars have built up a great deal of knowledge about the disputing process, that is, how people identify injuries or events as grievances, some of which turn into disputes, some of which ultimately end in trial. This process is commonly referred to as the "disputing pyramid" (Felstiner, Abel, & Sarat, 1980–1981). The pyramid illustrates that there are many fewer trials than there might possibly be because some potential cases fall out at each stage.

While the upper portion of the pyramid deals mainly with the final stages of disputes, the lower part captures what Felstiner, Abel, and Sarat call the "naming, blaming, and claiming" process. It examines if, how, and when people decide to mobilize the law, and is strongly associated with the literature on legal consciousness (see, for example, Ewick & Silbey, 1998; Merry, 1990; Nielsen, 2000). The foundation of the pyramid can be characterized as most concerned with questions of how people define events as troubles, particularly as legal troubles, and how, if at all, they attempt to resolve their disputes. At each subsequent step in the process, potential cases disappear from the pyramid. Not all people who have an injury, for example, think of it as a problem that can be remedied. Not all individuals identify who is to blame for that injury, and even fewer request compensation, and so on.

While the legal consciousness literature provides information about the early stages of disputes, and we know a great deal about their later stages (e.g., trials and outcomes of trials), we know very little about the stage of the disputing process that involves lawyers. In fact, all that we know for certain is that fewer cases are channeled from the lawyer's office into the legal system than came into it seeking redress. But how does this process work? What role does lawyer screening, whether for cases or clients, play in the disputing process? One reason so little is known about this stage is that most studies examine the disputing process from the perspective of the potential litigants, rather than from that of outside parties such as lawyers who ultimately "transform" the dispute. Consequently, studying how lawyers screen cases represents an important addition to the knowledge of the disputing process.

1. BACKGROUND ON CASE SELECTION AND PRODUCTS LIABILITY CASES

Previous studies of case screening suggest that lawyers make decisions about cases following a rational choice model, accepting cases which offer many rewards and few risks, and declining those which offer few rewards and many risks. Because plaintiffs' lawyers work on a contingency basis, they receive financial compensation only if they win a case. Should they lose, it is the lawyers – not the clients – who bear the entire cost of working up the case. These costs, particularly for complex cases such as those involving products liability or medical malpractice claims which require the use of expert witnesses, can easily approach $100,000 or more. As a result, lawyers' best interests require screening cases as carefully as possible, selecting only those which promise a return on their investments (Kritzer, 1996, 1997; Parikh, 2001).

While case selection is doubtless driven by lawyers' financial concerns, these decisions are embedded in broader social and legal environments that impact lawyers' evaluations of the potential risks and returns associated with cases. Thus, analyses of case screening should incorporate not only the financial aspects associated with cases, but also the broader contexts in which screening decisions are made. Tort reform, especially lawyers' perceptions of reform and the attitudes of potential jurors in their community, influence how lawyers decide which cases to accept and which to decline.

Given the financial costs associated with products liability cases, screening decisions for these cases are especially important. Most products liability cases require the use of expert witnesses, and often require that products be tested and redesigned, representing important cost centers for each case. There are no systematic, verifiable data on the use of or expenses associated with civil cases; nearly all the information legal scholars have gathered come from attorney self-reports (e.g., Daniels & Martin, 2001–2002; Grow, 2003), or from publicity surrounding particular cases. Lawyers in my interviews reported that they routinely spent $50,000–$100,000 on expert witnesses in products liability and medical malpractice cases – expenses that are only recouped if a case is won (or settled) for a large enough amount to cover expenses, attorney fees, and victim compensation. Given these investments, few lawyers would be inclined to invest tens or hundreds of thousands of dollars in a case unless they felt very strongly that the case had a better-than-average chance of winning.

Products liability cases also capture the influence of the wider culture. While they account for just a very small percentage of personal injury trials (2 percent according to the Bureau of Justice Statistics, see Cohen & Smith, 2004), many high-profile personal injury cases are products liability cases. The McDonald's hot coffee case, or prescription drug cases like Fen-Phen or Vioxx, make these cases prominent in the public consciousness due to media attention (Haltom & McCann, 2004; Lofquist, 2002; Vidmar, 1998). It is not surprising that many complaints about "frivolous lawsuits" which include warnings that lawsuits pose dangers to business and American free enterprise, and call for increased "personal responsibility" (all slogans of the tort reform movement), most often follow high-profile products liability cases (and medical malpractice cases), rather than cases in other areas of personal injury. As a result, lawyers' perceptions of how the local populace responds to such cultural shifts become an underlying factor in the case screening process, as lawyers working in these areas must contend with jurors' pre-existing attitudes and expectations of products liability cases in general as they work up and argue their particular case.

Another reason to focus on products liability cases is that state-level tort reforms are most often targeted at products liability cases (or medical malpractice cases), especially reforms that cap pain and suffering and/or punitive damage awards, change joint and several liability, and increase requirements for expert witnesses and scientific evidence (Baker, 2005; Koenig & Rustad, 2001; Zegart, 2004). Much of the previous research on personal injury lawyers has focused on those who specialize primarily in lower value cases such as auto accidents (Daniels & Martin, 1999, 2000; Kritzer, 1997; Parikh, 2001; Van Hoy, 1997, 1999). However, such lower value cases are relatively unaffected by these changes in the letter of the law. Studying cases and areas of practice affected by multiple aspects of culture, including the structure of law, represent a promising avenue for research on how tort reforms shape lawyer's case selection. For analytic leverage on the effects of tort reform on the case screening process, I interviewed lawyers selected from two kinds of states: two "restrictive" reform states (widely viewed as difficult states in which to practice personal injury law), and two "open" non-reform states, considered to be more "plaintiff friendly."

2. RESEARCH DESIGN

I focus my analysis on the evaluation of a hypothetical products liability case, assessed by lawyers who handle products liability and/or medical malpractice cases almost exclusively, the most specialized and complex sub-specialties of the broad field of personal injury. Unlike more routine personal injury cases such as car accidents, products liability cases are in a unique position to give us insight into the ways in which economics, culture, and law intersect in the case screening process, leading to a richer understanding of the disputing process as a whole.

Texas and Colorado are widely considered to be difficult states in which to practice personal injury law (ATRA, 2004; Daniels & Martin, 1999, 2000, 2001; Martin & Daniels, 1997; Schneyer, 2002). Both states are heavily dominated by conservative politics, and both have passed a large number of tort reforms which severely limit the rights of injured parties to seek redress. According to the American Tort Reform Association (ATRA, 2004), Colorado has passed more tort reforms, in more issue areas, than any other state since 1986, and the pro-reform Colorado Civil Justice League boasts that Colorado is "noted as a national leader on reform" (2004). Texas follows as the state with the second most reforms in all issue areas. These include modifications on economic damages, punitive damages, scientific and technical evidence, products liability, medical malpractice, class actions, and others.

In contrast, Massachusetts and Pennsylvania are considered by both plaintiff and defense attorneys to be "friendlier" toward plaintiffs than to corporations (Boynton, 1999; Harris Interactive, 2004). Philadelphia is one of only 13 areas in the United States named as a "judicial hellhole" by ATRA and its members (ATRA, 2003), and, along with Boston, is listed as one of the 25 local jurisdictions with the "least fair and reasonable litigation environments" by a poll of corporate attorneys (Harris Interactive, 2004). Massachusetts and Pennsylvania have each passed very few tort reform measures. Massachusetts has passed a small-scope modified rule of joint and several liability which applies only to public accountants, and has modified attorney's fees in medical malpractice cases. Pennsylvania has passed just two reforms: a similarly small-scope joint and several liability rule and a venue change for medical malpractice cases (all cases must be filed in the county where the malpractice occurred).

I conducted in-depth, face-to-face interviews with equivalent numbers of plaintiffs' lawyers from each of the four states regarding their screening practices. To minimize intra-state variation, I sampled lawyers from a single large city in each state (San Antonio, Denver, Philadelphia, and Boston). The sample is restricted to lawyers who specialize in plaintiffs' products liability or medical malpractice, and those who have practiced for at least five years in order to capture a sense of changes over time. I interviewed a total of 83 lawyers (20 in Boston and 21 in each of the other three cities).

3. THE VIGNETTE

During each interview, I gave each lawyer[3] a hypothetical products liability case to evaluate. In this vignette, a 12-year-old child became permanently paralyzed from the waist down after losing control and being thrown from a hypothetical toy called a "roller stick." Roller sticks, the vignette explains, are "something of a cross between in-line roller skates and pogo sticks" – that is, they travel at a high velocity and can make vertical leaps into the air. Based on a law school examination question,[4] the vignette gave a limited set of purposefully ambiguous facts that lawyers could use to evaluate the case: it described the history of the product, the extent of the injury, the conduct and characteristics of both the victim and the defendant, and the feasibility of an alternative design of the roller stick.

After giving a brief description of the toy itself, the vignette reveals that roller sticks have been associated with a number of previous injuries: in the three years since roller sticks have been in the market, two children have been killed, 10 seriously injured, and 50 slightly injured in roller stick accidents, caused by excessive speed or jumps over 3 ft off the ground. The reader then learns that an add-on safety feature, a "damper," can limit the speed and height at which roller sticks can travel, and virtually eliminate all accidents associated with it. Dampers are required for all roller sticks sold in Europe.

At this point, the vignette explains the price differential associated with the safety device. Normally sold for $150, dampers add an extra $50 to the overall cost of roller sticks. Moreover, American children prefer the velocity and jumping ability of models without roller sticks, making the higher-costing, safer alternative difficult or impossible to sell. As a result, the manufacturer of the roller stick in question, "Star Toy Corporation," added warnings to their entire roller sticks and owner's manuals, "clearly and adequately" cautioning about the dangers of excessive speeds or jumps. The child, in question, however, was not aware of these warnings – he/she[5] was so eager to play with the roller stick that he/she did not read the warnings on the stick or those in the owner's manual, and was soon thrown from the roller stick after losing control, resulting in permanent paralysis from the waist down. The vignette concludes with the child and his/her family wanting to sue the Star Toy Corporation and asking if the reader will accept the case.

The vignette was well-received by the lawyers I interviewed, and many remarked that it was a good hypothetical in that it had interesting facts and covered all the factual points that they thought about when evaluating cases. This is an important point, for, in order for vignettes to be maximally useful, the stories must appear real and plausible to those who are responding to it (Barter & Renold, 1999; Neff, 1979).

4. ACCEPTING AND DECLINING PLAINTIFF'S CASES

When asked if they would accept the hypothetical case, lawyers responded in a variety of ways. While the majority of lawyers gave clear "yes" or "no" answers to the question of whether they would accept the case described in the vignette, a significant number gave "middling" responses such as

Table 1. Hypothetical Case Acceptance Patterns.

Would You Accept This Case?	Number of Respondents (% of Sample)
No	12 (15)
Probably not	2 (2)
Refer the case to another lawyer	5 (6)
Maybe	8 (10)
Probably/seriously consider	12 (15)
Yes	42 (52)
Total	81 (100)

"probably," "probably not," or "maybe." Table 1 shows these responses along with the number and percentage of lawyers who fell into these different response categories.

As shown in Table 1, most lawyers accepted the case outright (52 percent) or felt that they probably would (15 percent), while only 14 (17 percent) absolutely rejected or said that they would likely not accept the case. While those who said they would refer the case to another lawyer technically did not accept the case, they are excluded in the following analyses because their reasons for personally declining the case are ambiguous. For example, those who referred the case may have felt that it was a good case, but perhaps not closely aligned enough with their particular expertise in products liability work to justify pursuing it themselves. Other interpretations are also possible. I also exclude lawyers in the "maybe" category. These lawyers were so ambivalent, seeing both the positives and the negatives of the various aspects of the case, they really felt they could not make a decision without a great deal of further investigation. These two categories of responses, "refer to another lawyer" and "maybe" were evenly distributed among potential clients (name of the child injured in the vignette) and cities in which lawyers worked (analyses not shown). Removing "maybe" and "refer" cases does not affect interpretation of potential gender, race, or geographic influences on responses. This leaves a sample size of 68, analyzed by collapsing "Probably Not" and "No" into a single "No – decline" category, and "Probably/Seriously Consider" and "Yes" into a single "Yes – accept" category. These are shown in Table 2. The analytic decision to eliminate the middle categories from further analysis improves interpretability of the potential role of legal culture on decisive lawyer's responses to the hypothetical vignette.

As Tables 1 and 2 show, most lawyers in the sample said they would accept the hypothetical case (about 80 percent). Yet lawyers gave varying

Table 2. Acceptance Rates of Hypothetical Case (Collapsed Categories).

Would You Accept This Case?	Number of Respondents
Decline	21% ($n = 14$)
Accept	79% ($n = 54$)
Total	100% ($n = 68$)

reasons for accepting the case; different constellations of factors led lawyers to evaluate the case positively.

The analyses that follow show how lawyers interpreted the different case components that were presented in the vignette, beginning with the legal issues surrounding the damper and warnings, followed by lawyers' various interpretations of the conduct and other characteristics of the defendant, and then how lawyers interpreted the behavior and characteristics of the potential plaintiff. I also consider how interpretations of these case components and lawyers' acceptance or rejection of the hypothetical case are related, noting differences between lawyers in reform states and non-reform states.

5. INTERPRETATIONS OF CASE COMPONENTS

The main portions of the vignette were written in such a way that they could each have been interpreted in a variety of ways. I had anticipated that some lawyers would see some features as being strong deterrents to taking the case, while others would interpret those same elements more favorably. I describe the different interpretations that lawyers had of three sets of elements: (1) the legal issues surrounding the dampers and warnings; (2) the characteristics and conduct of Star Toy Corporation, the potential defendant; and (3) the characteristics and conduct of the injured child and his/her family, the potential plaintiff.

5.1. Warnings, Dampers, and the Legal Hierarchy of Product Safety

The main theory surrounding U.S. products liability law is that unless a product is defective, no manufacturer or distributor of that product may be held liable for any harm caused by that product (Dobbs, 2000). There are three primary ways that a product may be legally found defective: (1) through its *design*, meaning that every product in that line is defective or unreasonably dangerous in the same way (the Ford Pinto, for example, had a design defect, in that the gas tank for every Pinto was located near the rear bumper, causing the car to explode when impacted); (2) through its *manufacture* or production, meaning that the flaw is random, and does not affect every product in the line (for example, a single candy bar that contains shards of glass); or (3) through its *marketing* or *warnings* to consumers, meaning that if a product may be harmful when used improperly, it should contain a warning explaining proper and improper usage (a hairdryer that failed to warn about dangers when used in/near water, for example, might have a warning defect). States then have different thresholds that products must meet (or fail to meet) in order to legally be defined as defective in their particular jurisdiction.

In their evaluation of the case, the majority of lawyers made arguments as to why roller sticks should – or should not – be considered defective products under law using one of these main theories of liability. No lawyer made the argument that roller sticks had a *manufacturing* defect, since by design, *all* roller sticks are compromised by too much speed and height. Many lawyers, however, argued that roller sticks had a *design* defect, since all roller sticks without dampers could result in accidents when traveling very high or very fast. As one San Antonio lawyer explained, "Roller sticks, when operated the way they can be normally operated by children, can kill them. So that's an unreasonably dangerous product by definition" (SA-1).

Some lawyers argued that roller sticks had a *marketing* defect. They questioned whether the warnings were "clear and adequate" as the vignette had suggested. Typically, lawyers mentioned that the wording and placement of the warnings, as well as the sophistication and comprehension of their intended recipient might all be problematic for the manufacturer, as this Denver lawyer suggests: "What's a clear and adequate warning? Is that a clear and adequate warning to a twelve-year-old, or the twelve-year-old's parents?" (D-19). For this lawyer, the very definition of "clear and adequate" warning depends on who is the intended reader of the warning. A San Antonio lawyer echoes this concern about the intended audience and elaborates on other issues that warnings raise. He says,

> Even if a product has warnings, those warnings need to take into account the factors of readability, visibility and target audience. In other words, are the warnings the type a user is prone to see, understand, and follow. The last point can be difficult, but there are some instructions that, if followed, would make the product unusable. The manufacturer

> knows nobody is going to follow such a warning, and putting it on the product does not shield them from liability if they know the product is going to be used in a fashion that is customary for the product, even though the directions say otherwise. (SA-4)

Several other lawyers voiced similar concerns about warnings that will not be followed due to incompatibility with the use of the product (e.g., a diving board which warns users to "not dive"), thus making the warnings "useless" and "ineffective" safety improvements.

Many of the lawyers found the warnings issue attractive because of the "engineering hierarchy" of product safety. This hierarchy says that manufacturers should do their best to eliminate risks associated with products, which they can do in a variety of ways, as this Philadelphia lawyer explains:

> If a product has a risk, the first thing you do is design the risk out. If you can't design the risk out, you install a guard on the product that prevents people from being exposed to the risk. If you can't install a guard, then you warn about the risk. (P-16)

For manufacturers, warnings are the simplest, cheapest, and some lawyers would argue, least effective way to make a product safe, while designing a risk out of the product is the most difficult and typically the most expensive. One reason that designing risk out of a product is so difficult, as many lawyers pointed out, is due to the importance of retaining a product's utility. Several gave examples of products in which designing out a hazard compromised the usability of a product, as did this Boston lawyer: "We can design the hazards out of a fan if we take the blades off, but now it doesn't work anymore as a fan" (B-10). Instead, he explained, fan makers *guard against* risk by putting cages around the blades and/or manufacturing blades out of rubber so that fingers and hands cannot be accidentally amputated.

For a safer alternative to be considered reasonable, it must be both practical and financially feasible. Many products carry some risks that cannot be designed away or guarded against in a practical or feasible manner. A Philadelphia lawyer shows this dilemma using the example of an automobile:

> I can make a car that will never allow any occupant to be injured in any accident. I'll just build it like a Sherman tank. I can do it. I can make it out of heavy gauge steel, I can put plates around it, and that person will never be hurt. Any product [can be safe] if you go crazy enough. But it's no longer functional, and people can't buy it because it's so expensive. So … it's an issue. The cost of safety and improvements is a factor. (P-16)

In the vignette, dampers were presented as a way in which to guard against the risk associated with roller sticks, and they increased the purchase price of the toy from $150 to $200. Some lawyers saw the dampers as a reasonable, affordable alternative, while others believed that the dampers both changed the utility of the product and raised the cost of the roller sticks so much that it was not a practical, financially feasible alternative.

Contrast the following statements made by two Boston lawyers. The first argues that dampers are not a reasonable solution to the risks associated with roller sticks because of the significant price increase and because consumers did not respond to the safer design, while the second thinks nothing of the increase in price:

> I'm sensitive to the fact that this particular safety device dramatically raises the price of the product and so that concerns me. Most safety devices that I have come in contact with are small, increase the product's price by a very small fraction. This is obviously a significant increase ... My biggest reservation is the cost because it's going to increase the price of the product by one-third, and that's a big chunk. And apparently ... there has been some effort by some manufacturers to market the device with dampers and they've gotten burned by it, so I think that is significant. (B-13)
>
> I certainly would not reject it out of hand because of this idea that the safety device would cost fifty bucks. Or that thus far the marketing of the safety device has not been effective ... This defense of the high cost of the safety device and its unacceptability, I've dealt with on numerous occasions. And it's very much a by-product of the marketing of the device itself. In other words, if they sell it as a safe device, if they sell safety as an important factor, ... then there will be greater acceptability. Most people are concerned about the safety of their children. Any failure of the market with respect to increased costs for a safety device that may protect a child is usually due to the fact that the company has not marketed well the idea of safety ... So even if I learned about these problems during the case, even if I learned this was the defense, I'm not buying it. (B-14)

These two different perspectives on the practicality and feasibility of the dampers come from lawyers who both practice in the same city. Previous studies of tort reform and the legal profession suggest that such changes in the legal environment lead to changes in lawyers' behaviors. The implicit assumption is that lawyers working in states with tort reform (and the accompanying social and cultural changes) behave similarly to other lawyers in their states and differently from lawyers in states without tort reform, including how they screen cases. As a result, the expectation is that lawyers within each city would have highly similar perceptions of the various components of the hypothetical case. While there were disagreements on the issue of feasibility of the dampers in all four cities (lawyers who accepted the case, regardless of reform status, were more likely to see the dampers as feasible), as well as disagreements about the adequacy of the warnings, and the conduct of both the defendant and the plaintiff, within subsamples of lawyers from particular cities, there were also patterns of overall differences between lawyers in reform versus non-reform states. I discuss each of these below, including their implications for acceptance of the case and access to justice.

5.1.1. Roller Sticks as Legally Defective

U.S. states have different definitions of product safety and different thresholds that manufacturers must meet to not be liable for any harm their products may cause. Pennsylvania courts, for example, instruct jurors that products are defined as defective under state law under the following conditions:

> The Manufacturer, Distributor, Wholesaler, etc. of a product is the guarantor of its safety. The product must be provided with every element necessary to make it safe for its intended use, and without any condition that makes it unsafe for its intended use. If you find that the product, at the time it left the defendant's control, lacked any element necessary to make it safe for its intended use, or contained any condition that made it unsafe for its intended use, then the product was defective, and the defendant is liable for all harm caused by the defect. (Pennsylvania Suggested Standard Civil Jury Instructions § 8.02)

A number of Philadelphia lawyers mentioned this law, which is generally interpreted as being tough on corporations and very favorable to plaintiffs. Consider the remarks of P-2. When asked if he would accept the hypothetical case, he replied, "That's easy. I'll take that case in a minute." Among other reasons he gave for his enthusiasm for the case was his restatement of the jury instructions given above:

> The test for defective products under our Supreme Court's decisions is if the item lacked any feature that would have made it safer, and that the safety device was known and feasible. That makes a defective product, that's all I need ... Pennsylvania law is that the product is on trial, the actor's conduct is not. Contributory negligence is not a defense. You want to look at this product and say, if this product had a fixed damper to it that was part of the product, and couldn't be removed, this accident never would have happened. That's the way it should have been sold, and that's the only way it could have been sold safely. And that's it. Whatever the 12-year-old did or didn't do has no relevance whatsoever to this. (P-2)

This lawyer, and many others in Philadelphia, interpreted the law as being on his side. For him, the case is simple: the law requires safety features, the roller stick lacked a safety feature, therefore the product is defective.

In contrast, a recent tort reform in Colorado provides that "a product liability action may not be taken if the product was improperly used or if the product provided warning or instruction that, if heeded, would have prevented the injury, death, or property damage" (Colorado Product Liability Reform, SB 03-231, 2003). Unlike in Pennsylvania, where the

Table 3. Reform Status and Case Acceptance.

Case Disposition	Reform State		Non-Reform State
Declines	26% ($n = 9$)		15% ($n = 5$)
Accepts	74% ($n = 25$)		85% ($n = 29$)
Total	$n = 34$		$n = 34$
		$\chi^2 = 1.425$	

$^{*}p<.05$, $^{**}p<.01$, $^{***}p<.001$.

product had to be rendered safe, in Colorado, warnings can be interpreted as an "absolute defense." Warnings absolve product manufacturers of all liability under all circumstances, provided that the warnings can be followed. Laws such as these are generally interpreted to be more favorable to corporations and less so to plaintiffs.

Given such differences in states' orientations to products liability cases, dramatic variation in the acceptance of the vignette based on whether a lawyer is practicing in a reform or a non-reform state is to be expected. Table 3 presents the relationships between acceptance rates and reform status.

As Table 3 shows, tort reform alone does not predict whether lawyers accept the case described in the vignette. While lawyers in non-reform states *appear* to be more likely to accept the case than those in the reform states, the differences between the two are not statistically significant.

5.2. Characteristics and Conduct of the Defendant

Just as lawyers interpreted the legal defectiveness differently, lawyers also interpreted the characteristics and conduct of the defendant in different ways. These interpretations were not always consistent within single cities, or even within the distinction between reform and non-reform states. Most lawyers commented one way or another on either the characteristics of the defendant (Star Toy Corporation), the conduct of the defendant, or both.

A number of lawyers commented – or made implicit assumptions about – the size of Star Toy Corporation. Generally lawyers assumed Star to be a large corporation, which, in their eyes, is a better defendant to have, as this San Antonio lawyer explains:

> The most practical consideration of all of this is, what are their assets? Is it a mom and pop operation? The fact that there are European sticks, maybe made by Star too, leads

> me to believe that it's a big corporation. Because obviously, this child, her injuries are way off the scale. So it's a multi-million dollar potential recovery. If it's a mom and pop company that doesn't have anything going for them, it'd be just like chasing, it'd be like trying to get blood out of a turnip. The most practical consideration is, what kind of assets and what kind of insurance coverage does Star have? (SA-17)

Lawyers preferred Star to be a large corporation because they believe that a larger recovery is more likely than with a small company because of financial holdings and assets. Moreover, some believed that there were likely several large corporations that could be sued in the case:

> There's probably a number of deep pockets to sue. There's the Star Toy Corporation. There's probably somebody else who distributed it. There may be parts that were manufactured by another company that sold them to Star. There may be, whoever sold it – whether it's Wal-Mart or K-Mart, or Target, whoever she bought this from. It could be in the line of distribution, so there's a *number* of potential defendants to sue. (D-8)

In this reasoning, even if Star Toy was not a large, multi-national corporation, there are likely some "deep pockets" to be found somewhere in the case. One Boston lawyer, combining both arguments made above, hypothesized that the case might be more successful by going after the retailer rather than the manufacturer, since retailers increasingly have a great deal of influence over the pricing of products. He says,

> You may have a better argument here arguing against the retailer. I'm thinking of a Wal-Mart or some big huge company where the money is just unbelievable and *they* are the ones that are dictating if these things have dampers on them or not, because they want to sell them at a certain price point, and they don't care about anything except the price point ... They wanted volume sales, and *that* a jury can identify with ... If it was a mom and pop operation [selling the product], even though the mom and pop organization is doing everything for the same reasons that Wal-Mart is doing it, you wouldn't get the chance ... They'd have no economic coercion over the manufacturer to tell them to sell them cheaper one versus the more expensive one. I mean, once it's in the marketplace, who can make them the fastest wins. And the retailer pretty much decides what they pay. (B-17)

But generally, lawyers focused less on the characteristics of Star Toy Corporation, and more on the corporation's conduct. By far, the most common way in which lawyers talked about the behavior of Star was by making a morality-based argument as to why the corporation's actions and motives would make a jury angry: lawyers argued that the Star Toy Corporation acted irresponsibly by choosing to prioritize their bottom line over the safety and well-being of American children. As one San Antonio lawyer put it, "There was obviously an alternative design, but because of the economics involved, they wouldn't profit as well. Profits over safety ... I think [the case] has a good piss-off factor" (SA-8). Lawyers liked the presentation of the hypothetical case because it allowed them to paint a dark portrait of Star, and a number of lawyers peppered their evaluation of Star's behavior and duty with emotional appeals and remarks to an imagined jury, as did this Denver lawyer:

> They can obviously design the hazard out with a safety device. They did so when the law required them to do so. When the law had made no such requirement of them, they eliminated that safety device ... But I think you got the jury, you got a lot of factors in any case that you take is their anger. Is their anger here? And I think the anger is, they're selling it to Europeans with this safety device and they're dumping their unprotected product on Americans. Americans! We're in America! I think it has great jury appeal ... The jury is going to get angry. If there's a law, they'll abide by the law to make it safe. But if the law doesn't make the manufacturer make the product safe, then they're not going to do it. (D-19)

Over half of the lawyers I interviewed (54 percent, $n = 44$) made an argument about corporate social responsibility(CSR) and what they believed to be Star's poor choices. Following this line of reasoning, it is not making a profit or the nature of the roller stick itself that makes Star liable, but because they prioritized profit over safety by providing only a warning about the dangers involved rather than doing something more tangible about it. The following Philadelphia lawyer explains this argument in greater detail, and extends the argument to automobiles – should auto manufacturers, he asks, be allowed to save money on safety features by just adding warnings to cars?

> In this scenario the industry decided [they're] not going to put this safety device on because [they] care more about money than about kids ... So they will sacrifice these kids at the altar of profit and I think that is wrong. You cannot have a feasible safety device that's going to prevent it and not put it on there because of money. I think that's morally wrong. You go tell this little paralyzed girl we had a safety device that would have protected her ... A warning is generally and usually a poor excuse for bad design. So, using this analogy in this case, car manufacturers shouldn't give you seat belts, airbags, bumpers that reduce the force of an accident, shatter-proof glass, they should give you none of that. They should just give you a warning – hey you could get hurt in an accident. You could get killed. If we put in an airbag and seatbelts it's going to cost us more money. We won't be able to sell as many cars. Tough luck! Your kid gets paralyzed even though we could have put in an airbag or a seatbelt. Tough luck for your kid. I think that's wrong. I think that's dead wrong. (P-20)

A number of lawyers made similar arguments, likewise filled with passionate anger about Star's behavior, as does this Denver lawyer, who also invokes the legal hierarchy of product safety discussed previously:

> American manufacturers have chosen not to put [dampers] on their machines even though they're successful [at preventing injuries]. They sell them as options, and they

know if they sell them as options people won't buy them. And they know that they're going to have cases like this. The question is not whether you're gonna have injuries, the question is when and where. It's a given. You're going to have injuries, they know it, and yet they are selling these products without safety devices. And they've made a conscious choice, knowing that they're going to face litigation. And they say, 'screw it.' That's what they've done here in this hypothetical. They said, 'We'll face the litigation because we think we can make enough profit.' Despite the fact that there is going to be a trade-off of dead and seriously injured children. And it is absolutely gross for them when they have a guard that is available. But instead of putting that on the machine, they put a warning on when they know damn well that the warning is going to be ineffective. They have a duty. They have duty when they have a product that is foreseeably hazardous – to design out that hazard if they can economically and ecologically do so. If they can't do that they have a duty to put a guard on it if they economically and ecologically can do so, which they can here. And thirdly, and *only if* they can't do the first two, should they use a warning. (D-5)

So how well does this argument predict lawyers' willingness to accept the hypothetical case? Table 4 presents results of case selection for lawyers making – or not making – arguments about CSR, regardless of reform status.

The results are striking. While making *no* argument about CSR makes little difference in case selection, *making* the CSR argument is significantly associated with case acceptance. Only a single lawyer (among 40) who argued that Star was irresponsible declined the case anyway.

Table 5 shows the interactions between a state's tort reform status and the CSR argument. The first panel presents results from reform states, whereas the second looks at CSR in non-reform states.

Analyzing acceptance rates separately by reform status shows that lawyers in *reform* states dominate in the observed pattern of accepting cases when arguments of corporate responsibility are made. Every reform state lawyer who made an argument about CSR accepted the case. More lawyers in non-reform states make no CSR argument, although that does not appear

Table 4. Corporate Social Responsibility and Case Acceptance.

Case Disposition	CSR Argument		No CSR Argument
Declines	2.5% ($n = 1$)		46% ($n = 13$)
Accepts	97.5%($n = 39$)		54% ($n = 15$)
Total	$n = 40$		$n = 28$
		$\chi^2 = 19.44$***	

*$p<.05$, **$p<.01$, ***$p<.001$.

Table 5. Corporate Social Responsibility and Case Acceptance by Reform Status.

Case Disposition	Reform States		Non-Reform States	
	CSR argument	No CSR argument	CSR argument	No CSR argument
Declines	0% ($n = 0$)	56% ($n = 9$)	5% ($n = 1$)	33% ($n = 4$)
Accepts	100%[a] ($n = 18$)	44% ($n = 7$)	95% ($n = 21$)	67% ($n = 8$)
Total	$n = 18$	$n = 16$	$n = 22$	$n = 12$
	$\chi^2 = 13.77$***		$\chi^2 = 5.13$*	

*$p<.05$, **$p<.01$, ***$p<.001$.
[a]Notably, 39 percent of reform state lawyers who made a CSR argument and who accepted the case ($n = 7$), and 29 percent ($n = 2$) of reform state lawyers who accepted the case *without* making a CSR argument did so believing that they had a very strong chance of losing. Only one lawyer in the non-reform states accepted the case thinking that they could very well lose.

to have a significant impact on their likelihood of accepting or declining cases. The pattern of overwhelmingly accepting cases where CSR arguments are made is evident among lawyers in non-reform states as well. Comparing lawyers from reform and non-reform states on the CSR factor indicates that they behave in broadly similar ways: when they argue that the Star "behaved badly," lawyers were likely to take the case regardless of their state's reform status.

Of course, not all lawyers made an argument about morality or CSR. Many lawyers instead focused on the characteristics and conduct of the potential plaintiff in the vignette, the 12-year-old child and his or her family.

5.3. Characteristics and Conduct of the Plaintiff

Of each of the core case components that I have discussed (legal issues surrounding the dampers and warnings, conduct of the defendant), none received as many mixed interpretations as did the conduct of the potential plaintiff. As they tried to guess how a jury would react to the case, lawyers were split as to whether the child would be perceived as blameless or as essentially at fault for the accident.

A number of lawyers felt that the age of the victim would work in their favor by eliciting sympathy from a jury. As one Denver lawyer explained, "A child is always a desirable plaintiff. It's very difficult for a jury to dislike any child." She further explained that while victims are often blamed for contributing to their own injury, "none of it applies to kids. They get the presumption of goodness and innocence in the minds of the jury and in the minds of the defense lawyer" (D-8). Many lawyers told me that the age of the child was a very significant factor for them in the evaluation of the case. "Now if you gave the same facts with an adult," a Boston lawyer told me, echoing the statements made by several others, "that would be a different story. I would expect the adult to read the warning. I would not expect a 12-year-old [to do so]" (B-7).

A few lawyers also made gendered arguments about the desirability of the case. For some, a paraplegic girl was an especially good client because of the loss of the chance of future motherhood, making her even more sympathetic to a potential jury, as this Philadelphia lawyer explains:

> This little girl's going to be a sympathetic plaintiff. She's got a horrible injury, paralysis from the waist down. She won't have a normal life. She won't have a normal marriage. And she won't be able to bear children, probably. It's going to be a horrible future that she's going to have, and she deserves fair compensation for that. (P-5)

In addition, some lawyers made gendered arguments with regard to boys. Not only can children be "forgiven" for not reading warnings, but this is especially true for boys, some lawyers said, making a "boys-will-be-boys" argument. "He's not like you and I who are full-grown adults and we can make up our own minds as to whether we want to accept that risk," a Denver lawyer told me. "He's, you know, sort of overwhelmed by his youthful enthusiasm and the fact that every 12-year-old boy thinks that they're indestructible" (D-11).

Not all lawyers were convinced that the child's age would work in their favor. Several expressed concerns that by age 12, a child should know better and be able to behave in a more reasonable manner. As one Boston lawyer put it, "My [own] son is twelve, so I have a concept of what twelve-year-olds do and what they understand. So I don't think that the jury is going to let a 12-year-old off the hook they way they would let a 3- or a 6-year old off the hook" (B-3). In other words, this lawyer is concerned about "contributory negligence," a legal term which means that the plaintiff is partially to blame for his or her injury (Dobbs, 2000). In some states (including both Colorado and Massachusetts), if a plaintiff is found to be more than 50 percent at fault for the injury in question, the defendant cannot be held liable or made to pay any damages whatsoever. Of the lawyers I interviewed, 42 percent ($n = 34$) expressed concerns about contributory negligence. Some worried about the fault that would be assigned to the child, as B-3 expressed earlier. Others, however, were concerned that the *parents* of the child would be blamed by a jury for lack of supervision, rather than blaming Star Toy Corporation for the lack of safety provisions. A Denver lawyer describes how he imagines a jury would react to this case. He says,

> The parents would basically be put on trial for, 'How could you let your son do this, use this dangerous device, why didn't you read the warnings, why didn't you monitor your son's use? It's really *your* fault and not the manufacturer's.' ... A jury would say personal responsibility should be that people should be held to warnings. And if it says don't do something, don't do it, and don't hold the manufacturer responsible for doing something you're told not to do. And if you didn't read the warnings, that's your own stupidity. A jury could certainly come against you on the plaintiff. (D-1)

In other words, D-1 argues that jurors in his community would not assign liability to the manufacturer of the roller stick. Instead, they would find the parents to be at fault for essentially being a bad parent – for not reading the warnings to their child, for not supervising their child's play, or even for being the one to purchase an obviously dangerous product for their child. Thus, the behavior of the plaintiff, like the behavior of the defendant, and the meaning of the dampers and warnings, is fraught with multiple meanings and interpretations by the legal actors who must evaluate them.

When lawyers described their concerns over "personal responsibility," that is, whether a jury would believe that the client was partially to blame for his or her injuries, it appeared that such a belief would be strongly associated with declining the case. If lawyers believe that a jury will find their client responsible for their own injury, it makes sense that they would decline the case. For example, a Denver lawyer suggests that the issue of personal responsibility makes the hypothetical a "case [that] could easily be lost" (D-9). Believing that jurors would prefer to place responsibility on the parents of the child rather than on the manufacturer in order to create distance between the injury and the possibility of a similar injury occurring to their own child, he explains,

> Most jurors are looking for a way to explain how this could never happen to them or their kid. Most jurors will say, 'Well this wouldn't happen to me because I would have read the warnings myself.' 'This wouldn't happen to me because my kid reads warnings.' 'This wouldn't happen to me because my kid wouldn't do this excessively.' 'This wouldn't happen to me ... blah, blah, blah, blah, blah.' Nobody wants to embrace the fact or admit the fact that this could happen to them. It's too scary. It's too scary to embrace the fact that I as a juror have a 12-year-old, and next week I might have a 12-year-old that's a paraplegic. That's too much to emotionally handle, so everybody comes in and they try to mentally, in their own mind, explain away how this couldn't happen to them. And when they explain how it couldn't happen to them, they're finding some reason why they are different than the plaintiffs in front of them. (D-9)

Given D-9's careful consideration of a potential jury's reaction to the plaintiffs' behavior, and his own admission that the case might not win, one would expect him to decline the case. Yet he did not. D-9 accepted the case, as did many other lawyers who recognized the potential for the personal responsibility argument.

As shown in Table 6, believing that a jury might find his client to be at fault seems to matter little whether or not the lawyer accepted or declined the case. It is *not* worrying about personal responsibility that is strongly associated with accepting the case. In the following tables, the presence of a personal responsibility argument indicates that lawyers raised the issue of potential responsibility by a plaintiff, while "no personal responsibility argument" means that the issue was not even raised in their discussion of the hypothetical.

Several patterns are obvious in the interaction of reform status and personal responsibility. Table 7 shows the influence of "personal

Table 6. Personal Responsibility and Case Acceptance.

	Personal Responsibility Argument	No Personal Responsibility Argument
Declines case	44% ($n = 12$)	5%($n = 2$)
Accepts case	56% ($n = 15$)	95% ($n = 39$)
Total	$n = 27$	$n = 41$
	$\chi^2 = 15.57$***	

*$p<.05$, **$p<.01$, ***$p<.001$.

Table 7. Personal Responsibility and Case Acceptance by Reform Status.

Case Disposition	Reform States		Non-Reform States	
	Personal responsibility argument	No personal responsibility argument	Personal responsibility argument	No personal responsibility argument
Declines	38% ($n = 8$)	8% ($n = 1$)	67% ($n = 4$)	4% ($n = 1$)
Accepts	62% ($n = 13$)	92% ($n = 12$)	33% ($n = 2$)	96% ($n = 27$)
Total	$n = 21$	$n = 13$	$n = 6$	$n = 28$
	$\chi^2 = 3.804^+$		$\chi^2 = 15.715$***	

$^+p<.10$, *$p<.05$, **$p<.01$, ***$p<.001$.

responsibility" in how lawyers accept and decline cases in reform and non-reform states.

Lawyers in reform states are much more likely to believe that jurors in their state might blame the victim for their injury than they were to believe that jurors would regard their victim as "innocent." The majority of lawyers who mentioned the idea of contributory negligence were from reform states (21 reform state lawyers did so, whereas only six non-reform state lawyers did), suggesting that this mantra of the tort reform movement has certainly hit home with lawyers practicing in those states. The results suggest that lawyers in non-reform states are driving the dominant relationship between *not* mentioning personal responsibility and accepting the case. Lawyers in reform states were about equally likely to accept the case regardless of whether they mentioned personal responsibility or not.

6. SUMMARY AND CONCLUSION

When someone is harmed, who is ultimately responsible? Corporations that make dangerous products, or the consumers who use them? Answers to these questions have profound impacts on the case screening process and how justice is framed and experienced by lawyers in the aftermath of injury. This process, in turn, impacts the ultimate trajectory of disputes. Among the important findings in this research is that while lawyers in reform states and non-reform states were about equally likely to accept the hypothetical case with which they were presented, they approached the case in different ways, used different theories, and made different arguments in order to justify their acceptance of the case.

Lawyers in non-reform states had little concern over the jury blaming the victim for their injury, and readily accepted the case. In order for lawyers in reform states to accept the case, however, they *had* to make an argument about the irresponsibility of the product manufacturer. They had to focus on what their defendant did wrong by stressing the duty that corporations have to ensure and promote safety and well-being, especially the safety of children. The product manufacturer's behavior had to be called into question, characterized as compromising children's safety not out of necessity, but out of a motivation for profit and increased sales.

These findings are consistent with those from my research on the process by which lawyers screen cases and clients (Trautner, 2006). There I argued that tort reform leads plaintiffs' lawyers to change the party on which they select cases, from a focus on plaintiffs to a focus on the defendants. Because tort reformers have been successful in linking corporations and victimhood in a narrative that focuses on runaway juries and astronomical damage awards, to win cases in a reform state lawyers believe that it is corporate defendants that must be shown to be villains, *not* victims. Plaintiff's lawyers appear to be responding less to changes in law than to perceived changes in public attitudes and beliefs. Thus, plaintiff's lawyers want cases in which defendants can be easily shown to have been bad (negligent) and both legally and factually responsible for the outcome (liability). The important change is a shift from a traditional focus on plaintiffs to a new focus on defendants. The findings from this analysis are consistent with other findings that emphasize the characterization of defendants as critical to lawyers in reform states. Every reform state lawyer who made an argument about CSR accepted the case. However, there was no discernable pattern that distinguished reform state lawyers with regard to personal responsibility.

What, if any, are the implications for these different styles of case screening for the broader questions of how lawyers mediate access to the civil justice system? If lawyers are accepting roughly the same number of cases in reform and non-reform states (an arguable claim, to be sure), and are even accepting some of the same kinds of cases, as I have shown here, does it make any difference if they are doing so using different approaches and theories of liability?

One thing I have tried to show is the importance of studying lawyer decision-making and the case screening process comparatively. While scholars have long recognized the importance of legal environments for organizational and individual decision-making (e.g., Edelman, 1990, 1992; LoPucki, 1996; Sutton, Dobbin, Meyer, & Scott, 1994), and the effects of tort reform on lawyers' practices and access to justice (Baker, 2005; Daniels & Martin, 2000, 2001; Haltom & McCann, 2004; Van Hoy, 1999), most previous studies of personal injury lawyers and case screening have focused on lawyers in only one city or state (Daniels & Martin, 1999, 2000, 2001; Kritzer, 1997, 2004; Parikh, 2001; Van Hoy, 1999). Although Van Hoy (2004) argues that such studies are helpful because such analysis avoids getting bogged down in jurisdictional details, there are several obvious merits of comparative studies like the one I conducted.

Plaintiffs' trial lawyers across the United States, regardless of legal regulations or jurisdiction, screen cases carefully and attempt to accept "winnable" cases and decline "non-winnable" ones. Analyzing lawyers' responses to vignettes, I show that if acceptance rates alone are considered, lawyers do seem rather similar across jurisdictions. But as I have shown here and elsewhere (Trautner, 2006), how lawyers define cases as "good" and "bad" varies significantly by legal environment. The lack of comparative design in many previous studies appears to have masked some of the localized subtleties and nuances of lawyers' approaches to case screening, as well as the effects of tort reform on the case selection process. Comparative analysis that holds particular background "facts" comparable (as using vignettes does in this contrast between lawyer's case selections in reform and non-reform states does) can demonstrate how localized legal environments shape the ways lawyers frame cases. Beyond issues of case selection, those ways of framing cases and presenting them to juries can have dramatically different effects on the success, value, and overall impact of the case to the vitality and health of tort law in general.

To return to a theme raised earlier, this study also addresses the general disputing process. Fewer cases leave the lawyer's office than come into it, but we know very little about how that winnowing process occurs – especially from the perspective of lawyers themselves. I have tried to fill this gap. Understanding more about what happens in the office – that lawyers frame cases in ways they expect to appeal to what they believe the jury will find compelling in the context of their own localized legal cultures matters, both analytically and substantively. In reform states, that means lawyers frame their cases by downplaying sympathy and characteristics of the client and emphasizing the social irresponsibility of the defendant. In non-reform states, cases are framed by appealing to emotion, either by orchestrating sympathy for the plaintiff or by making a jury angry at the irresponsibility of the defendant.

My findings also suggest that more research is needed on the relationship between the practices of personal injury lawyers and a more complex and nuanced idea of legal environments. Following the work of Edelman (2008) and Edelman and Suchman (1997), among others, the legal environments of organizations (including law firms) are composed of more than legal rules and the direct cultural changes that accompany them. Lawyers and law firms interact with and interpret those legal rules in ways that transform the laws in action. As organizations respond to laws and legal changes, that is, they are simultaneously constructing new legal regimes and new institutionalized norms. I have begun to show here how lawyers actively construct the meaning of tort law and tort reform through their practices, including case evaluation. Formal changes to tort law, such as caps on non-economic damages, do not carry with them prescriptions of how lawyers are to respond to a newly enacted legal culture. Rather, lawyers give tort reform meaning through their interpretation of and response to those legal changes.

NOTES

1. I use "tort law" and "personal injury law" interchangeably. "Tort law" is a broad term that encompasses a wide range of wrongs, not all of which are physical. As Dobbs (2000) says, "Tort law is more than injury law because it includes rules for wrongs that cause economic and emotional injury even when no physical harm of any kind has been done" (pp. 9–10), for example, slander or libel. In contrast, people usually refer to "personal injury law" as the portion of tort law which deals directly with physical injuries caused by another (Dobbs, 2000).

2. Dobbs (2000, p. 1052) lists several activities that diminish one's quality of life, such as no longer being able to "see a sunset, or hear music, or engage in sexual activity."

3. Two lawyers did not receive the vignette due to time constraints, and neither responded to follow-up emails requesting their evaluation of the hypothetical case.

4. The vignette was written for a law school torts examination by Harry S. Gerla, Professor of Law, University of Dayton, who generously gave me permission to use the case in my interviews with lawyers.

5. Four different children's names were used in the vignette, which were then randomly assigned to lawyers. The names used were Greg or Anne Baker, or Tyrone or Tamika Jackson. These particular names were chosen based on previous research on names and labor market discrimination (Bertrand & Mullainathan, 2003).

ACKNOWLEDGMENTS

This research was made possible with funding from a Dissertation Improvement Grant from the National Science Foundation (SES #0451762). I am grateful to Debra Street and Rebecca Sandefur for their discerning feedback and suggestions. I also wish to thank Sarah Soule, Ronald Breiger, Calvin Morrill, and Patricia MacCorquodale for their comments on earlier drafts of this chapter.

REFERENCES

American Tort Reform Association (ATRA). (2003). Bringing justice to judicial hellholes. Available at www.atra.org/reports/hellholes/. Accessed 10 June 2004.

American Tort Reform Association (ATRA). (2004). Tort reform record. Available at www.atra.org/files.cgi/7802_Record6-04.pdf. Accessed 15 July 2004.

Baker, T. (2005). *The medical malpractice myth*. Chicago, IL: University of Chicago Press.

Barter, C., & Renold, E. (1999). The use of vignettes in qualitative research. *Social Research Update*, Issue 25. Department of Sociology, University of Surrey. Available at www.soc.surrey.ac.uk/sru/SRU25.html

Bertrand, M., & Mullainathan, S. (2003). *Are Emily and Greg more employable than Lakisha and Jamal? A field experiment on labor market discrimination*. Working Paper 03-22. Department of Economics, Massachusetts Institute of Technology.

Bogus, C. T. (2001). *Why lawsuits are good for America: Disciplined democracy, big business, and the common law*. New York, NY: New York University Press.

Boynton, P. D. (1999). Study: Massachusetts near the bottom in civil verdicts. *Massachusetts Lawyers Weekly*, December 13. Available at www.masslaw.com/reprints/breakstone 121399.htm. Accessed on 15 July 2004.

Burke, T. H. (2002). *Lawyers, lawsuits, and legal rights: The battle over litigation in American society*. Berkeley, CA: University of California Press.

Cohen, T. H., & Smith, S. K. (2004). Civil trial cases and verdicts in large counties, 2001. *Bureau of Justice Statistics Bulletin*. U.S. Department of Justice, Washington, DC.

Daniels, S., & Martin, J. (1999). 'It's Darwinism – Survival of the fittest': How markets and reputations shape the ways in which plaintiffs' lawyers obtain clients. *Law and Policy, 21*, 377–399.

Daniels, S., & Martin, J. (2000). 'The impact that it has had is between people's ears': Tort reform, mass culture, and plaintiffs' lawyers. *DePaul Law Review, 50*, 453–496.

Daniels, S., & Martin, J. (2001). 'We live on the edge of extinction all the time': Entrepreneurs, innovation and the plaintiffs' bar in the wake of tort reform. In: J. Van Hoy (Ed.), *Legal professions: Work, structure, and organization* (pp. 149–180). New York, NY: JAI Press.

Daniels, S., & Martin, J. (2001–2002). It was the best of times, it was the worst of times: The precarious nature of plaintiffs' practice in Texas. *Texas Law Review, 80*, 1781–1828.

Dobbs, D. B. (2000). *The law of torts*. St. Paul, MN: West Group.

Edelman, L. B. (1990). Legal environments and organizational governance: The expansion of due process in the American workplace. *American Journal of Sociology, 95*, 1401–1440.

Edelman, L. B. (1992). Legal ambiguity and symbolic structures: Organizational mediation of law. *American Journal of Sociology, 97*, 1531–1576.

Edelman, L. B. (2008). Overlapping fields and constructed legalities: The endogeneity of law. In: W. W. Powell & D. Jones (Eds), *Bending the bars of the iron cage: Institutional dynamics and processes*. Chicago, IL: University of Chicago Press.

Edelman, L. B., & Suchman, M. (1997). The legal environments of organizations. *Annual Review of Sociology, 23*, 479–515.

Ewick, P., & Silbey, S. S. (1998). *The common place of law: Stories from everyday life*. Chicago, IL: University of Chicago Press.

Felstiner, W. L. F., Abel, R. L., & Sarat, A. (1980–1981). The emergence and transformation of disputes: Naming, blaming, claiming .... *Law and Society Review, 15*, 631–654.

Finley, L. (1997). Female trouble: The implications of tort reform for women. *Tennessee Law Review, 64*, 847–880.

Grow, B. (2003). Expert witnesses under examination. *Chicago Tribune*, 23 July.

Haltom, W., & McCann, M. (2004). *Distorting the law: Politics, media, and the litigation crisis*. Chicago, IL: University of Chicago Press.

Harris Interactive. (2004). State liability systems ranking study: Final report. Conducted for the U.S. Chamber of Commerce and the U.S. Chamber Institute for Legal Reform (released on 8 March).

Kessler, D., & McClellan, M. (1996). Do doctors practice defensive medicine? *Quarterly Journal of Economics, 111*, 353–390.

Koenig, T. H., & Rustad, M. L. (2001). *In defense of tort law*. New York, NY: New York University Press.

Kritzer, H. (1996). *Rhetoric and reality ... Uses and abuses ... Contingencies and certainties: The American contingent fee in operation, Disputes Processing Research Program*. Working Paper 12-2. Institute for Legal Studies, University of Wisconsin Law School.

Kritzer, H. (1997). Contingency fee lawyers as gatekeepers in the American civil justice system. *Judicature, 81*, 22–29.

Kritzer, H. (2004). *Risks, reputations, and rewards: Contingency fee legal practice in the United States*. Stanford, CA: Stanford University Press.

Lofquist, W. S. (2002). Closing the courthouse door: Constructing undeservingness in the tort and habeas corpus reform movements. *Sociological Spectrum, 22*, 191–223.

LoPucki, L. M. (1996). Legal culture, legal strategy, and the law in lawyers' heads. *Northwestern University Law Review, 90*, 1498–1556.

Martin, J., & Daniels, S. (1997). Access denied: Tort reform is closing the courthouse door. *Trial, 33*, 26–31.

Merry, S. E. (1990). *Getting justice and getting even: Legal consciousness among working-class Americans*. Chicago, IL: University of Chicago Press.

Michelson, E. (2006). The practice of law as an obstacle to justice: Chinese lawyers at work. *Law and Society Review, 40*, 1–38.

Neff, J. A. (1979). Interaction versus hypothetical others: The use of vignettes in attitude research. *Sociology and Social Research, 64*, 105–125.

Nielsen, L. B. (2000). Situating legal consciousness: Experiences and attitudes of ordinary citizens about law and street harassment. *Law and Society Review, 34*, 201–236.

Parikh, S. (2001). *Professionalism and its discontents: A study of social networks in the plaintiff's personal injury bar*. Doctoral dissertation, Department of Sociology, University of Illinois at Chicago.

Schneyer, T. (2002). Empirical research with a policy payoff: Market dynamics for lawyers who represent plaintiffs for a contingent fee. *Texas Law Review, 80*, 1829–1838.

Sharkey, C. M. (2005). Unintended consequences of medical malpractice damage caps. *New York University Law Review, 80*, 391–512.

Sutton, J. R., Dobbin, F. R., Meyer, J. W., & Scott, W. R. (1994). The legalization of the workplace. *American Journal of Sociology, 99*, 944–971.

Trautner, M. N. (2006). *Screening, sorting, and selecting in complex personal injury cases: How lawyers screen cases and clients*. Doctoral dissertation, Department of Sociology, University of Arizona.

Van Hoy, J. (1997). *Franchise law firms and the transformation of personal legal services*. Westport, CT: Quorum Books.

Van Hoy, J. (1999). Markets and contingency: How client markets influence the work of plaintiffs' personal injury lawyers. *International Journal of the Legal Profession, 6*, 345–366.

Van Hoy, J. (2004). Can we generalize about plaintiffs' personal injury lawyers? Paper presented at the Law & Society Association annual meeting, Chicago, IL.

Vidmar, N. (1998). Maps, gaps, sociolegal scholarship, and the tort reform debate. In: P. Ewick, R. A. Kagan & A. Sarat (Eds), *Social science, social policy, and the law* (pp. 170–209). New York, NY: Russell Sage Foundation.

Zegart, D. (2004). The right wing's drive for 'tort reform'. *The Nation*, 25 October. Available at www.thenation.com/doc/20041025/zegart. Accessed on 1 January 2006.

WHEN BAD THINGS HAPPEN: TOWARD A SOCIOLOGY OF TROUBLES☆

Jennifer Earl

ABSTRACT

This article argues that troubles – including how they are identified, how responsibilities for their creation and remedy are assigned, and the actions people pursue to resolve them – are a central sociological concern that runs across a wide array of sub-fields. This article illustrates this point by examining how troubles are discussed in literatures including the sociology of law (or, more broadly, law and society), social movement studies, social problems, and organizational quality and conflict. Furthermore, this article argues that more is being lost by parceling these questions into disconnected sub-fields chosen based on the resolution process (i.e., use a court to resolve the problem, use a social movement, use policy-making) than is being intellectually gained. To make this point, common findings, questions, and quandaries that emerge from a broader examination of a sociology of troubles are discussed. The article recommends that a broader sociology of troubles be developed, bringing

☆This manuscript benefited from comments by Calvin Morrill, Rebecca Sandefur, Mayer Zald, and an anonymous reviewer, as well as from conversations with Robert MacCoun, and Stephen Hilgartner.

Access to Justice
Sociology of Crime, Law and Deviance, Volume 12, 231–254

ISSN: 1521-6136/doi:10.1108/S1521-6136(2009)0000012013

the welter of sub-fields studying troubles into smoother conversation, and recommends analyses that consider multiple resolution alternatives (e.g., filing a lawsuit, versus protesting, versus "lumping it").

Individuals and communities face a wide variety of problems, or "troubles." The processes of apprehending and assigning blame for troubles are complex and not well understood even though a number of areas of inquiry are concerned with them. When individuals and communities are able to identify troubles and potential causes, a wide array of potential solutions await them: they can "lump it" (i.e., not act to address their troubles); file a lawsuit; use self-help techniques; pursue psychological counseling; use available organizational processes for dispute resolution such as union bargaining, grievance hearings, or ombuds services; start or join a social movement; turn to their church for aid; or lobby their elected officials, among other options. Indeed, scholars from many other sub-fields could add means of redress that individuals and communities may use to deal with troubles and their perceived causes.

In some ways, all these may seem to state the obvious. Yet, this basic insight – that many sociologists and other social scientists share a central concern for troubles – is entirely side-stepped by the disciplinary structure of how we study troubles, which involves breaking trouble up by forms of redress and researching those forms of redress in isolation. For instance, the law and society literature wonders when individuals will "lump it" versus using folk or formal legal systems to address their woes and tries to understand how the "naming, blaming, claiming," process works (Felstiner, Abel, & Sarat, 1980–1981). Similarly, troubles, and collective attempts to address them, lie at the heart of the study of social movements. Although students of social movements often ask what will lead to the formation of a social movement, or to vacillations in support and/or mobilization of social movements, these questions boil down to questions about whether individuals and groups will realize a grievance and then pursue it through social movements or not. The industrial relations literature considers the role of unions and grievance proceedings in addressing troubles. The social problems literature considers when individual and community-wide problems will be re-interpreted as larger social problems. The sub-literature on moral panics asks when moral hysteria will affect the understanding of problems and the solutions to problems. The policy literature considers how institutional and government authorities realize troubles and then use institutional or legal policies to address those issues.

In this article I argue that we as scholars are losing more than we are gaining by divvying up troubles and forms of resolution into fairly discrete sub-fields instead of seeing this work as connected through a sociology of troubles.[1] I argue for continued research on troubles in related sub-fields, but with a much more explicit sense of connection to one another and sensitivity to emerging common findings, to potential ideas and mechanisms that might be imported into these conversations based on larger dialogues, and to the development of a sociology of troubles literature. To make this case, I make several related claims in this article:

(1) Trouble is a cross-cutting concept that appears in a number of sociological fields. I make this case by focusing on four large areas of inquiry: the sociology of law (or law and society literature more broadly), social movement studies, the study of social problems, and research on organizational quality and conflict.
(2) When findings are read through the larger lens of a sociology of troubles, common findings emerge that indicate fundamental, shared questions. For instance, why is inaction (i.e., lumping it) such a common response to troubles?
(3) When findings are read through the larger lens of a sociology of troubles, common gaps in understanding emerge that pose important challenges. For example, why is the study of "naming" so stunted across so many fields?
(4) By realizing the variety of areas that could sit around a common research table, we are also able to see the importance of asking questions that involve comparing multiple action alternatives. It seems likely that our collective understanding of how blaming and claiming works would change if we regularly studied types of redress competing against one another, such as filing suit versus joining a social movement versus lobbying for policy change. Currently, scholars tend to study how a single alternative such as filing a lawsuit competes against doing nothing (i.e., lumping it).
(5) When we begin to compare multiple action alternatives, we also open the possibility of being able to understand and explain choices between action alternatives such as explaining the conditions under which lawsuits might be more likely outcomes than social movements.

I argue that these five claims together represent a strong case for the development of a sociology of troubles and for the re-orientation of relatively discrete research areas to a collective dialogue on the sociology of troubles.

TROUBLE AS A CROSS-CUTTING CONCEPT

Sociologists acknowledge several central concepts – social organization, social stratification, social change, and social control, to name a few of the most prominent – as major concepts that bind the discipline and its research together. These concepts cannot be adequately studied by a small set of researchers constituting a particular sub-field. Indeed, these are themes that run through many sociological sub-fields and inform and are connected to contributions in "generalist" journals. Appeals to the general concepts are appeals for the applicability of ideas and research to other sub-fields, using these concepts as conduits through which research and theoretical innovations are imported and exported.

This article argues that troubles, and how they are realized and addressed, are cross-cutting concerns for sociologists, and, as such, troubles should be added as a general concern to our repertoire of overriding concepts. More to the point, this article calls for the manufacture of a sociology of troubles, which would run through and across the discipline, attempting to at least somewhat mitigate the intellectual costs associated with pretending that troubles can be cleanly cut into legal troubles, policy troubles, mental troubles, etc. and can be studied adequately without some ongoing discipline-wide discussion of troubles.

Following Felstiner et al.'s (1980–1981) lead, any study of troubles or reactions to troubles should share several central questions: (1) how do people and/or organizations come to assign negative subjective meanings to actions or situations (i.e., "naming"), (2) how do people and/or organizations assign responsibility for negatively defined actions or situations (i.e., "blaming"); and (3) how do people pursue grievances once they have been named and responsible parties identified (i.e., "claiming"). The following brief review of the four literatures demonstrates: (1) the importance of trouble and reactions to trouble in each of the fields focused on in this article and (2) the variability in theoretical and empirical answers provided by each literature to the three questions introduced by Felstiner et al. (1980–1981).

Law and Society Scholarship

The centrality of trouble to law and society scholarship is inescapable. Indeed, at their bedrock, folk and formal legal systems are systems designed to help people avoid trouble, and when that fails, to control and/or resolve troubles. Thus, if one looks at major works in the field, it is easy to spot the role of troubles in those works. For instance, in Ewick and Silbey's (1998) study of legal consciousness and the law in everyday life, they find that people use the legal system to try to address their troubles, whereas others attempt to avoid the legal system and the troubles it brings into their everyday lives. Merry (1990) examines the ways in which people attempt to transform "non-legal" troubles into legal issues in hopes of resolving their problems. Contributions to Sarat et al.'s (1998) edited volume, *Everyday Practices and Trouble Cases*, illustrate this same point across a broad range of law and society concerns.

Anthropologists of law have engaged trouble in a different way by famously using the "trouble case" as a methodological window into folk and unfamiliar, formal legal systems. Introduced by Llewellyn and Hoebel's (1941) *The Cheyenne Way*, and then further popularized in Nader and Todd's (1978) edited volume *The Disputing Process*, this methodology encourages analysts to look for signs of trouble and then follow how the trouble is handled through a social process.

"Naming, Blaming, and Claiming"

Felstiner et al. (1980–1981) build on the rich law and society history of work on trouble in their examination of dispute transformations. They argue that dispute transformation is the path between trouble and disputing and that this transformative process can be broken into three stages: naming, blaming, and claiming.

The naming process begins with the occurrence of an unperceived injurious experience (unPIE), which must be transformed into a perceived injurious experience (PIE) for a dispute to eventually occur. More generally, the authors are arguing that all disputes are social constructs whose parameters are defined by subjective understandings loosely tethered to objective happenings.[2] Thus, any objective happening can become the subject of a dispute, although not all, or even many, actually go through such a transformation.

Felstiner et al. (1980–1981) offer the example of a shipworker whose industrial contact with asbestos has caused undiagnosed cancer. This worker has an unPIE: the cancer exists but is not perceived. Once a diagnosis is made, there may be a PIE. However, the worker may feel the cancer is an expected and tolerable result of his/her labor in which case the unPIE would remain unchanged, even after the diagnosis. If the unPIE does become a PIE, then the first stage of the process has been accomplished: naming.

Felstiner et al. (1980–1981) argue that the naming process is not heavily studied because it poses several methodological problems. For instance, researchers' inquiries into unPIEs may unintentionally facilitate the transformation of an unPIE into a PIE. Additionally, it is not clear what categories of objective happenings constitute the grounds for a PIE.

Blaming is the next step, and it occurs when people assign responsibility for the creation and/or maintenance of a PIE. Felstiner et al. (1980–1981) argue that this stage is critical because many people are unable to attribute a cause for their PIE. Blaming may be impacted by a range of factors. For instance, Felstiner et al. (1980–1981) suggest that more highly educated persons or persons with extensive networks may be able to attribute fault to a concrete entity more easily than less educated persons or persons with lesser networks.

The third stage, claiming, occurs when people make claims against the allegedly responsible actor(s) for redress. Informal and formal legal disputing results only after claims are rebuffed by the allegedly responsible actor. At this point in the process, the dispute has been prefigured and need only fail to be resolved in order to advance.

Felstiner et al. (1980–1981) argue that there are at least five characteristics of the naming, blaming, and claiming process: (1) the process is subjective in the sense that actions or situations need not change physically (or "in reality") to change in meaning; (2) the process is unstable in the sense that meaning can change many times and at any time; (3) the process is reactive in that meanings often change in response to "communications, behavior, and expectations of a range of people, including opponents, agents, authority figures, companions, and intimates" (Felstiner et al., 1980–1981, p. 638); (4) the process is complex in that disputing involves "ambiguous behavior, faulty recall, uncertain norms, conflicting objectives, inconsistent values, and complex institutions" (Felstiner et al., 1980–1981, p. 638); and (5) the process is incomplete in that a dispute can always continue or be renewed.

Several scholars have built on or supplemented Felstiner et al.'s (1980–1981) basic argument. For instance, Conley and O'Barr (1998) argue that the naming stage should be broken into articulation and labeling, which reflects the authors' emphasis on linguistic process. This would change the framework from naming, blaming, and claiming to articulation, labeling, blaming, and claiming.

Miller and Sarat (1980–1981) empirically model the original naming, blaming, and claiming process with data from the Civil Litigation Research Project. This project conducted telephone surveys regarding legal needs and usage. However, Miller and Sarat's (1980–1981) findings suggest that the variables they are able to incorporate into each model account for only a small fraction of the total variation.[3]

Finally, Coates and Penrod (1981) attempt to identify psychological theories that could augment explanations of the identification of grievances. Specifically, they review relative deprivation, perceived control, equity, and attribution theories and conclude that each offers some possible contribution to a study of the psychological determinants of grievance identification.

Social Movement Studies

The study of social movements is concerned with unpacking what causes people to participate in collective change-oriented action, among other questions. Even though McCarthy and Zald (1973, 1977) so famously argued that grievances are virtually ubiquitous and yet social movements are not, leading one to believe grievances may be necessary but insufficient conditions for protest, troubles and their relationship to collective action remain at the heart of social movement studies.

In considering a sociology of troubles, though, two areas of inquiry within social movement studies seem particularly promising: the study of grievances themselves (e.g., Useem, 1985; Useem, 1980; Walsh & Warland, 1983) and the study of framing, which examines how subjective understandings are created and transformed (e.g., Snow & Benford, 1988; Snow, Rochford, Worden, & Benford, 1986). Both areas in the study of social movements have tried to explain participation patterns and differential recruitment in social movements.[4] Fig. 1 maps this and other literatures onto the naming, blaming, and claiming process.

Grievances

Early explanations of social movements were simple: people with grievances and psychological dispositions geared toward protest joined movements, whereas people who lacked grievances and/or psychological dispositions for movement action steered clear of protest (Garner, 1997). However, the unquestioned role of grievances in social movement mobilization was attacked by the resource mobilization (RM) school. RM researchers argued that since grievances seemed to be more ubiquitous than either social movements or social movement participation, grievances alone could not explain the rise of social movements or the motivation for social movement participation (McCarthy & Zald, 1977). Furthermore, RM and other major

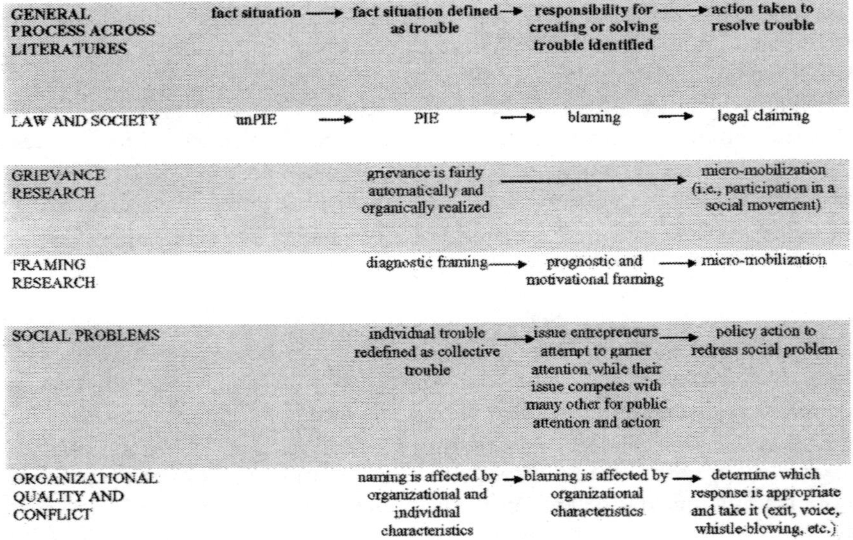

Fig. 1. Summary of Naming, Blaming, and Claiming across Literatures.

theories, such as the political process approach, eschewed the psychological and "irrational" orientation of prior research in favor of more rationalistic, sociological models (Garner, 1997).

As RM and political process came to dominate the social movements literature, research increasingly questioned the direct connection between grievances and protest involvement and focused instead on alternative determinants of movement mobilization. However, three lines of research continued to directly consider grievances (Buechler, 2004). First, Useem's work on Boston's anti-busing movement (1980) and a New Mexico prison riot (1985) argue for a breakdown model where increasing grievances lead to protest activity. Useem (1980) describes two versions of breakdown theory in the literature: (1) the mass society version where social disorganization directly increases protest and (2) the discontent version where social disorganization increases discontent and discontent then increases protest. Useem's (1980) anti-busing work doesn't support the mass society version of breakdown theory. However, his research does support relative deprivation models of grievances, indicating that grievances are important to the movement mobilization process (Useem, 1980). His later work offered more support for a breakdown model. Useem (1985) finds support for the discontent version of the breakdown model in his study of a major New Mexico prison riot. He argues that a change in the social organization of the prison, ushered in by a change in wardens, created distrust and anger between inmates. According to Useem, the tight fit between grievances and protest activity is demonstrated not only by the occurrence of the riot but also by the form as well: "The fragmenting of bonds among inmates appears to have contributed to the weak and chaotic structures of leadership among inmates during the riot, as well as to the brutal attacks of some inmates against other inmates" (Useem, 1985, p. 685).

Walsh and his collaborators represent a second line of grievance research that is focused on "suddenly imposed grievances." Walsh and Warland's (1983) study of Three-Mile Island (TMI) area anti-nuclear activists and free-riders finds that a key difference between activists and free-riding supporters is that activists are far more likely to have been evacuated from their homes than free-riding supporters. The intense and sudden nature of evacuation is a special type of grievance that spurs people to join anti-nuclear protest groups. Thus, while in general grievances may not lead to social movement participation or mobilization, Walsh and Warland (1983) argue that the occurrence of suddenly imposed grievances will lead to social movement involvement.

A final group of researchers argue that the grievance models of both Useem (1980, 1985) and Walsh and Warland (1983) can be subsumed under another model of grievances: grievances which involve quotidian disruption (Snow, Cress, Downey, & Jones, 1998). Quotidian disruption occurs when either cognitive scripts used in daily life are disrupted or behavioral scripts (or patterns) used in daily life are disrupted. Snow et al. (1998) argue that grievances founded in quotidian disruption lead to protest, whereas other types of grievances may have less of an effect on social movement involvement. In discussing previous work on grievances, Snow et al. (1998) argue that Useem's (1985) prison riot was not spurred by social disorganization per se but rather by the sudden disruption of inmate routines by a new warden. With respect to Walsh and Warland's (1983) research, Snow et al. (1998) argue that evacuation represents a major disruption to daily behavioral routines.[5]

To summarize, traditional grievance research and more recent grievance research focus on the effect of trouble in movement mobilization, although approaches differ in whether they argue all grievances, or only certain types of grievances, lead to protest participation. Importantly, these works tend to treat troubles as more or less objectively existing and motivating action without a great deal of interpretative work. In Felstiner et al.'s (1980–1981) parlance, the transition from an unPIE to a PIE is relatively unexamined by this work; instead, the focus is on the impact of a PIE (or certain types of PIEs) on action.

Framing

Research on framing complicates the connection between grievances and social movement participation by problematizing the processes by which potential movement actors come to apprehend trouble, understand what can be done about trouble, and motivate themselves and others to react to trouble. This line of research suggests that in any given situation, grievance or trouble must be subjectively understood and interpreted before action can occur. In Felstiner et al.'s terms, framing is concerned with the interpretative processes that transform an unPIE to a PIE and that shape how people believe they should blame and claim about that PIE.

Frame theorists argue that a key determinant of social movement participation is the resonance of movement frames with would-be participants or "frame alignment" in the literature's parlance. Snow and Benford (1988, p. 198) argue that frames "assign meaning to and interpret ... relevant events and conditions in ways that are intended to mobilize potential adherents and constituents, to garner bystander support, and to demobilize antagonists." When frame alignment occurs, movement mobilization results (Snow & Benford, 1988, p. 198).

In an earlier paper, Snow et al. (1986) detailed four processes through which frame alignment could occur: frame bridging, frame amplification, frame extension, and frame transformation. Frame bridging occurs when two or more previously unconnected frames regarding a problem or issue are linked together into a single, new frame, or when social movement organizations connect with popular concerns through outreach efforts. Frame amplification occurs when an existing frame that relates to a problem or issue is clarified or invigorated. The authors suggest frame amplification is empirically found in one of two forms: value amplification or belief amplification. Value amplification occurs when a personal value becomes more important and is highlighted by movement framing. Belief amplification happens when relationships between two things (e.g., a problem and the believed cause of the problem) are strengthened through social movement framing. Frame extension occurs when social movements include already held values or interests of potential adherents in movement frames even where they would otherwise be non-essential. For instance, Snow et al. (1986) cite the use of rock-and-roll bands at peace rallies to increase attendance and garner support from otherwise uninterested or unaffiliated people as an example of frame extension. Finally, frame transformation occurs when existing individual beliefs are incongruent with movement aims and new values or beliefs must be nurtured by movement frames in order to transplant previously held beliefs or values in potential participants. Snow et al. (1986) suggest that religious movements might be common users of frame transformation.

No matter how frame alignment is achieved, three core framing tasks exist and must be successfully executed if participation is to be encouraged: (1) frames must diagnose the grievance or trouble to which change-oriented action is directed (i.e., "diagnostic framing"); (2) frames must propose solutions to the grievance or trouble identified (i.e., "prognostic framing"); and (3) frames must motivate action (i.e., "motivational framing"; Snow & Benford, 1988).

At the broadest level, these core framing tasks resemble Felstiner et al.'s naming, blaming, and claiming arguments: Snow and his collaborators' work suggests that trouble may not be immediately identifiable and that grievances have to be framed so that they can be apprehended and then acted upon. Furthermore, action requires a guide such that even when trouble is apprehended, frames need to suggest what is to be done to rectify a situation. However, in the details, there are some differences: diagnostic frames include both naming and some blaming elements, whereas prognostic frames include both blaming and claiming elements, and motivational frames are not considered at all by Felstiner et al. (1980–1981).

The Study of Social Problems

The study of social problems has also fundamentally concerned itself with trouble and reactions to trouble. Although objectivists and constructivists dispute whether particular troubles or social problems have always "existed" or are "constructed" (Best, 1987; Woolgar & Pawlunch, 1985), many researchers assume that situations or actions can at some times be understood as troubled whereas at other times the same situation or action is accepted unproblematically. For instance, in Pfohl's (1977) classic work on child-abuse, it is clear that where child-abuse is now understood to be a social problem, the same physical acts were once understood to be a normal form of discipline or, at least, the subject of private parental discretion. Thus, a central question in the literature is under what conditions will actions or situations have negative subjective meanings attached to them and what are the action-oriented results of such meanings (e.g., Hilgartner & Bosk, 1988; Kingdon, 1995).

Theoretical answers to these questions vary broadly. Instead of giving an overview of the entire theoretical space of social problems research, I illustrate this point with reference to several major works. Best (1987) argues that social problems are identified by key claims-makers who use public story-telling techniques such as atrocity tales to publicize the breadth and severity of particular social problems. Fineman (1991) elaborates on the role of atrocity tales in the development of contemporary divorce practices as a feminist social problem. Other theorists stress the role of the media (e.g., Kingdon, 1995), "focusing events" (e.g., Kingdon, 1995), social interaction (e.g., Maynard, 1988), language (e.g., Maynard, 1988), or moral or movement entrepreneurs (e.g., Jenkins, 1983).

In contrast to many of the models based on claims-making and the skillfulness with which claims-making is completed, Hilgartner and Bosk (1988) suggest a public arenas model of social problems where social problems are seen as competing with one another for scarce public attention and resources. Although Hilgartner and Bosk agree that individuals concerned with social problems must make claims to capture scarce public attention, what determines the rise and fall of specific social problems on the public agenda is not the quality of claims-making per se, but rather the relative effectiveness of particular claims and problems in competing with other social problems for limited public attention.

Across this field of research, attention tends to focus on the individual process of coming to view one's own problems as social problems, and the collective process of taking notice, and then potentially addressing social problems. Read in relation to the areas that I have already reviewed, this literature has much in common with the social movements framing literature in that they both examine how to frame a PIE as a collective concern – something we might think of as a form of collective or social naming – versus the potentially individual naming Felstiner et al. (1980–1981) discuss. However, although the questions social problems scholars and some social movement scholars ask are similar, the theoretical answers have differed in these two literatures.

Organizational Quality and Conflict

Although Hirschman's (1970) ground-breaking *Exit, Voice, and Loyalty* is perhaps the most noted book on these topics, a number of industrial relations and organizational resistance researchers have asked how customers apprehend and react to goods and services of poor quality and/or declines in quality over time (Best & Andreasen, 1977; King & McEvoy, 1976; McNeil, Nevin, Trubek, & Miller, 1979; Nader, 1980; Ross & Littlefield, 1978; Warland, Heirman, & Willits, 1975) and how employees apprehend and react to various problems in their workplace (Edelman, 2005; Farrell & Rusbult, 1992; Hebdon & Stern, 1998; Higgibotham & Weber, 1999; Hoffmann, 2005; LaNuez & Jermier, 1994; Marshall, 2003, 2005; Martin & Meyerson, 1998; Rothschild & Miethe, 1994; Saunders, Sheppard, Knight, & Roth, 1992). Instead of reviewing this sprawling area generally, I focus my review on research that speaks to the naming, blaming, claiming process specifically.

Research on consumer dissatisfaction has examined what Felstiner et al. (1980–1981) would refer to as the naming process (e.g., Best & Andreasen, 1977; King & McEvoy, 1976; McNeil et al., 1979; Ross & Littlefield, 1978; and Warland et al., 1975). Researchers in this area tend to generate a list of possible grievances and ask whether respondents have experienced any of the grievances in a given amount of time. Then, using variables such as age, education, income, or socio-economic status, analysts try to explain which respondents reported such grievances. However, the research design does not allow for an understanding of grievance-related processes, simply an understanding of either who is most likely to actually have problems or who is most likely to understand any given situation as a problem.

Similarly, research on employee grievances has until recently assumed that employees can readily identify problems. That is, the literature had assumed that naming and blaming happened unproblematically and the real decision facing employees was about claiming. However, recent work by authors examining sexual harassment and employment discrimination more broadly have found that organizational structures can affect how naming occurs. For instance, Marshall (2003) examines how workplace polices and practices affect how women come to identify sexual harassment in their workplace. Similarly, Edelman (2005, p. 349) argues that managers can shape employees conceptions of legal rights, or employees' legal consciousness, such that "events that might otherwise seem problematic may be viewed as normal, proper, and fair." Thus, organizations may shape whether problems are identified and how problems are understood.

Research on claiming has also been conducted. Hirschman (1970), for instance, suggests that employees who are loyal to an organization are less likely to exit the organization and more likely to voice concerns over quality declines in hopes of rectifying the decline. Saunders et al. (1992) examined Hirschman's claims and argued that managerial openness to employee voice also impacted the level of employee reports of dissatisfaction. Specifically, when supervisors where thought to be responsive to prior complaints, approachable, and had longer tenures, employees were more likely to raise complaints. Farrell and Rusbult (1992) found that (1) job satisfaction increased employee voice and loyalty and decreased exit and neglect; (2) alternative employment opportunities increased exit and voice and decreased neglect; and (3) high investments in jobs or organizations increased voice and loyalty and decreased neglect. Tucker (1993) argued that temporary employees were less likely to voice complaints than more long-term employees because they lacked organizational aspirations, loyalty, or commitment; they had less time to accumulate grievances; they lacked strong alliances that could protect them from vengeful and unreceptive supervisors; and they were often organizationally marginalized.

Other researchers studying claiming have gone beyond "voice." Rothschild and Miethe (1994) argue that whistle-blowing usually occurs after an employee voices concern to a supervisor and is either ignored or persecuted for the complaint. In contrast to the portrait painted by companies, whistle-blowers according to Rothschild and Miethe (1994) are often dedicated employees who begin the whistle-blowing process by reporting a problem to their supervisor with the expectation that the problem will be remedied. It is only when the problem remains or when the employee is persecuted that those employees become whistle-blowers.

Marshall (2005) and Hoffman (2005) examine how organizational structures, practices, and policies affect both the blaming and the claiming processes. Hoffman (2005), for example, suggests that in relatively egalitarian organizational structures, women tend to use formal grievance procedures whereas men have access to informal remedies. Marshall (2005) shows that where women feel managers are not open to sexual harassment claims that women are less likely to complain about harassment and are more likely to have a narrower vision of their legal rights than either organizational policies or laws provide. This, in turn, affects how women pursue remedies for sexual harassment.

Perhaps closest to the broad comparative concerns of this article, Hebdon and Stern (1998) argue that a trade-off exists between striking and grievance arbitrations such that when strikes are prohibited, grievance arbitrations increase. As discussed in more detail below, they more broadly argue that scholars should be studying trade-offs between types of actions in claiming.

Summary Comparison of Research Traditions

Although this division of labor between sub-fields may be necessary in the course of everyday scholarship, this article argues that a more general awareness of trouble as being a central sociological concept and an orienting concern would have numerous benefits for sociology as a discipline and, conversely, that the continuing failure to explicitly orient research findings, at least at some minimal level, to the thread of trouble has a number of serious theoretical costs.

Identifying Common Findings: "Lumping It" Dominates

Taking a step back from the details of these sub-fields allows one to identify common findings across areas. The first and most obvious convergence of findings is that people most often tend to take no ameliorative action in the face of troubles. In Felstiner et al.'s (1980–1981) parlance, most unPIEs and even most PIEs never eventuate into lawsuits (Hensler, 1998), social movement participation (Oegema & Klandermans, 1994), policy solutions or other forms of public recognition and address of social problems (Hilgartner & Bosk, 1988), or organizational redress (Hirschman, 1970; Nader, 1980). One thing a sociology of troubles must aim to account for is why doing nothing is the most common option across all of these areas.

Furthermore, having noticed the prevalence of inaction as a finding across divergent sub-fields, some area-specific explanations for inaction likely deserve further inspection and interrogation. For instance, social movement scholars have argued that a key problem for mobilizing participants is overcoming the free-rider problem (Marwell & Oliver, 1993). Because social movements tend to produce public goods, it is argued that it is individually rational to free-ride off of others' efforts and enjoy the public good that is produced despite one's own non-participation. Selective incentives or other types of personal motivators are seen as necessary to overcome this dilemma (Olson, 1998 [1965]).

However, even forms of trouble resolution that have direct, personal rewards show high levels of lumping it. For instance, Hensler (1998) reviews research on torts, arguing that the clear finding in this literature is that the vast majority of potential plaintiffs lump it. Furthermore, seeking personal gain does not seem to be the only and perhaps not even the primary motivator for pursuing tort litigation. Instead, Hensler (1998) points to research showing that seeking a sense of fairness, an apology, and prevention of similar troubles for someone else in the future weigh as heavily, if not more heavily, in plaintiffs' minds as they pursue their suit (although fees weigh heavily in most attorneys' minds according to this same research).

If Olson's free-rider logic were correct, one would expect higher action rates where personal gain would result, as would be true in tort litigation. And yet, not only is the rate not high for tort litigation, plaintiffs that do go forward highlight other rationales for their suits beyond personal or monetary gain. Thus, although the free-rider dilemma seems to make sense in the limited context of non-participation in social movements, it does not fit with more general non-participation rates in the face of trouble. Parsimony would favor any explanation that could explain the prevalence of "lumping it" generally, not just failing to participate in a social movement. Scholars working on a sociology of troubles should work toward such a parsimonious explanation.

Identifying Common Gaps in Theory and Research

A common focus on a sociology of troubles would also help to reveal which points in the naming, blaming, and claiming process are relatively understudied and/or what kinds of explanations or dynamics have received too scant attention across sub-fields. To illustrate, I briefly discuss three shortcomings that a broader sociology of troubles should attempt to address.

First, although most of the literatures make a nod to the subjectivity and recursiveness of the naming, blaming, and claiming process, few researchers have tackled this tough issue. Felstiner et al. (1980–1981) halt their discussion of the subjective and possibly recursive nature of naming, blaming, and claiming after merely acknowledging that dispute transformation is inherently unstable and unfolding. Similarly, social movement scholars studying frames have acknowledged that a dialogic process may be at work, but little published work has examined this in more detail (save notable examples such as Steinberg, 1999). The social problems literature takes as given that a social problem's definition will change over time, but the literature has an almost uniform focus on the rise of social problems and rarely examines the fall of social problems (save the classic by Hilgartner & Bosk, 1988). Industrial conflict theorists' emphasis on claiming has exempted them from even having to handle the naming and blaming process as of yet.

Second, the transition from an unPIE to a PIE may be the least understood part of the naming, blaming, claiming process. Felstiner et al. (1980–1981) note that this transition has to occur, but do not theorize much beyond that. Scholarship on grievances in social movements don't problematize the naming process, instead they focus on what types of PIEs will produce subsequent action. The framing literature does address naming, but it assumes that some people (often movement organizers) already acknowledge a PIE, leaving naming questions to focus on how others may be persuaded to see the same PIE. The same could be said of the social problems literature, where the focus is on how individuals redefine their PIEs as social problems and how moral entrepreneurs encourage others to acknowledge that a social PIE exists. Work on organizational quality and conflicts doesn't focus on naming explicitly, making most of its contributions instead around claiming processes. Perhaps as Felstiner et al. (1980–1981) suggest, this might be due to the methodological problems that face researchers interested in that transition. Yet, if a larger sociology of troubles were striving to make progress on these issues, certainly methodological progress, and then theoretical and empirical progress, would follow from those collective efforts.

Third, the social psychology of trouble is not well-developed. Although some work has been completed (e.g., Coates & Penrod, 1981; Snow et al., 1998), no systematic theoretic statements have been developed. One promising lead might be Coates and Penrod's (1981) discussion of attribution theory. They argue that whether or not a person assigns blame to him or herself or to others is critical in the blaming process. If blame is assigned to oneself, no further dispute is likely.[6] Conversely, if blame is assigned to some other identifiable actor or agent, a dispute has a higher likelihood of progressing. They also argue that this process of self- or other-blaming will turn on the stability of grievances (infrequent and sporadic grievances versus constant grievances) and on the intentionality attributed to the grievance (the grievance resulted from a willful act or an accident).

Another promising lead might be drawn from Snow et al.'s (1998) incorporation of Kahneman and Tversky's (1979) work on risk assessment and loss. Kahneman and Tversky (1979) argue that losses weigh more on people's minds than gains, leading Snow et al. (1998) to suspect that the threat of loss should spur action more than the possibility of gain. Snow et al. (1998) limit their application to grievances and social movement mobilization, but Kahneman and Tversky's work might contribute to a larger social psychological approach to naming, blaming, and claiming processes. Although these two arguments are potential starting points for needed inquiries, an emerging sociology of troubles could benefit from the development of a more refined social psychology of troubles.

Understanding Whether and How Alternative Forms of Redress Compete

An advantage of a larger, consolidated study of trouble would be the consideration of competing claiming and action options. In their study of strike bans and grievance arbitrations, Hebdon and Stern (1998) argued that studies in industrial conflict rarely consider trade-offs between different forms of conflict, resistance, and voice. This oversight prompted their study of the effect of strike bans on the level of grievance arbitrations. They found that such a trade-off exists, at least in the sectors they studied.

If trade-offs and competition are rarely considered within the industrial conflict literature, they are almost never considered *between* literatures. For instance, when social movements scholars discuss movement mobilization and participation, they often ask the question such that free-riding (i.e., no action) and movement participation are the only options available to interested or concerned persons. Only rarely have social movement scholars clarified in a more realistic way the set of actions that individuals are choosing from (see McVeigh, 1999 for a comparison of institutionalized action and protest). Other social movement scholars consider frames that either make claims for movement participation or do not. Similarly, legal scholars assume formal legal redress, informal disputing, or avoidance/withdrawal are the only alternatives available to aggrieved parties.

Hebdon and Stern (1998) argue that such oversights in the industrial conflict literature may have resulted in incomplete or mis-specified theories. Furthermore, the authors argue that "if various conflict forms are in fact linked, the failure to take these relationships into account in empirical work may cause errors in ... estimation" (Hebdon & Stern, 1998, p. 205). Applied more broadly, it is reasonable to assume that various types of claims compete (claims for social movement action, claims for organizational action, claims for legal action) and that various types of action compete with one another (social movement participation, legal redress, organizational sabotage). Thus, if Hebdon and Stern (1998) are correct, the theoretical and empirical insights of several literatures may presently be partial at best and mis-specified at worst.

Explaining Likelihoods of Different Forms of Redress

Not only does the omission of competition between types of claims and actions open the possibility of mis-specification, this omission also represents an untapped area for theoretical innovation. If there is competition between types of claims and actions, it is reasonable to assume that with future research efforts, scholars could develop and test hypotheses explaining this competition.

As an example, the following hypothesis speaks to this issue:

H1. Individual lawsuits are more likely as forms of claiming and action when relatively unambiguous legal rights and procedures exist for a specific type of dispute, whereas claims for collective action or claims regarding the existence of a social problem are more likely when legal rights and/or legal procedures in an area are unclear.

This hypothesis is likely because one-shot legal litigants are not likely to play for rules, but rather are likely to rely on the existing state of case law and statutes to make their claims (Galanter, 1974). Furthermore, social movements are often attempting to gain further legal rights, or clarify existing uncertainty in order to make legal gains (Rosenberg, 1991). Finally, without relatively unambiguous legal rights and/or procedures for handling an issue, litigants can face a great deal of trouble in transforming their non-legal troubles into legally actionable claims (Merry, 1990). But, whether one agrees with this particular hypothesis or not, the ability to generate and test such a hypothesis will lead to scholarly gains in a more consolidated study of troubles and also develop each distinct literature more fully.

CONCLUSION

The first claim of this article was that trouble is a cross-cutting concept in sociology, illustrated here by discussions of troubles in four sub-fields. I argue that academic progress would be best served by considering this research part of a larger sociology of troubles, which draws on and contributes to these four sub-fields, among others.

Through a review of relevant work from these four sub-fields, this article has also demonstrated that a fair amount of variation exists between these four literatures in terms of their theoretical and empirical attentions and findings. Where some literatures are stronger in explaining naming and blaming, other literatures have excelled in researching claiming. Where some questions have been handled well by all four literatures, some questions have been little touched by any literature.

The simultaneous overlap and variation demonstrated by these literatures further supports my call for the development of a sociology of troubles. Whether construed as a scholarly conversation informally carried out or as a formal scholarly project, consolidating studies of trouble and reactions to trouble would have many advantages. In this article, I outlined four such advantages: (1) the ability to identify common, robust findings across sub-fields addressing troubles, such as the prevalence of lumping it, and the consequent hope of explaining these findings more parsimoniously once they are identified; (2) the ability to identify common gaps in the theorizing and research across sub-fields addressing troubles, such as identifying the need for the development of a social psychology of troubles and more research on core naming processes; (3) the potential to compare action alternatives to one another in research versus comparing a single form of redress to lumping it as occurs in most sub-fields now; and (4) the potential to hypothesize about and more broadly explain choices between different action alternatives.

Additionally, a sociology of troubles would help each sub-field as well. For instance, the consolidation of studies of trouble should allow literatures to more easily poach major empirical or theoretical insights from one another. A researcher in industrial conflict interested in embarking on research regarding the naming of industrial problems would be well-served by reading research on framing, social movement grievances, and legal dispute transformation processes. However, without a consolidated conversation about studies of trouble, this enterprising industrial conflict researcher may not soon locate relevant existing research.

I close by considering the implications of progress on a sociology of troubles – and the naming, blaming, claiming questions that would be a touchstone for the area – for improving "access to justice." Felstiner et al. (1980–1981) make this connection in their work on dispute transformation, arguing:

> the waiver of court costs, the creation of small claims courts, the movement toward informalism, and the provision of legal services ... The ostensible goal of these reforms is to eliminate bias in the ultimate transformation: disputes into lawsuits. If, however, as we suspect, these very unequal distributions have skewed the earlier stages by which injurious experiences become disputes, then current access to justice efforts will only give additional advantages to those who have already transformed their experiences into disputes. (p. 637)

This is similar to the concern raised by Galanter (1974) when he described the "legal iceberg": so much of what could be producing unequal access to justice happens before people arrive at a lawyer's office or courthouse. If there are processes that lead people to never see themselves as potential litigants, access to the courts is immaterial.

Although sociologists of law often mean access to formal and fair legal dispute resolution when they discuss access to justice, it is possible to expand what we mean by this term through a sociology of troubles. Indeed, each of the non-legal fields that I discussed has important orientations to some sense of personal or social justice or fairness. Social movements are often oriented toward some sense of social justice, as are people working to raise awareness of, and to address, social problems. People in disputes with organizations – whether over products they have purchased or the conditions of their employment – are also seeking a sense of fairness, or justice. Understanding and improving access to fairness and justice in this broader context – where justice might be delivered by a court, a mediator, or a policy-maker who responds to a social movement or the rise of a social problem, or may be delivered in an office building to customers or workers – would be an important contribution of an emerging sociology of troubles.

NOTES

1. I am not using the "sociology of trouble" as Emerson and Messinger (1977) intended. Whereas Emerson and Messinger specifically limit their call to the study of individual troubles and deviance, I allow the "level of trouble" to vary from individual problems to collective troubles. This article will also move away from Emerson and Messinger's "micro-politics" approach and examine the macro- and meso-politics of trouble.
2. Objective and subjective are not juxtaposed to make a philosophical claim about the nature of apprehension and reality. I acknowledge an ongoing debate within philosophy (and many other disciplines) as to the possibility of objectivity. Rather, the use of the terms is meant to suggest that while a factual situation can remain constant, the subjective understanding of that factual situation can change.
3. The other literatures reviewed in this article suggest additional variables that could be included to improve these kinds of analyses, and the literatures also suggest that alternative outcomes beyond litigation need to be considered.
4. Differential recruitment examines why some people participate in movements and others do not, assuming ideological compatibility with a movement.
5. Studying the relative importance of "threats" to mobilization has been increasingly important in the study of social movements (e.g., Einwohner, 2003; Goldstone & Tilly, 2001), but elaborating the relationship between threats, grievances, and troubles is beyond the scope of this article.

6. Several social movement scholars also acknowledge that self-blame stymies mobilization while blaming others increases mobilization (for instance, Snow et al., 1998). However, how people come to blame themselves or others is not specifically problematized in the literature.

REFERENCES

Best, A., & Andreasen, A. (1977). Consumer response to unsatisfactory purchases: A survey of perceiving defects, voicing complaints, and obtaining redress. *Law and Society Review, 11*, 701–742.

Best, J. (1987). Rhetoric in claims-making: Constructing the missing children problem. *Social Problems, 34*, 101–121.

Buechler, S. M. (2004). The strange career of strain and breakdown theories of collective action. In: D. A. Snow, S. A. Soule & H. Kriesi (Eds), *The blackwell companion to social movements* (pp. 47–66). Oxford: Blackwell Publishing.

Coates, D., & Penrod, S. (1981). Social psychology and the emergence of disputes. *Law and Society Review, 15*, 655–680.

Conley, J. M., & O'Barr, W. (1998). *Just words: Law, language, and power*. Chicago: University of Chicago Press.

Edelman, L. B. (2005). Law at work: The endogenous construction of civil rights. In: L. B. Nielsen & R. Nelson (Eds), *Handbook of employment discrimination research* (pp. 337–352). The Netherlands: Springer.

Einwohner, R. L. (2003). Opportunity, honor, and action in the warsaw ghetto uprising of 1943. *American Journal of Sociology, 109*, 650–675.

Emerson, R. M., & Messinger, S. L. (1977). The micro-politics of trouble. *Social Problems, 25*, 121–134.

Ewick, P., & Silbey, S. S. (1998). *The common place of law: Stories from everyday life*. Chicago, IL: University of Chicago Press.

Farrell, D., & Rusbult, C. E. (1992). Exploring the exit, voice, loyalty, and neglect typology: The influence of job satisfaction, quality of alternatives, and investment size. *Employee Responsibilities and Rights Journal, 5*, 201–218.

Felstiner, W. L. F., Abel, R. L., & Sarat, A. (1980–1981). The emergence and transformation of disputes: Naming, blaming, claiming. *Law and Society Review, 15*, 631–654.

Fineman, M. A. (1991). *The illusion of equality: The rhetoric and reality of divorce reform*. Chicago: University of Chicago Press.

Galanter, M. (1974). Why the haves come out ahead: Speculations on the limits of legal change. *Law and Society, 9*, 95–160.

Garner, R. (1997). Fifty years of social movement theory: An interpretation. In: R. Garner & J. Tenuto (Eds), *Social movement theory and research: An annotated bibliographical guide* (pp. 1–58). Lanham, MD: Scarecrow.

Goldstone, J. A., & Tilly, C. (2001). Threat (and opportunity): Popular action in state response in the dynamics of contentious action. In: R. Aminzade, J. A. Goldstone, D. McAdam, E. J. Perry, W. H. J. Sewell, S. Tarrow & C. Tilly (Eds), *Silence and voice in the study of contentious politics* (pp. 179–194). Cambridge: Cambridge University Press.

Hebdon, R. P., & Stern, R. N. (1998). Tradeoffs among expressions of industrial conflict: Public sector strike bans and grievance arbitrations. *Industrial and Labor Relations Review, 51*, 204–221.

Hensler, D. R. (1998). The real world of tort litigation. In: A. Sarat, M. Constable, D. Engel, V. Hans & S. Lawrence (Eds), *Everyday practices and trouble cases* (pp. 155–176). Chicago: Northwestern University Press.

Higgibotham, E., & Weber, L. (1999). Perceptions of workplace discrimination among black and white professional-managerial women. In: I. Browne (Ed.), *Latinas and African-American women at work: Race, gender, and economic inequality* (pp. 327–353). New York: Russell Sage Foundation.

Hilgartner, S., & Bosk, C. L. (1988). The rise and fall of social problems: A public arenas model. *American Journal of Sociology, 94*, 53–78.

Hirschman, A. O. (1970). *Exit, voice, and loyalty*. Cambridge: Harvard University Press.

Hoffmann, E. A. (2005). Dispute resolution in a worker cooperative: Formal procedures and procedural justice. *Law and Society Review, 39*, 51–82.

Jenkins, J. C. (1983). Resource mobilization theory and the study of social movements. *Annual Review of Sociology, 9*, 527–553.

Kahneman, D., & Tversky, A. (1979). Prospect theory: An analysis of decision under risk. *Econometrica, 47*, 263–291.

King, D. W., & McEvoy, K. A. (1976). *A national survey of the complaint handling procedures used by consumers*. Rockville, MD: King Research.

Kingdon, J. W. (1995). *Agendas, alternatives, and public policies*. New York, NY: HarperCollins Publishers.

LaNuez, D., & Jermier, J. M. (1994). Sabotage by managers and technocrats: Neglected patterns of resistance at work. In: J. M. Jermier, D. Knights & W. R. Nord (Eds), *Resistance and power in organizations* (pp. 219–251). London: Routledge.

Llewellyn, K., & Hoebel, E. A. (1941). *The cheyenne way*. Norman, OK: University of Oklahoma Press.

Marshall, A.-M. (2003). Injustice frames, legality, and the everyday construction of sexual harassment. *Law and Social Inquiry, 28*, 659–689.

Marshall, A.-M. (2005). Idle rights: Employees' rights consciousness and the construction of sexual harassment policies. *Law and Society Review, 39*, 83–123.

Martin, J., & Meyerson, D. (1998). Women and power: Conformity, resistance, and disorganized coaction. In: R. M. Kramer & M. A. Neale (Eds), *Power and influence in organizations: Structures and processes* (pp. 311–348). Thousand Oaks, CA: Sage.

Marwell, G., & Oliver, P. (1993). *The critical mass in collective action: A micro-social theory*. New York, NY: Cambridge University Press.

Maynard, D. W. (1988). Language, interaction, and social problems. *Social Problems, 35*, 310–334.

McCarthy, J. D., & Zald, M. N. (1973). *The trend of social movements in America: Professionalization and resource mobilization*. Morristown, NJ: General Learning Press.

McCarthy, J. D., & Zald, M. N. (1977). Resource mobilization and social movements: A partial theory. *American Journal of Sociology, 82*, 1212–1241.

McNeil, K., Nevin, J. R., Trubek, D. M., & Miller, R. E. (1979). Market discrimination against the poor and the impact of consumer disclosure laws: The used car industry. *Law and Society Review, 13*, 695–720.

McVeigh, R. (1999). Who protests in America: An analysis of three political alternatives-inaction, institutionalized politics, or protest. *Sociological Forum, 14*, 685–702.

Merry, S. E. (1990). *Getting justice and getting even: Legal consciousness among working-class Americans*. Chicago, IL: University of Chicago Press.

Miller, R. E., & Sarat, A. (1980–1981). Grievances, claims, and disputes: Assessing the adversary culture. *Law and Society Review*, *15*, 525–565.

Nader, L. (Ed.) (1980). *No access to law: Alternatives to the American judicial system*. New York, NY: Academic Press.

Nader, L., & Todd, H. F. (Eds). (1978). *The disputing process: Law in ten societies*. New York, NY: Columbia University Press.

Oegema, D., & Klandermans, B. (1994). Why social movement sympathizers don't participate: Erosion and nonconversion of support. *American Sociological Review*, *59*, 703–722.

Olson, M. (1998 [1965]). *The logic of collective action: Public good and the theory of groups*. Cambridge, MA: Harvard University Press.

Pfohl, S. (1977). The discovery of child-abuse. *Social Problems*, *24*, 310–324.

Rosenberg, G. N. (1991). *The hollow hope: Can courts bring about social change?* Chicago: The University of Chicago Press.

Ross, L. H., & Littlefield, N. O. (1978). Complaint as a problem solving mechanism. *Law and Society Review*, *12*, 199–216.

Rothschild, J., & Miethe, T. D. (1994). Whistleblowing as resistance in modern work organizations the politics of revealing organizational deception and abuse. In: D. Knights, J. M. Jermier & W. R. Nord (Eds), *Resistance and power in organizations* (pp. 252–273). London: Routledge.

Sarat, A., Constable, M., Engel, D., Hans, V., & Lawrence, S. (Eds). (1998). *Everyday practices and trouble cases*. Evanston, IL: Northwestern University Press.

Saunders, D. M., Sheppard, B. H., Knight, V., & Roth, J. (1992). Employee voice to supervisors. *Employee Responsibilities and Rights Journal*, *5*, 241–259.

Snow, D. A., & Benford, R. D. (1988). Ideology, frame resonance, and participation mobilization. *International Journal of Social Movement Research*, *1*, 197–217.

Snow, D. A., Cress, D. M., Downey, L., & Jones, A. W. (1998). Disrupting the 'Quotidian': Reconceptualizing the relationship between breakdown and the emergence of collective action. *Mobilization*, *3*, 1–22.

Snow, D. A., Rochford, E. B., Worden, S. K., & Benford, R. D. (1986). Frame alignment processes, micromobilization, and movement participation. *American Sociological Review*, *51*, 464–481.

Steinberg, M. W. (1999). The talk and back talk of collective action: A dialogic analysis of repertoires of discourse among nineteenth-century English cotton spinners. *American Journal of Sociology*, *105*, 736–780.

Tucker, J. (1993). Everyday forms of employee resistance. *Sociological Forum*, *8*, 25–45.

Useem, B. (1980). Solidarity model, breakdown model, and the Boston anti-trust movement. *American Sociological Review*, *45*, 357–369.

Useem, B. (1985). Disorganization and the new Mexico prison riot of 1980. *American Sociological Review*, *50*, 677–688.

Walsh, E. J., & Warland, R. H. (1983). Social movement involvement in the wake of a nuclear movement: Activists and free riders in the TMI area. *American Sociological Review*, *48*, 764–780.

Warland, R. H., Heirman, R. O., & Willits, J. (1975). Dissatisfied consumers: Who gets upset and who takes action. *Journal of Consumer Affairs*, *9*, 148–163.

Woolgar, S., & Pawlunch, D. (1985). Ontological gerrymandering: The anatomy of social problems explanations. *Social Problems*, *32*, 214–227.

COMMENT: A REVIVAL OF ACCESS TO JUSTICE RESEARCH?

Bryant G. Garth

Access to justice is both a topic of engaged social-legal research and a key component of legal professional ideology. There is a relationship between the two. The more committed the organized legal profession to the issue of access to justice, the higher the profile of scholarly research on topics that relate in one form or another to access to justice. The organized bar's commitment peaked in the 1960s and 1970s, waned in the 1980s, and has not regained the position it once had on the domestic U.S. agenda. In contrast, however, access to justice has recently emerged strongly on the reform agenda that U.S. and multilateral foreign aid organizations – along with the U.S. legal profession – are promoting abroad as part of the renewed post Cold War effort to build the rule of law.

It takes very little Internet searching to see the centrality of access to justice rhetoric in the law and development world. The World Bank statement on legal and judicial reform includes an assertion that "Improving, facilitating and expanding individual and collective access to law and justice supports economic and social development. Legal reforms give the poor the opportunity to assert their individual and property rights; improved access to justice empowers the poor to enforce those rights" (World Bank, 2008). A World Bank concept paper on "legal empowerment" contains the following statement on the need to awaken rights consciousness: "There are many instances in which relatively poor and vulnerable people take on rights consciousness. But under what conditions do they

Access to Justice
Sociology of Crime, Law and Deviance, Volume 12, 255–260

ISSN: 1521-6136/doi:10.1108/S1521-6136(2009)0000012014

adopt this perspective? The ideas rooted in transnational human rights documents need to be translated into terms that make sense in local contexts. This requires the work of intermediaries, such as local organizations, human right activists, academics, journalists" (World Bank, 2006).

Similarly, a document of the OECD states that "The rule of law and access to justice are crucial to the immediate upholding of law and order, and to human security imperatives, stability and development. Assistance in this area is, therefore, vital to build and sustain peace" (OECD, 2008). The UNDP similarly takes the position that "Access to justice is a vital part of the UNDP mandate to reduce poverty and strengthen democratic governance. Within the broad context of justice reform, UNDP's specific niche lies in supporting justice and related systems *so that they work for those who are poor and disadvantaged*" (emphasis in original) (OECD, 2004). Finally, the American Bar Association recently promoted its high profile World Justice Forum with a headline stating that "Access to Justice is the Key to Advancing the Rule of Law, Experts at World Justice Forum Agree at ABA World Justice Initiative" (ABA, 2008).

This international revival of concerns with access to justice so far involves more professional ideology than scholarly research. Consistent with the dominance of economists in the world of developmental assistance, it draws substantially on the literature from law and economics emphasizing the importance of property rights as key bases to legal empowerment. The UNDP's Commission on Legal Empowerment of the Poor, led by Madeleine Albright and Hernando de Soto, thus emphasized the linkage between secure property rights and access to justice before concluding its work in the summer of 2008 (UNDP, 2008).

The literature mobilized on behalf of this focus also included references to U.S. works on legal needs and to British studies of civil justice problems and solutions (e.g., Genn, 1999). Much of this work and certainly the conceptual framework reflect studies done in the earlier period, and the recent cited literature in any event is relatively sparse. It may be that here, as elsewhere, international developments will provide some impetus to raise the value of discourses that have lost their position on the mainstream research and reform agendas at home. My simple question for this new collection of works on access to justice is whether the new body of literature exemplified in this collection portends a potential revival of research on the topic both nationally and internationally.

I start with a personal reflection. I lived through and experienced the vicissitudes of this research agenda focused on access to justice. After law school, I took a research fellowship in Florence to work on the Ford

Foundation sponsored "Access to Justice" Project, which led to several volumes making the case for legal services, court reforms, and alternative dispute resolution in order to "make rights effective." (e.g., Cappelletti & Garth, 1978a, 1978b). The project also provided a vehicle to cooperate with the then burgeoning interdisciplinary scholarship on legal needs, disputing behavior, legal aid, and even social movements. The still relatively new Law and Society Association was a home where these groups could come together in the interests of a progressive social reform agenda (Garth & Sterling, 1998). The general essay that I co-authored with the General Editor of the project, Mauro Cappelletti, argued that there were waves of reforms all directed toward the social progress that would come with implementing the rights of ordinary people – rights that were the product of the "rights revolution" of the 1960s and more generally the welfare state (Cappelletti & Garth, 1978a, 1978b).

My period of active research into these questions for the most part ended in the early 1980s. I was not alone in my shifting focus. The topic of access to justice as a research question practically disappeared at that time. The Reagan era coincided with a shift toward law and economics, deregulation, and markets, and there was almost no public policy interest in the social problems that had consumed scholars in the prior decade. Alternative dispute resolution continued with a different agenda, the rights revolution came to a halt, and scholars moved on to other topics typically far from the rights-oriented legal idealism that attracted many to the legal profession in the first place. Only a sprinkling of researchers who had focused on access to justice in the 1960s and 1970s sustained that interest.

The move away from access to justice as a state priority paralleled a shift in the organized bar from the spirited defense of activist lawyers funded by the state to voluntary pro bono handled mostly by young corporate lawyers. As Scott Cummings observed, "Pro bono's institutionalization bears important features of this reaction against centralized governmental power – a fact made clear by way of comparison with the federal legal services program, which symbolized both the promise and perils of the government-centered approach" (Cummings, 2004, p. 20). Academic research has understandably followed the bar's turn to pro bono as *the* key vehicle to improve access to justice. And much of that research is very much tied into professional ideology, taking the bar to task, for example, for an insufficient commitment to pro bono as a group or within certain elite sectors – notably the corporate bar (cf. Rhode, 2004).

The link between access to justice research and the organized bar's agenda at home and abroad is therefore clear, with the agendas at home and abroad also relating to larger issues of politics and foreign relations. But the key to advancement of any access to justice agenda in my opinion is its relationship to critical scholarship informed by the theories and methods of social science, especially sociology. Sociology has a particular focus on hierarchy and inequality, which makes its methods well designed for taking on issues that are too easily defined by a professional agenda and ideology. Law without the sociology of law easily slips into the reiteration of legitimating rhetoric.

To oversimplify a basic point that is both obvious and often neglected, law and lawyers are deeply embedded in relationships of economic, political, and social power. As rational choice scholars note, even if somewhat too crudely, law serves power, or the powerful would not invest in law. The holders of economic and political power have ceded – over time and in ways that are no longer readily visible – a little of their instrumental power in order to make that power more legitimate. The rules necessarily have a tilt to them (Dezalay & Garth, 1996).

It is not surprising, therefore, that legal elites have always had to respond to the criticism that the law serves the advantaged. The most famous critical statement to this effect is the one by Anatole France: "The law, in its majestic equality, forbids rich and poor alike to sleep under bridges, to beg in the streets, and to steal their bread." Learned Hand's equally famous "Thou shalt not ration justice" provides the profession's response that the legitimacy of the legal system requires that those who cannot afford legal services should be provided access to legal rights and remedies. Since legal rights and remedies are generally tied to the problems and interests of the advantaged, however, there is always a built in contradiction in an access to justice program offering more lawyers to the disadvantaged. One British critic from the 1970s thus argued that lawyers need the poor more than the poor need lawyers (cited in Garth, 1980).

The contradiction between the position of law and the legal profession close to power and an ideology that promotes equal access as a key to formal and substantive justice can be frustrating. It leads lawyers to think that only legal solutions to social problems are good ones. And it leads to simplistic exhortations that the unmet legal needs of relatively vague categories of the "poor" or the "middle class" require that lawyers try harder to fulfill those needs. At the same time, considerable energy and idealism goes into the access to justice programs, and access to law is not a trivial benefit for countries where the law purports to protect property and the rights of citizens.

The coming together of professional idealism, sustained by longstanding professional ideology, and critical social science, is to my mind vital to the enterprise of developing some positive reform agenda that can actually help ordinary people, including those who are disadvantaged. Rebecca Sandefur's (2007) work provides that kind of critical stance grounded in empirical research and sociological theory. Among other insights, she has shown that familiarity with the legal system can be a recipe for inaction and discouragement rather than an assertion of legal rights (2007), that what lawyers provide is often simply a signal to the legal or administrative system to follow its own norms – whether the lawyer is competent or not (Sandefur, forthcoming), and that the general supply of helping resources – not just access to law – has a major impact on how people act to remedy their problems. The research in this collection is part of this welcome new research trend as well.

I will highlight just a couple of the insights that I think come from these articles. One is that law as a potential solution to any kind of social problem should not be taken for granted. Authors in this volume examine cascades of social problems (Ab Currie) and look toward a more general sociology of troubles that goes well beyond legal needs (Jennifer Earl). They question perceptions of problems (Pascoe Pleasence, Nigel Balmer, and Tam) and offer novel insights about how race and ethnicity affect what access to justice might mean (Mary Rose, Kwai Hang Ng). Furthermore, instead of focusing on gaps in the provision of legal services and exhortations to close the gap through good works, the authors look at the way that pro bono lawyers act in relation to the professional, economic, and career incentives that they face (Stephen Daniels and Joanne Martin, Marie Nell Trautner). Daniels and Martin, in particular, provide the first detailed examination of the landscape of pro bono, showing the relationship between the provision of legal services and the incentives and hierarchies in a very competitive world both of non-profits and corporate law firms in Chicago. It has very little to do with so-called legal needs.

This kind of critical empirical work is essential to enlighten some of the work taking place abroad, and it also has the potential to reenergize this research line at home. Without empirical work informed by sociological theory, the access to justice movement, however much legal rhetoric goes into it, is bound to do very little for the ostensible beneficiaries of the programs. One of the strengths of the movement in the 1960s and the 1970s was that the professional program was criticized, held accountable, and to some extent informed by social science theories attuned to questions of hierarchy, inequality, and organizational legitimacy. My own history, of course, links me with legal idealism and professional ideology, and I therefore hope for this kind of critical combination. Whether it materializes or not, however, this new research promises to give us a far better understanding of what law means and does not mean in people's everyday lives. It will be immensely valuable when the time finally does come of a renewed focus on the problems of individuals and how best to ameliorate them.

REFERENCES

American Bar Association. (2008). World Justice Forum, July 2–5, 2008, News from the World Justice Forum. Available at http://www.abavideonews.org/ABA517/news_printables/Access_to_Justice.html

Cappelletti, M., & Garth, B. G. (1978a). *Access to justice: A world survey*. Leyden and Boston/Milan, Sijthoff/Giuffre (Vol. I of the Florence access-to-justice project series).

Cappelletti, M., & Garth, B. G. (1978b). Access to justice: The newest wave in the worldwide movement to make rights effective. *Buffalo Law Review*, *27*, 181–292.

Cummings, S. L. (2004). The politics of pro bono. *U.C.L.A. L. Rev.*, *51*, 1–149.

Dezalay, Y., & Garth, B. G. (1996). *Dealing in virtue: International commercial arbitration and the construction of a transnational legal order*. Chicago, IL: University of Chicago Press.

Garth, B. G. (1980). *Neighborhood law firms for the poor: A comparative study of recent developments in legal aid and in the legal profession*. Sijthoff: Alphen aan den Rijn.

Garth, B. G., & Sterling, J. (1998). From legal realism to law and society: Reshaping law for the last stages of the social activist state. *Law and Society Review*, *32*, 409–472.

Genn, H. (1999). *Paths to justice: What people do and think about going to law*. Oxford: Hart Publishing.

OECD. (2004). Access to justice practice note 9/3/2004 CONTENT. Available at http://www.undp.org/governance/docs/Justice_PN_En.pdf

OECD. (2008). Development Assistance Committee, Issues brief, equal access to justice and the rule of law. Available at http://www.oecd.org/dataoecd/26/51/35785471.pdf

Rhode, D. L. (2004). *Access to justice*. New York, NY: Oxford University Press.

Sandefur, R. L. (2007). The importance of doing nothing: Everyday problems and responses of inaction. In: P. Pleasence, A. Buck & N. Balmer (Eds), *Transforming lives: Law and social process*. London: HMSO.

Sandefur, R. L. (forthcoming). Elements of expertise: Lawyers' impact on civil trial and hearing outcomes.

UNDP. (2008). Commission on legal empowerment of the poor. Available at http://www.undp.org/legalempowerment/

World Bank. (2006). Legal empowerment of the poor: An action agenda for the world bank (prepared by Ana Palacio). Available at http://siteresources.worldbank.org/INTLAWJUSTINST/Resources/LegalEmpowermentofthePoor.pdf

World Bank. (2008). Law and justice institutions, access to justice for the poor. Available at http://web.worldbank.org/WBSITE/EXTERNAL/TOPICS/EXTLAWJUSTINST/0,,contentMDK:20745998~menuPK:1990386~pagePK:210058~piPK:210062~theSitePK:1974062,00.html

SUBJECT INDEX